I0796943

A FOREST OF GRANITE

Union Monuments at Gettysburg 1863–1913

BRENDAN HARRIS

Havertown, Pennsylvania

Brookline Books is an imprint of Casemate Publishers

Published in the United States of America and Great Britain in 2025 by
BROOKLINE BOOKS
1950 Lawrence Road, Havertown, PA 19083
and
47 Church Street, Barnsley, S70 2AS, UK

Hardback Edition: ISBN 978-1-955041-51-5
Digital Edition: ISBN 978-1-955041-52-2

A CIP record for this book is available from the British Library

Printed and bound in the United Kingdom by CPI Group (UK) Ltd, Croydon, CR0 4YY

Typeset in India by Lapiz Digital Services, Chennai.

For a complete list of Brookline Books titles, please contact:

CASEMATE PUBLISHERS (US)
Telephone (610) 853-9131
Fax (610) 853-9146
Email: casemate@casematepublishers.com
www.casematepublishers.com

CASEMATE PUBLISHERS (UK)
Telephone (0)1226 734350
Email: casemate@casemateuk.com
www.casemateuk.com

All images and maps Brendan Harris unless credited otherwise.

The Publisher's authorised representative in the EU for product safety is Authorised Rep Compliance Ltd., Ground Floor, 71 Lower Baggot Street, Dublin D02 P593, Ireland.
http://www.arccompliance.com

To all veterans who saw the elephant.

Contents

Introduction

My fascination with Gettysburg's Union monuments began when I was a young boy in northern Virginia. I did not need to read American history books to understand where the roots of our country started and grew; I was fortunate enough to live in an area surrounded by those roots. Growing up in northern Virginia allowed me close access to many of the sites that were pivotal to the founding of the United States during its first century as a nation. By the time I reached grade school, my maternal grandfather could see that I enjoyed history and took me to the nation's capital to tour the different Smithsonian museums and the monuments and statues that dotted the National Mall. Returning from one of these visits, I saw a sign that read "Exit: Manassas National Battlefield Park," and asked my grandfather what it meant. My grandfather nonchalantly stated, "Oh, that is where one of the first major battles of the Civil War started, and you had ancestors who fought in it."

It took a while to wrap my head around the information I had just received. At that point I was familiar with America's recent wars; the First Gulf War had just ended, and I had heard many stories from my paternal grandfather and other family friends about the Vietnam War, in bits and pieces, but nothing beyond that. I understood that a civil war meant that groups of people who were under the same government fought one another, but it shocked me that the United States had fought one, let alone with people in my own family participating. My follow-up question was whether other battlefields were around, which made my grandfather laugh. He said, "Of course there are, and one of the big ones is near where we have family in Pennsylvania."

The following weekend saw my first trip to Gettysburg. I was amazed by the number of monuments and gawked at the informative state markers that dotted the landscape. On one of the statues I was shown the name of a family member who fought in the battle, his name etched on a plaque with the rest of his regiment. The battlefield surrounded the town itself, and I could not believe that so many men fought and died in such a small area over three days. Little did I know that my first trip to Gettysburg in the spring of 1992 would precede a keen interest in the battle in broader popular culture the following year.

When the film *Gettysburg* debuted on October 8, 1993, interest in the battle and the American Civil War reached a vast new audience. Using local reenactors and Hollywood special effects, filmmakers told the story of the battle by drawing on Michael Shaara's historical novel, *The Killer Angels*. Ken Burns's 1990 documentary *The Civil War* had also captured audiences by bringing the conflict to life on screen. The popularity of both productions sent people flocking to Gettysburg to see battle sites such as Little Round Top, the Devil's Den, and Cemetery Ridge, the "high water mark" of the Confederate assault on the battle's third day. To deal with the increased interest in these sections of Gettysburg National Military Park, the National Park Service (NPS) updated its infrastructure.

The addition of better roads dealt with the influx of vehicles, and paved walking paths replaced dirt and gravel trails. However, these infrastructure improvements changed the look of the battlefield from what combatants saw in 1863. Many modern visitors do not understand why the park is preserved differently from other battlefields in the United States. The goal of veterans who fought at Gettysburg was to place monuments in a way that tells a story about the actual location of where a unit fought and the outcome of their area of the battle. The monuments also explain why placing the monument at Gettysburg and not at other battlefields was essential to the unit's survivors. Another difference is that veterans took great pains to ensure the monument's placement aligned with where they fought on the battlefield. The attention to detail at Gettysburg would become a template for other battlefields because Gettysburg became a focal point of Union veterans as a place of monumentation for their families and future generations to understand their war experience. What was it about the battle outside this small Pennsylvania town that was so important that a popular mainstream documentary and a major Hollywood production were filmed about it? After all, battles that were fought in the Civil War before and after the Gettysburg campaign concluded.

Gettysburg is also unique among other battlefields because of its "to the victor go the spoils" mentality of monument placement. When touring many of the Civil War battlefields in the South, visitors see monuments mostly dedicated to rebel units, with little in the way of Union unit monuments. Aside from many of these rebel monuments being placed during the height of the "Lost Cause Narrative," which will be discussed later, Union veterans did not want to place monuments at battlefields where they lost. Instead,

Union veterans looked to place monuments where they either had a stalemate with a rebel army, or won outright. Union veterans wanted people to visit where they showed success and not defeat.

The three days of fighting in and around Gettysburg, from July 1 to July 3, 1863, left a lasting impression on combatants and civilians. Geographic names synonymous today with the battlefield, like Cemetery Ridge, the Round Tops, the Wheatfield, and Cemetery Hill, were once innocuous parts of a thriving community in rural southern Pennsylvania. Today, those names are known for struggle and sacrifice, because when July 3 ended, the battle had cost the Union and Confederate armies over 50,000 casualties (killed, wounded, and missing). Most reports place Union casualties alone at over 23,000 men. Repelling the Confederate army from northern soil at this point of the war was not only a boost to the Union army and how they would remember the battle in later years but also to the civilian population of the North. General George Meade, commander of the Union army, stated in his official report:

> It is impossible in a report of this nature to enumerate all the instances of gallantry and good conduct in such a hard-fought field as Gettysburg … the heroic bravery of the whole army, officers and men, which under the blessing of divine providence, enabled a crowning victory to be obtained, which I feel confident the country will never cease to beam in grateful remembrance.[1]

The importance of the Union victory resonated beyond commanders and echoed amongst the lower ranks of the Union army.

Letters and reports from officers and soldiers illustrate how individual units experienced and interpreted the battle. In a letter to his wife, Sergeant Calvin Haynes of the 125th New York Infantry wrote that Gettysburg was "the hardest campaign the army of the Potomac ever had … the sight of the dead and dying on the field is such a sight I never wish to see again."[2] The sentiments of Sgt. Haynes are echoed by the regiment's acting Adjutant-General, Lieutenant Harry Haskell. His report stated that the enemy "made a desperate charge on our position and was repulsed with heavy loss. All prisoners agree that it was by far the most desperate battle of the war."[3]

Though Union armies were consistently advancing in the Western Theater, Northerners had grown accustomed to news of Union defeats in the East. From July 1861 until the battle of Gettysburg, Union armies operating in the East lost more than they won. This losing streak was of great concern to civilians who, by 1863, had reservations about what would happen to the country if the Confederacy continued to triumph. The Union victory at Gettysburg helped change civilian perceptions of the capability and strength of the Army of the Potomac. The *Burlington Daily Times* noted that the Army of the Potomac, "won a victory unsurpassed in the history of the war."[4] Within a week, newspapers as far as California were reporting the importance of what occurred at Gettysburg.

One of the first California newspapers to break the news about Gettysburg was the *Placer Herald*, which described the Union victory as "a great battle … fought at Gettysburg, fighting to be of the most desperate character and the most severe of the war."[5] The news of the victory helped quell secession talk within California just as a convention was set to meet in Sacramento to decide if a secession vote was needed. After the news that General Robert E. Lee's invasion of the North had been repulsed, the measure was quickly defeated.[6] The broad coverage of the Union victory at Gettysburg would help establish the battle as a key victory during the Civil War. Another reason for Gettysburg becoming a place for Union memorials and monumentation is the effect of the battle on the civilians living in Gettysburg at the time.

Despite popular belief, the first efforts to memorialize Civil War battles did not occur at Gettysburg. Union cavalry troopers under General William Gamble erected two monuments on the battlefields of Manassas in the summer of 1865, more than a decade before Union veterans would begin memorialization at Gettysburg. The first monument was erected near Henry Hill on the First Manassas battlefield, and the other near the railroad cut that was the center of action at Second Manassas. Both monuments are designed similarly: 27-foot-tall obelisks atop pedestals constructed of sandstone bricks.[7] The monuments also have the same inscription: "In memory of the patriots who fell," and the dates of the respective battles. These two monuments influenced the designs used by Union veterans to commemorate their dead at Gettysburg.

The First Manassas monument is one of the first monuments I visited as a young child. The battlefield is located barely a stone's throw from where my grandparents lived. There was a path through their neighborhood between houses that led to the stream called Bull Run, which, if I followed, would put me right on the edge of the battlefield. The obelisk sits near the heaviest fighting at the first battle of Manassas, within sight of where Thomas "Stonewall" Jackson, a professor from Virginia Military Institute, got his famous nickname. While the monuments are simple in design, their importance for what they meant to the Union soldiers who built them needs to be understood.

Neither battle at Manassas left a good taste in the mouth of the Union army. In both cases on that field, first in July 1861 and then in August 1862, the Union army was defeated and driven back toward Washington. One of the first things done by Gen. William Gamble's Union cavalry at the end of

First Manassas Monument, Manassas National Battlefield.

hostilities in 1865 was to throw up memorial obelisks to honor their dead that fell on the ground they had lost twice. The meaning of these monuments can be found in their inscriptions, which would eventually be reflected in the feelings expressed on monuments at Gettysburg over the next 50 years. Ironically, many of the men who helped build the Manassas monuments would be involved in building regiment-specific monuments over the next 30 years at

Second Manassas Monument, Manassas National Battlefield.

Gettysburg. Their focus was on the dead and how they fell as patriots fighting for the United States. The focus on honoring the fallen would be a common theme for monuments at Gettysburg and battle sites throughout the country.

On an early fall day in 1889, people came together near Gettysburg for a day of remembrance. The group gathered to dedicate a group of monuments to men from Maine who fought in the battle 26 years earlier. Ceremonies centered around monument dedications followed a standard pattern, and this day would be no different. Bands played patriotic music and dignitaries gave speeches and a benediction to the monument. One of the men asked to provide a dedication speech this day was General Seldon Connor, a former governor of Maine who, when younger, had commanded troops at Gettysburg.

The speech talked about the sacrifices of the men fighting that day and described why they were willing to enlist and fight in the army during the war. General Connor stated, "We are not waiting for the historian to arise, but we may well fear that the casualties of time are daily taking from us many a man who leaves untold the heroic sagas of his share in those eventful July days."[8] In his speech, Connor made it clear that these monuments needed to be built to preserve the experiences of individual soldiers for future generations. The speech also highlighted the importance of individual states providing funding for monuments to mark the placement of troops on the battlefield. Maine thought so highly of the sacrifices made by men from its state that money was provided for individual unit monuments at Gettysburg. Each monument was made from granite and chiseled with identifying information about what happened at each site.

General Connor's dedication speech exemplifies the hundreds of speeches and benedictions given to dedication monuments at Gettysburg. Union regimental monuments highlight the sacrifices of soldiers during the battle and what surviving veterans remembered in later years. While this book's title draws inspiration from one such dedication speech, the book goes beyond single regiments of Union soldiers at Gettysburg. Throughout the coming chapters, this book will examine how Union veterans used monuments to explain their battle and wartime experiences. Examining Union unit monumentation at Gettysburg serves two purposes. The first shows the Union army's complex individual makeup through memorialization on the battlefield. Gettysburg National Military Park contains roughly 1,300 monuments, markers, and tablets dedicated to both sides of the battle.

The second purpose is to analyze why veterans revered Gettysburg more than other battles fought during the Civil War. Even with the Union victory on that field, the war continued for two more years. The battle cost both armies a combined casualty count of over 50,000 men, and it did not conclude the war. Yet, every state that sent men to fight in the Army of the Potomac dedicated at least one monument on the battlefield. Visitors can see monuments for miles while visiting Gettysburg National Military Park and the town. The monuments mark where battle lines were formed and where sacrifices were made to defeat the enemy.

Union veterans spent thousands of dollars and exerted much political influence to create and dedicate their monuments at Gettysburg. The questions in this book focus on why Gettysburg, more than other battles fought during the Civil War, was the focus of veterans and memorialization decades after the battle. Research questions will focus on the political and social climate in the United States during Reconstruction and into the early 20th century. This period is essential to the Union veterans' memorialization at Gettysburg because it is when they gained political clout and the economic influence to build monuments. Memorialization of what Union veterans fought for and wanted people to remember was the focus of monumentation in the United States. However, with the passing of Union veterans, different voices about what Gettysburg and the Civil War meant to the nation would emerge. As the country moved farther away from the conflict, deep feelings against the enemy who wanted to break up the Union gradually gave way to reconciliation.

American society allowed both sides to memorialize their dead and explain their actions during the war. Historians defending the honor of the South during the Civil War found a foothold over time. Explaining the Civil War from the Southern perspective muddied the waters about why the war occurred. Shifting feelings about the reasons for the Civil War would eventually allow Confederate monuments to be dedicated at Gettysburg. Southerners began pushing for the addition of Confederate monuments at all Civil War battlefields as the country came out of Reconstruction and into the late 19th and early 20th centuries. Adding Confederate monuments reflected a change in public perception of the conflict. Included in this change in perception were the veterans themselves. An eventual rift occurred between veterans and younger generations regarding what monuments meant on the battlefield. Veterans wanted to build monuments based on their experiences, while younger generations wanted to move the nation forward into a new era of inclusivity that highlighted the deeds of both sides.

Focusing on Union veterans, Gettysburg, and a specific period helps identify specific primary source material. Using veterans' personal diaries and correspondence will help explain their views on Gettysburg and the war. The source material also helps focus on why Gettysburg was important for memorializing veterans. Official battle reports, veterans organizations' meeting notes, and monument commission documents lay the groundwork for why Union veterans wanted to memorialize their experiences at Gettysburg. Using these primary sources provides insight into how Union veterans felt about their combat experiences. These experiences endured in their memory and helped individuals produce Gettysburg's monuments and dedication speeches. Each monument provides a snapshot of feelings about the war at the time of the monument's completion.

Viewing the monuments through a modern lens as mere objects that were erected in the late 19th and early 20th centuries does not explain their creation or their context. Instead, a wholistic approach is needed; they should be examined alongside the records and correspondence at the time of their creation.

Eventually, once former Confederates were allowed to participate in monument creation, monuments dedicated at Gettysburg shifted away from what Union veterans had intended. This book will focus on the earlier monumentation period, from 1863 to 1913. The first monument dedicated to a former Confederate state at Gettysburg did not occur until 1917. Examining the era before Confederate monuments became commonplace establishes the Union veterans' perspective on the Civil War.

The battle of Gettysburg is a topic that historians have analyzed and researched since July 1863. A vast amount of literature has covered tactical decisions by commanders as well as strategic maneuvers, and examined the overall impact of the battle in the context of the war. Interest in the battle has also led to focusing on the histories of individual units and their experiences during the three days of fighting. The focus on these units includes biographies of their leaders and soldiers' personal recollections to explain what happened on the battlefield in July 1863.

American Civil War remembrance is a relatively new topic being examined by historians. Discussing memory is a key element in this book because gaps exist in the current literature about monuments placed at Gettysburg. The park's original bylaws allowed private entities to control the placement of monuments. Until the federal government took possession of Gettysburg in 1895, only Union units could have monuments placed on the field. After federal possession, Confederate battle line markers and monuments were allowed. This process, over time, helped bridge a reconciliatory gap between North and South and provided historical context for events on the field. Historical memory—how people remember history and their modern interpretation of events—has been discussed in the literature usually only in general terms.

This book contains stories about what motivated veterans to place monuments at Gettysburg. While no specific text has been written about motivations, there is literature about veterans organizations and monumentation regarding the Civil War as a whole. After the Civil War ended, the Grand Army of the Republic (GAR) was one of the largest Union veterans organizations. The group had membership through every state of the Union, consisting of veterans who served honorably during the war. While military operations are a common theme in historical literature, this book goes beyond discussing the battle itself. For this reason, the following section will define terms that will be part of the discussion. As its title suggests, this book will focus on units within the Union Army of the Potomac, their experiences at Gettysburg, and the subsequent building of monuments to memorialize their sacrifices.

The regiment is one of the standard organizational units that focus on monuments at Gettysburg. A typical Union regiment was authorized to consist of 1,000 men.[9] However, as the war progressed, attrition in battle casualties and disease weakened regimental totals. Instead of using new recruits to strengthen old regiments, Union policy was to form new ones. As such, regimental totals shrank as the war continued.

By the time the Army of the Potomac moved toward Gettysburg, the average size of preexisting regiments was between 200 and 400 men.[10] Regiments belonged to a larger organizational unit called a brigade. A typical brigade consisted of three to five regiments, and divisions consisted of two to four brigades. The corps was the next highest organizational unit, consisting of two to four divisions. At Gettysburg, seven Union corps deployed to face the Confederates. Almost all troop movements were conducted through these types of units, and for this reason, they are the focus of most Union army monuments at Gettysburg.

Infantry units were not the only type memorialized at Gettysburg, as cavalry and artillery units also have monuments that dot the landscape. Like the infantry, Union cavalry was organized into regiments, brigades, divisions, and corps levels. Cavalry regiments could theoretically number approximately 1,000 troopers,[11] but like the infantry, mounted units were severely undersized and not at full strength by the time of the battle. While the cavalry was similar to the infantry in its organization, artillery units had a different structure. The primary organizational unit of an artillery unit is the battery, consisting of four to six cannons, worked by 40–100 men and around 70 horses.[12] Most monuments dedicated to cavalry and artillery units were constructed at the regiment and battery level.

There are two words commonly used in the literature: memorialization and monumentation; both of which will be used throughout this book. While both seem interchangeable, they refer to two different and distinct ideas. Memorialization focuses on written words and speeches about an event or person, whereas monumentation focuses on a physical item left on a battlefield to mark where a significant event occurred. While sculptures are a typical example of monumentation, tablets and markers also fall under this category. The Union monuments discussed in subsequent chapters take on different shapes, focuses, and meanings from one another. Monuments at Gettysburg are unique and as varied as the states and men they commemorate. While a deeper examination of the uniqueness of each monument occurs in later chapters, we can provide basic definitions of each. Union monuments at Gettysburg are generally classified as funerary, individuals, memorials, sentinels, places, and reconciliatory.

While all monuments located at Gettysburg are memorials, I separate memorial-type monuments from other types based on the information provided on the sculpture. In this book, *memorial* monuments only provide unit identifiers and placements during the battle. *Funerary* types also include memorializing the dead and sacrifices made by the unit or person. Funerary monuments often provide specific figures of casualties suffered at the battle. *Sentinel* monuments are typical on Civil War battlefields and are popular among veterans. These monuments have a sculpture of a soldier standing guard over a location where a unit fought. The statue of the soldier is usually a generic form created by the sculptor. However, some of the sentinel monuments depict a particular unit, based on a uniqueness in its uniform or other indicator. Sentinels are different from monuments dedicated to an individual because the information provided on the monument indicates a particular unit's accomplishments.

Almost all the monuments discussed in the following chapters include the corps insignia to which the person or unit was assigned during the battle. While unit insignia seem commonplace for today's military, they were new to the Army of the Potomac in 1863. Unit insignias were created that spring to help identify units faster in the field. The insignia of the seven infantry corps at Gettysburg included a round disc for the I Corps, a trefoil (cloverleaf) for the II Corps, and a diamond for the III Corps. The V Corps had a Maltese Cross and the VI Corps a Greek Cross. The insignia of the XI Corps was a crescent moon, and the XII Corps was represented by a star.

The remaining monument types are unique because they focus on a specific person or place in the memorialization. Monuments dedicated to individuals are what the name implies and help memorialize the person's importance to a unit. The monument can include a likeness of the individual and the deeds that the veterans wanted to memorialize. Similarly, monuments dedicated to places memorialize a particular moment or event on the battlefield. While this monument type may seem redundant, it serves an essential purpose. When veterans decided to build monuments at Gettysburg, they expanded beyond their fellow soldiers. Some events within the battle stood out clearly in the memory of all who participated in them. For this reason, several of these types of monuments exist on the battlefield.

Finally, the *reconciliation* type of Union monuments on the battlefield differ from other types in that their dedications did not occur until many years after the war. The purpose of reconciliation monuments was to help seal the breach in arguments about what caused the Civil War. Instead of memorializing one side, reconciliation monuments instilled joint commemoration for both armies. Most of these monuments came to Gettysburg because they mirrored society's feelings. The research provided throughout this book will show how reconciliation was not part of the original plan for the Union monument placement at Gettysburg National Military Park.

Although reconciliation was discussed in dedication ceremonies by Union veterans, reconciliation monuments were allowed on the battlefield only after most Union veterans had passed away. While other authors have used sentinels and funerary types to describe the physical formation of monuments, they have not explained what the monument meant to the veterans. The monument type definitions described here will be used to explain the physical formation of the monument as well as what type of dedication speech was given for the monument. A regimental association could dedicate a monument for multiple reasons, and while the physical monument may have one theme, the dedication speech could have others.

One of the unique tasks when writing about Union monuments at Gettysburg and what they mean is deciding the scope of the writing. While most works focus on the narrative and linear progression of the battle of Gettysburg, this book will be different. This work examines the motivations of the Union veterans who built the monuments at Gettysburg. Due to the focus on monumentation and not battle tactics, we will not follow a day-by-day analysis of the battle. Each chapter will examine a specific monument type and give examples of each type at Gettysburg. Another feature of this book is its scope, discussing examples from every Northern state with monuments on the battlefield. Even though I focus on Union monuments, Confederate monuments are mentioned. Early Confederate monuments and proposals affected how Union veterans wanted to build their own monuments. Understanding how both armies interpreted the battle also helps explain why parts of the field were memorialized later.

The book follows a chronological path from 1863 to 1913. The use of chronology instead of thematic analysis is necessary for three reasons. The first is to show the change in Union veterans' thoughts about their experiences at Gettysburg. Second, a chronology explains the challenges veterans faced when building monuments at Gettysburg in the Reconstruction and Gilded Age periods of the United States. Finally, a chronological approach shows the shift of the nation's attention away from the Civil War and instead beginning to look to the future. This shift would change perspectives on the war and explain why future generations pushed a reconciliatory tone with living veterans. We will also discuss a few monuments outside of the 50-year timeframe to see the importance of the battlefield as a historic landmark in United States history.

Each chapter will cover the different eras of veteran monumentation. These eras include 1863–77, 1878–86, 1885–87, 1888–94, and 1895–1913. Due to the scale of monument placements at Gettysburg, a separate chapter will focus on monuments constructed and dedicated by the states of New York and Pennsylvania between 1887 and 1897. Analysis of monumentation from 1863 to 1913 is crucial for Civil War and its memory because most veterans could then provide firsthand accounts of their experiences. How veterans discussed their war service and why they fought would set the tone for remembrance traditions around the Civil War for future generations.

I want to refer to the primary sources cited in this text at this point. As mentioned previously, I strived to curate primary sources from the men on the battlefield when describing events as they remembered them. Whilst some of the sources will be familiar to some; I relied on letters and diaries for battle references, framing these accounts with the voluminous *Official Records of the War of The Rebellion*. Regarding unit strength and casualty counts during the battle, I relied on *Regimental Strengths and Losses at Gettysburg*, an informative and helpful resource.

The Union monuments dedicated at Gettysburg did not happen by chance. Veterans created them to preserve and honor the sacrifices of their compatriots. The monuments are a product of how Union veterans wanted to remember the American Civil War, as well as how they wanted it remembered by others. Eventually, the country grappled with how to remember the war, and both sides wanted to tell their story. Even though the Union veterans associations were initially the only groups allowed to place monuments on the battlefield, this would change over time. The federal government would eventually purchase the land, move monumentation toward a healing narrative, and include both armies. However, many Union veterans rejected placing Confederate monuments on the battlefield. Memorializing the other side of the battle changed the national perception of what the Civil War meant to the country. While the beginning stages of monumentation saw this ideal being carried out since there were enough veterans who had a voice, this would change over time. Eventually, what future generations wanted for memorialization would take hold since there would be no more veterans left alive to stand by their convictions.

CHAPTER I

Preserving the Battlefield, 1863–77

By the end of June 1863, residents of Gettysburg understood that Confederate and Union forces were concentrating near their town. Dispatches from Harrisburg, the state capital, had been sent statewide since the middle of June, warning of the approaching enemy.[1] What town residents would witness during the first three days of July 1863 would change the makeup of the community. William Bayly, a young boy living in Gettysburg, waited to see the approaching troops along the main roads leading into town. Bayly stated, "Our gallery seats, although good for the whole show, began to show signs of discomfort with the approach of glistening rifles."[2] Another account of what civilians felt came from citizens who lived on the outskirts of town during the first day of battle. Amelia Harmon, who lived on the Immanuel Harmon farm, described her experience on July 1. Harmon stated, "We were between the lines; to go forward into town would be to walk into the jaws of death."[3] While most citizens heard or observed the fighting from their homes, other residents became part of the battle itself.

Even as the Union army lost over 20,000 men as casualties at Gettysburg, the resident population of Gettysburg suffered losses as well. On the first day of battle, west of Gettysburg, War of 1812 veteran John Burns took his weapon and walked to the sound of the fighting. He joined the I Corps line of battle and fired at the Confederate advance. Burns was one of the oldest residents of Gettysburg at the time of the battle. He was eventually wounded and left alone by Confederates, eventually making his way back to his home. Surviving his wounds, Burns attended the dedication of the National Cemetery in November 1863. The other civilian casualty of Gettysburg, widely reported, was Virginia "Jennie" Wade. On July 2, Wade was caring for her sister on the south side of town near Cemetery Hill when a bullet entered the home and passed through a door and interior wall before striking her in the back,

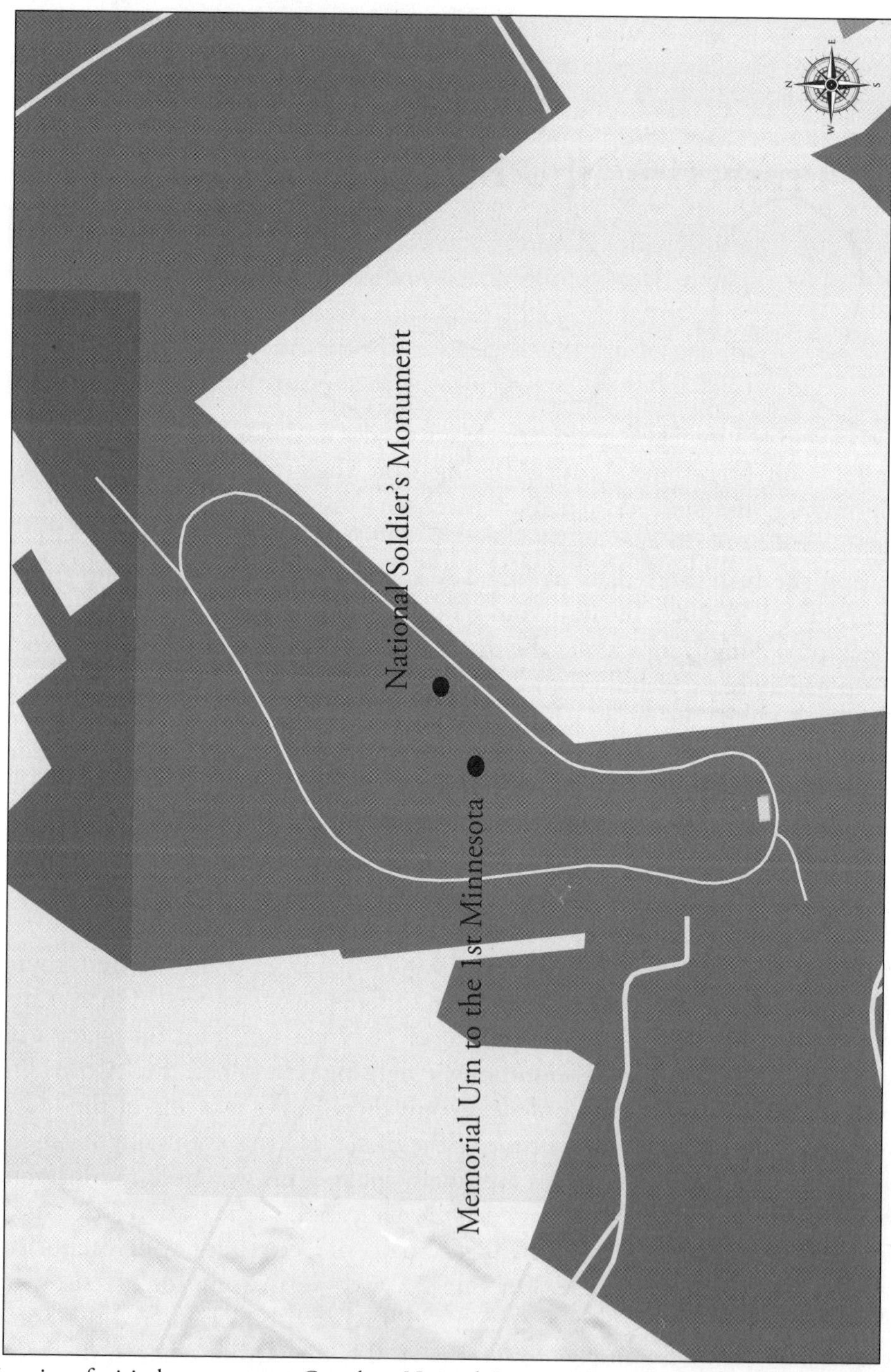

Location of original monuments at Gettysburg National Cemetery. (Created using ArcGIS Pro by Esri)

killing her. While Jennie Wade was the most famous civilian fatality of the battle, untold numbers of civilians became casualties in the weeks and months following due to unexploded ordnance.[4] A man named Russell Briggs picked up an unexploded ordnance shell found near Cemetery Hill, and as he attempted to disassemble the shell, it exploded in his hands. Briggs was taken to a local hospital where he had to have his hands amputated, which fortunately saved his life. However, not everyone near Briggs when the shell blew up was spared. The explosion cut a young boy named James Allen Frazer in half, killing him instantly. Civilian casualties were not the only losses for the townspeople of Gettysburg after the battle. The destruction of town buildings, farms, crops, and other sources of income in the surrounding area wrecked the local economy. Damage to the region required help from the government to fix, and requests for pensions poured in almost immediately after the battle ended. Civilians applied for these pensions to help fix buildings and recoup losses due to war damage or army confiscation. For example, Union soldiers destroyed the building of the Bliss family farm on the outskirts of town to prevent Confederate troops from occupying a favorable position against the center of the Union line on Cemetery Ridge. The Bliss family requested funds to rebuild their destroyed property, and William Bliss eventually sent a notarized damage claim for his property of $1,256.08.[5] Unfortunately, Bliss was denied his claim by the government. Bliss sold his farm to recoup some of his losses and moved his family out of the area. The damage to Gettysburg pushed many people out of the area to look for other places to live and rebuild their lives.

Another problem facing the town was what to do with the dead and wounded on the Gettysburg battlefield. Several field hospitals dotted the landscape, including Camp Letterman, the Seminary College, and other smaller sites to help care for wounded soldiers of both armies. Unfortunately, burials of dead soldiers, if they were buried at all, were in shallow graves dug where the men fell—leaving corpses out in the open or barely covered with dirt. This created problems in identifying the deceased as well as sanitation concerns for the community. Farmers could not tend their fields due to dead soldiers being there or buried just below the topsoil. After the battle, the combination of not knowing what to do with the dead and how to bring the local economy back to Gettysburg combined to create the genesis for battlefield preservation and monumentation that came to dominate the region for the next fifty years.

The need to remove bodies from farm fields and other hastily dug, shallow graves became a top priority for the townspeople of Gettysburg. Burial duty fell to the Union army's provost guard. However, the military lacked the manpower to carry out the task effectively. Officials appealed to civilians through newspaper advertisements to help with burials.[6] Unfortunately, very few citizens volunteered as they were occupied with repairing their properties from the damage sustained in the battle. Burial details from the Union army indicated they would hastily dig trenches and dump men into the trenches. Visitors could see limbs and skulls sticking out of the ground within a month of the battle.

Burying bodies quickly was not a cure-all to help the civilians live with the damage the battle had done to the town. Townspeople began to look at their lives differently and what the war meant to them. The quiet central Pennsylvania town had been turned into a war zone, and within 72 hours, both armies marched away, leaving the townsfolk to pick up the pieces. At the same time, the citizens were thrilled that the enemy was defeated and that on July 4, 1863, they retreated. While dealing with corpses of dead men was a problem for the town, perhaps worse was the stench of hundreds of dead animals, most of which had to be burned before burial. There was also the problem of cleaning the streets filled with leftover war material and reconstructing fences so that livestock could again be confined. Citizens later recalled the scene as "a picture of destruction which will never fade from the mind."[7]

While the town dealt with the detritus of both armies, farmers had to deal with more than just bodies. The amount of shelling done south of town during the second and third days of the battle destroyed farm roads and land tilled for crops.[8] Government funds could not cover this type of damage. Several farmers would have to wait and hope that their land could recover enough to be helpful. While civilians took stock of how they would rebuild the damage done to the town, the importance of the battle fought on its outskirts would need time to take hold. Once newspapers outside the region began trickling into the town, all who lived in Gettysburg felt the scope of the battle and what had been lost. This feeling would be further cemented by a published account of the battle by Michael Jacobs, a professor at Pennsylvania (now Gettysburg) College during the battle. Jacobs wrote that the battle of Gettysburg was more important than the Union victories at Vicksburg and Port Hudson, which occurred about the same time, because those battles were "not equal in its influence on the breaking of the power of an army which was striking a blow at the heart of the nation."[9] However, the initial concern of the entire Gettysburg region was removing bodies so that they could begin rebuilding their lives without the sight and smell of corpses.

Due to the war effort, local undertakers did not have enough wood to prepare proper coffins for the dead. The result was burying men as they were. Instead of leaving these bodies in the region's fields, prominent Gettysburg citizens discussed a centralized location for the dead. A new cemetery for Union burials would benefit the town for several reasons. It would allow the farm's fields to be cleared and so remove the possibility of contamination of future crops. In addition, family members of the dead and survivors of the battle would have a central location to visit and honor the fallen.

Governor Andrew Curtin. (National Archives)

What became a local issue would eventually begin to work its way up through the political machine of Pennsylvania. Besides the invasion of Maryland by the Army of Northern Virginia in September 1862, no other major battle was fought in the North during the entire course of the Civil War. Something had to be done to not only help the local citizenry but to maintain the honor and dignity of the Union soldiers who fell during this momentous event. Governor Andrew Curtin, a close political ally of President Abraham Lincoln, sent aides and even traveled to Gettysburg to understand the scope of the damage. Concerned with the damage done to the area, Curtin ordered the 36th Pennsylvania Volunteer Militia to move to Gettysburg to assist the townspeople in rebuilding. Curtin went as far as to name the unit commander, Colonel Hiram Clay Alleman as military governor of Gettysburg.[10]

Governor Curtin also understood that the state legislature had to do something about the conditions in Gettysburg. During the same visit, he named a military governor of Gettysburg and asked town officials what was needed from the state government. Unlike modern times, where a governor can declare an emergency and receive federal funds, Curtin would have to use state funds to help Gettysburg. The property damage to the town and casualties around Gettysburg were detrimental to the citizens' well-being, prompting the state legislature to allocate funds to help clean up and remove the dead and wounded from Gettysburg. The caveat to releasing the funds was that Pennsylvania would only pay for moving Pennsylvanians who died at Gettysburg. The Pennsylvania state legislature did not want to have to foot the bill for other states to collect their fallen. It would be up to the other states to send delegations to identify and remove bodies from Gettysburg on their own dime. The only other alternative concerning other states' dead would be to leave them where

David Wills. (National Archives)

they were currently buried. To assist other states, Governor Curtin tasked a lawyer from Gettysburg, David Wills, to be the state's point of contact with other state delegations.[11] The task before Wills would be to find a way to honor the Union dead scattered through Gettysburg and to address town sanitary concerns. Also included in his charge was working with other states to memorialize the dead in the most appropriate way possible. Wills started his work even before the Gettysburg campaign was over, and the enemy had still not crossed the Potomac back to Virginia.

Governor Curtin's naming of David Wills as the agent in Gettysburg was not made haphazardly. Wills was one of the town's prominent citizens who grew up not far from Gettysburg as a child. After college, Wills spent time in Alabama as a teacher, eventually moving back to Pennsylvania to work in the law office of Thaddeus Stevens, a prominent abolitionist. When Curtin visited Gettysburg after the battle, Wills acted in part as a tour guide and in part as a spokesman for the town to the governor. When Curtin decided that all Union dead should be moved together in one location, he immediately tapped Wills as his agent to the rest of the Union.

By July 16, 1863, representatives from several states had descended on Gettysburg for inquiries about the whereabouts of their dead Union soldiers. Unfortunately, the haphazard burying of the dead made the task of identifying specific soldiers daunting. Unless the burial detail placed an identification marker at a given site, it was impossible to identify soldiers without exhuming the bodies. The idea of disinterring bodies did not sit well with the townspeople of Gettysburg unless there was a plan to remove the bodies and put them in a central location. Several representatives began discussions about the best course of action. In a letter, New York representative Theodore Dimon stated, "The ground should be purchased near the Union line of battle on Cemetery Hill to facilitate a central burial place of the dead by all the states that wanted to contribute."[12]

Financially, a central cemetery for all was more manageable than incurring the cost of separately moving bodies back to individual states. David Wills became the spokesman for the rest of the state representatives in Gettysburg. He proposed to Governor Curtin that Pennsylvania should purchase ground on Cemetery Hill; that is, "on the Baltimore Turnpike opposite the cemetery where our army saw action. Pennsylvania should purchase the ground at once to furnish a place for the friends of those seeking permanent burial of their fallen loved ones and the hundreds dying in hospitals."[13] While purchasing land for a military cemetery seemed straightforward to Wills and Curtin, some townspeople had other ideas for a cemetery to honor the Union dead.

David McConaughy. (Adams County Historical Society, Gettysburg, PA)

Like David Wills, David McConaughy practiced law in Gettysburg and was a member of the Republican Party. However, McConaughy also had a hand in the battle of Gettysburg. During the Antietam campaign, McConaughy oversaw the Adams Rifles. The militia group, comprised of citizens from Adams County, acted as a scout and reconnaissance party that assisted Union forces working on the border between Pennsylvania and Maryland. In the last week of June 1863, McConaughy and his group determined the Confederate army's routes into southern Pennsylvania. The information was deemed credible enough for McConaughy to be mentioned in official reports.[14] When McConaughy was not scouting the enemy, he also chaired organizations in Gettysburg. One of these, Evergreen Cemetery, occupied the location of the planned National Cemetery. Like David Wills, McConaughy had designs for a soldiers' cemetery adjacent to the town's existing one.

In the year leading up to the fight at Gettysburg, McConaughy shared his idea in a newspaper article on June 24, 1862. The *Adams Sentinel* quoted McConaughy as saying that the land near Evergreen Cemetery is "an eligible site that should include a large marble statue in the center of the ground with interred remains of all the glorious dead who died in defense of the nation."[15] While Wills wanted to focus on building a cemetery to bury Union dead so they could be remembered collectively, McConaughy had grander ideas. McConaughy wanted to preserve and memorialize the battlefield and have a national cemetery blended with the existing civilian cemetery. The reason for this was simple: he already owned the town's prominent cemetery and wanted the national cemetery attached to it. However, Wills and Governor Curtin did not want to build an extension of Evergreen Cemetery. Another problem for Wills was McConaughy's reluctance to cooperate on land purchases around Cemetery Hill. His resistance jeopardized the plans for a national cemetery and monumentation at Gettysburg.

Infighting between Wills's group and McConaughy climaxed in August 1863. Due to the inability to acquire the land needed, other state agents began to back out of the deal with Pennsylvania and look for alternatives to deal with their military dead. David McConaughy would not sell the land next to Evergreen Cemetery, even with an increased offer from David Wills. Discussions between town leaders, state agents, Wills, and McConaughy eventually created a plan that gave everyone what they wanted. The plan created by compromising allowed the cemetery to come to fruition and kept personal egos intact. Governor Curtin asked both sides to come to an agreement that would keep the national cemetery in Gettysburg. The Evergreen Cemetery Association agreed to sell the disputed land on Cemetery Hill to the National Soldiers' Commission, stipulating that shared property lines would have an iron fence defining its borders and not a stone wall.[16] The board of Evergreen Cemetery concluded that visitors would see one continuous cemetery, not two divided parcels of land. With that agreed upon and the land purchased, David Wills tasked William Saunders, an employee of the Department of Agriculture, with designing the cemetery.

Saunders was one of the architects of Central Park in New York City. Saunders's design for the cemetery included continuous circles of gravesites that would radiate out from a central monument. With the design in place, Wills hired James Townsend as the Supervisor of Burials for the cemetery. Wills also hired Frank Biesecker to move Union bodies from their graves around Gettysburg to the new cemetery for $1.59 each.[17] There is no exact record of how many men were used to move the dead. However, it is estimated that at the peak of moving bodies, thirty to fifty men were in the employ of Biesecker to assist with moving bodies. The final burial team lead, Samuel Weaver, would document and catalog the bodies that Biesecker moved. The work of moving bodies began on October 26, 1863. Also during this time, David Wills prepared Gettysburg and the nation that was still at war for one of the first large-scale memorializations of Civil War dead.

By early fall 1863, the soldiers' cemetery had taken its physical form, and David Wills and Governor Curtin explored ways to dedicate the cemetery. Wills's first choice for a keynote speaker was Edward Everett, a popular orator at the time.[18] Both men focused on inviting individuals who helped make the cemetery a reality. Wills and other prominent Gettysburg citizens began inviting dignitaries from Pennsylvania and other states. Nearly as an afterthought to fill out the speaking list, Wills sent a letter to President Abraham Lincoln. Wills requested that Lincoln visit Gettysburg to deliver a few appropriate remarks during the ceremony.[19] The oversight was not that Wills or anyone else did not want the president at the ceremony; "... it was more our inference that he was still prosecuting the war." Lincoln agreed to speak at the dedication; however, he would give his address after Edward Everett at the November 19, 1863 ceremony.

Lincoln had much to keep him occupied with the war through the fall of 1863. In the east, the Union Army of the Potomac had pursued the Confederate Army of Northern Virginia into central Virginia. However, the Confederates could move faster than their counterparts, exposing the Union army to a possible flank attack. Due to its position, lack of supplies, and the need to send units elsewhere, the Army of the Potomac pulled back to Washington. To protect the withdrawal, a Union corps was left in the rear to stall a Confederate advance. On October 14, 1863, the Battle of Bristoe Station occurred between the Union II Corps and A. P. Hill's Corps of the Confederate army. The Army of the Potomac stymied the Confederate advance before needing to pull back to Washington due to the rest of the Confederate army moving forward. Bristoe Station would be the last significant engagement of the year between the armies in the east.

In the west, Union forces had been routed at the battle of Chickamauga in Georgia, and pulled back to take up defensive positions in Chattanooga, Tennessee. Confederate forces following the Union Army of the Cumberland to the city were able to lay siege and slowly cut off supplies. The goal of the Confederates was to force a surrender of the Union army and level the playing field in the region. However, support for the besieged Union forces came from General Ulysses Grant and his Army of the Tennessee. With the help of two Union corps dispatched from the Army of the Potomac, Grant ultimately lifted the siege, but the defeat of the Confederates would not occur until the end of November 1863.

Despite the precarious situation of the Union war effort that fall, President Lincoln agreed to come to Gettysburg for the cemetery's dedication ceremony. The trip and the remarks Lincoln would make at the ceremony solidified what the battle of Gettysburg meant to Union veterans and to the nation. Lincoln's visit to Gettysburg on November 18, 1863, was one of the rare times that he left Washington during the war. He occasionally traveled to the front lines to visit the Army of the Potomac, but he rarely wanted to be away from the War Department, where he could stay informed of all that transpired with the war.

People traveled to Gettysburg to witness the dedication ceremonies even while the war was raging. News accounts reported that the crowds were so large that people occupied every available spot on the principal streets of the town. The ceremonies started with a procession from the main square to the cemetery south of town on the Baltimore Pike, nearly a mile away. The town constructed an elevated platform for the dignitaries and the speakers to sit. Edward Everett took the stage after an opening prayer and an arrangement of music played for the crowd.

Everett spoke for nearly two hours, comparing Gettysburg to other famous battles in history. He lamented the secession of the Southern states and proclaimed that the men buried in the cemetery were martyrs against treason.[20] The crowd expected Lincoln to speak briefly, and the president did not disappoint with an address of only 270 words. President Lincoln described the battle of Gettysburg and the men buried in the cemetery within the context of the war by stating:

> Four score and seven years ago our fathers brought forth on this continent a new nation, conceived in liberty, and dedicated to the proposition that all men are created equal. Now we are engaged in a great civil war, testing whether that nation, or any nation so conceived and so dedicated, can long endure. We are met on a great battlefield of that war. We have come to dedicate a portion of that field as a final resting place for those who here gave their lives that that nation might live. It is altogether fitting and proper that we should do this. But in a larger sense we cannot dedicate, we cannot consecrate, we cannot hallow this ground. The brave men, living and dead, who struggled here have consecrated it, far above our poor power to add or detract. The world will little note, nor long remember, what we say here, but it can never forget what they did here. It is for us the living, rather, to be dedicated here to the unfinished work which they who fought here have thus far so nobly advanced. It is rather for us to be here dedicated to the great task remaining before us that from these honored dead we take increased devotion to that cause for which they gave the last full measure of devotion, that we here highly resolve that these dead shall not have died in vain, that this nation, under God, shall have a new birth of freedom, and that government of the people, by the people, for the people, shall not perish from the earth.[21]

When the president finished his address, he returned to Washington to continue the business of conducting the war. Lincoln's description of the battle and the

Four score and seven years ago our fathers brought forth on this continent, a new nation, conceived in Liberty, and dedicated to the proposition that all men are created equal.

Now we are engaged in a great civil war, testing whether that nation, or any nation so conceived and so dedicated, can long endure. We are met on a great battle-field of that war. We have come to dedicate a portion of that field, as a final resting place for those who here gave their lives, that that nation might live. It is altogether fitting and proper that we should do this.

But, in a larger sense, we can not dedicate— we can not consecrate— we can not hallow— this ground. The brave men, living and dead, who struggled here, have consecrated it, far above our poor power to add or detract. The world will little note, nor long remember what we say here, but it can never forget what they did here. It is for us the living, rather, to be dedicated here to the unfinished work which they who fought here have thus far so nobly advanced. It is rather for us to be here dedicated to the great task remaining before us— that from these honored dead we take increased devotion to that cause for which they gave the last full measure of devotion— that we here highly resolve that these dead shall not have died in vain— that this nation, under God, shall have a new birth of freedom— and that government of the people, by the people, for the people, shall not perish from the earth.

Executive Mansion,
Washington

November 19. 1863.

Abraham Lincoln.

Gettysburg Address (Bliss Copy). (National Archives)

sacrifices of the Union dead would serve as a guidepost for Union monuments and dedication speeches for the next 50 years.

While burials continued after the dedication and into early 1864, David Wills continued to work on the centerpiece of the cemetery. From April to June 1864, members of the National Cemetery Committee met to decide on a design for the Soldiers' National Monument. Designs had to appeal to the eye and work within the confines of William Saunders's recommendations. The monument should fit with the surroundings and not be ostentatious, while being grand enough for the subject it was to honor.[22] After considering several options, the committee selected a design by James Batterson. Batterson owned the New England Granite Works in Hartford, Connecticut, and was also president of the Travelers Insurance Company, which he founded in June 1863. The team building the Soldiers' Monument consisted of sculptor Randolph Rogers and architect George Keller.

Batterson's design centered around a granite pedestal with a sculpture depicting liberty. Surrounding the 60-foot-tall centerpiece at the base were statues and aspects of the war effort. The allegorical statues related to one another in the story of the battle of Gettysburg.[23] Randolph Rogers was picked as the lead sculptor due to his realism in creating life-like faces. One of Rogers's previous works, a Biblical statue called *Ruth Gleaning*, helped secure a commission for sculpting the bronze doors for the rotunda at the United States Capitol. To fulfill Rogers's designs, Batterson used one of the architects from his stonework's business, George Keller. David Wills had already secured funding for the monument by December 1863, with construction commencing by spring 1865. The architect would use the opportunity at Gettysburg to expand his resume, eventually creating several veterans monuments in New England after the Civil War. Like the cemetery where the monument would stand, funding was provided by private donations and appropriations from state governments. Before the monument was completed, the Civil War had come to an end, and the president was dead from an assassin's bullet. The man who had delivered one of the most famous speeches in American history to dedicate the ceremony never saw its final completion.

Union monumentation officially began at Gettysburg on July 4, 1865. When Lincoln came to Gettysburg in November 1863, tens of thousands had witnessed his dedication to the cemetery. An equal number of onlookers came to the cornerstone laying of the Soldiers' Monument. President Andrew Johnson declined an invitation to the ceremony, stating in a letter to David Wills, "I should have been pleased standing on the twice consecrated spot to share with you your joy at the return of peace."[24] Many in the crowd were

The Soldiers' National Monument, Gettysburg National Cemetery.

veterans of the battle. General Oliver O. Howard, who commanded the XI Corps at Gettysburg, was present to give an oration.[25] His remarks, similar in style to Everett and Lincoln two years earlier, described Howard's feelings about the country through his wartime experiences. He spoke of the monument as dedicated "to the soldier, embracing a patriotic brotherhood of heroes in its inscriptions and as an unceasing herald of labor, suffering, Union, liberty, and sacrifice."[26] Four statues on the monument's base represented war, history, peace, and plenty. On top of the 60-foot marble, the designers planned to mount a central sculpture depicting Liberty. Each statue depicted a Civil War soldier or civilian dressed in clothing styles appropriate for the monument's theme. The monument was completed over the next four years with few changes from the original design.

Dedication of the completed monument took place in July 1869. Once again, thousands of people crowded the cemetery and town to witness the

The Soldiers' National Monument—War, Gettysburg National Cemetery, Gettysburg National Military Park.

The Soldiers' National Monument—History, Gettysburg National Cemetery, Gettysburg National Military Park.

event. General George Meade, the commander of the Army of the Potomac at Gettysburg, was present and gave a short address. General Meade remarked that the creation of the monument and cemetery should be copied on other battlefields to honor the dead.[27] Another speech presented at the dedication was by Senator Oliver Morton, Governor of Indiana during the Civil War. Morton explained in his speech that many Union men died during the Civil War and at Gettysburg due to slavery. Morton pronounced that "the rebellion was madness; the people of the South were drunk with the spoils of the labor of four million enslaved people."[28] Morton's comments mark one of the first recorded instances when slavery was the theme of a dedication speech for a Civil War monument. While the central monument of the National Cemetery was the first such memorial dedication, several other monuments would be dedicated in the four years it took to complete the Soldiers' Monument.

The Soldiers' National Monument—Plenty, Gettysburg National Cemetery, Gettysburg National Military Park.

The Soldiers' National Monument—Peace, Gettysburg National Cemetery, Gettysburg National Military Park.

The Soldiers' National Monument—Liberty, Gettysburg National Cemetery, Gettysburg National Military Park.

Modern Soldiers' National Monument visitors can approach it from two different directions. The first is from the direction nearly everyone at the monument's dedication approached—through the gatehouse and past the circular planted graves. The second direction is from the back of the National Cemetery, where the parking lot is located. Regardless of the approach, visitors cannot miss the monument. It stands in the direct center of the cemetery, with graves radiating out from its base along the ground. In each of the four statues below, Liberty looks directly down over the final resting place of the Union soldiers buried there.

While the individual statues look down over the graves, the statue depicting Liberty looks toward the battlefield and keeps her gaze upon where the soldiers fell. While there is no evidence of this effect being purposefully designed by the sculptors or builders, it is very clear to see the sight lines of the figures, drawing visitors to look at what the statues are looking at. The figures look out at the cemetery as a subtle nod to appreciate the sacrifice of the Union dead. The monument is also one of the tallest on the battlefield. The large column can be seen from any approach to the cemetery, and it acts as a directional aid for anyone walking by. Due to the design and the growth of nearby trees, the rest of the monument is obscured until you pass through the cemetery's gates. The plan of the cemetery has been achieved in that even today it can be seen that it provides a peaceful final resting place for the thousands of Union soldiers buried there.

As the Soldiers' National Monument began taking shape, the first individual unit memorial was built in the cemetery by members of the 1st Minnesota Infantry, who wanted to commemorate the loss of their fallen in the battle. The regiment's survivors decided to place their memorial near the Minnesota section of the cemetery. The monument is urn-shaped, consisting of white marble, a pedestal, and a square base.[29] It is inscribed, "The surviving members of the 1st Minnesota Infantry Regiment, to the memory of their late associates, who died on the field of honor at Gettysburg 1863." The 1st Minnesota entered combat at Gettysburg with 269 officers and men on July 2, 1863. By the end of the day, 224 were killed, wounded, or captured.[30] While the survivors of the 1st Minnesota created a memorial for their dead within a few years of the Civil War's ending, they would not dedicate a monument to their actions in the battle for another 30 years.

When looking at the memorial urn, it almost seems out of place compared to the other gravestones in the cemetery. Nearly all graves are simple markers buried flush with the ground and grouped by state. However, as you look across the ground and get to the Minnesota section, you will see the flush graves on

Memorial Urn to the 1st Minnesota, Gettysburg National Cemetery, Gettysburg National Military Park.

the ground around the urn. The contrast of a tall object amongst the otherwise flat ground draws your immediate attention to the urn. While the design is simple, the large urn symbolizes the unit's collective loss during the battle.

Another interesting aspect of the placement of the urn is that it is the only one of its type in the cemetery. The 1st Minnesota was one regiment out of the hundreds that fought with the Army of the Potomac at Gettysburg. However, it was the only one from Minnesota, and was one of the first regiments to form when President Lincoln asked for volunteers from the states in 1861. Due to these factors, the 1st Minnesota is the only regiment with a specific memorial to its dead within the confines of the cemetery. This does not mean that no other monuments are located within the cemetery. As we work through the monumentation periods at Gettysburg, it is evident that monuments were placed on battle lines through different parts of the cemetery due to their tactical positions. However, the 1st Minnesota Memorial Urn is the only monument in the cemetery that was placed to honor the dead.

The ability of the 1st Minnesota and other Union regiments to build monuments at Gettysburg began to take shape in 1864. Fresh off his inability to secure the National Cemetery under local control, David McConaughy began his second attempt at battlefield memorialization. While David Wills developed the final stages of the cemetery, McConaughy expanded his ownership of Union battle lines around Gettysburg beyond the land around Cemetery Hill. McConaughy had purchased land around:

> … the Granite Spur of Round-top, on our left [some 30 acres] the position held by our Pennsylvania Reserves, with the wonderful stone defences constructed by them, & which shall remain undisturbed, as their monument of their heroic labors & valor. I am also in successful negotiation for about the exact extent of Wolf Hill [Culp's Hill], on our right, embracing the extensive timber breastworks & the equally wonderful exhibition of the withering effects of our musketry fire.[31]

The property McConaughy purchased in 1863 consisted of the Union army's left flank (the Round Tops) and right flank (Culp's Hill) during the battle of Gettysburg. McConaughy's goal with these land purchases was to keep these parts of the battlefield "in their actual form and condition, [as] the most eloquent memorials of their glorious struggles and triumphs."[32] Even though McConaughy lost the fight to control the National Cemetery on Cemetery Hill, he began preserving land on which Union veterans would build numerous monuments to their units' actions.

As the Civil War continued into 1864, McConaughy created the Gettysburg Battlefield Memorial Association (GBMA). The association was incorporated in April 1864 by the Pennsylvania State Legislature. The

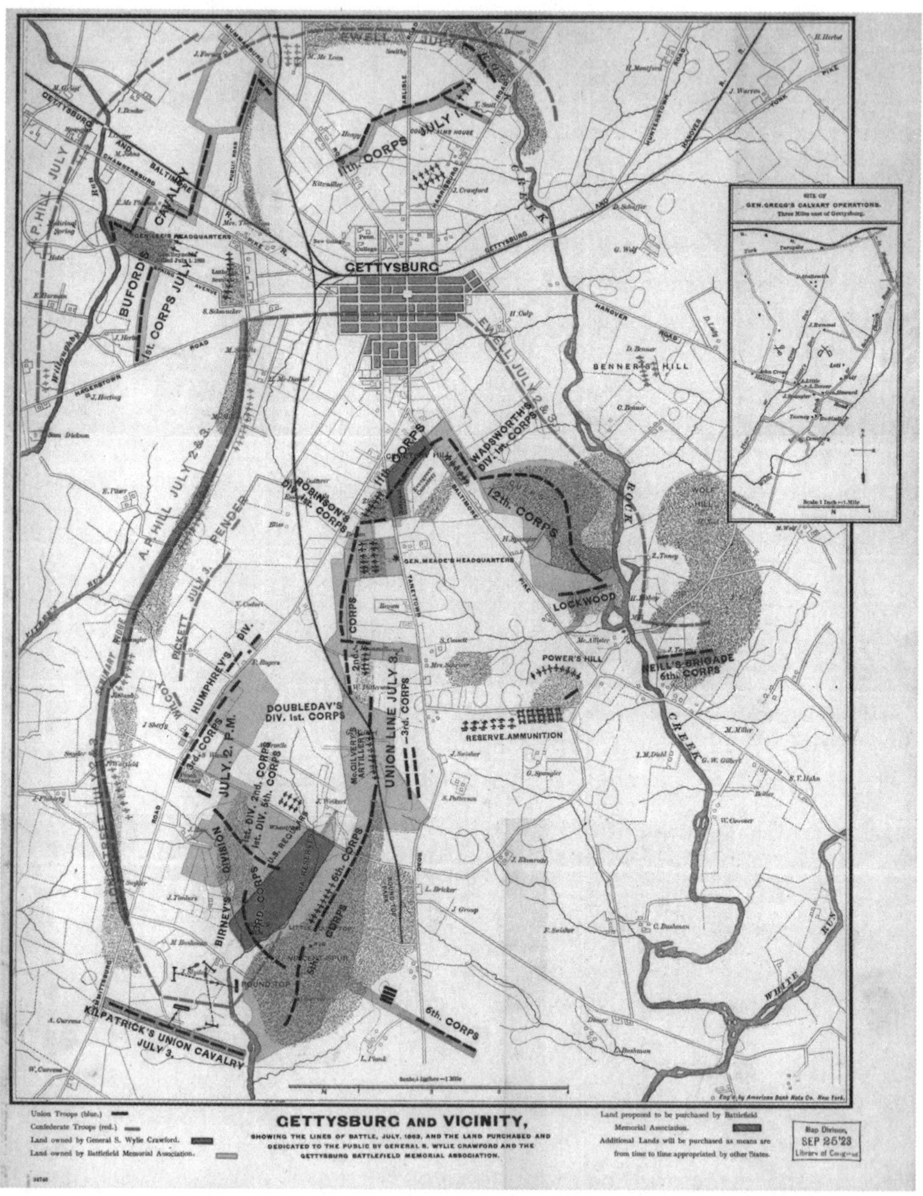

Map of Gettysburg Battlefield Memorial Association Holdings. (Gettysburg National Military Park Archives)

overall goal of the GBMA was to "… hold and preserve, the battle-grounds of Gettysburg with the natural defences, as they were at the time of said battle … to commemorate the heroic deeds, the struggles, and the triumphs of their brave defenders."[33] The initial plots of land preserved by the GBMA at its inception were the only work the association did until 1867. The principal reason for this was the reality of the war still being fought. The spring of 1864 saw the battles of the Wilderness, Spotsylvania Courthouse, and Cold Harbor. Each battle pushed the Confederates back toward Richmond, the Confederate capital. By the summer of 1864, the Union and Confederate armies were locked in siege positions around Petersburg, Virginia. The focus of the GBMA on the "defenders" at Gettysburg (the Army of the Potomac) would be the organization's sole focus until it ceded the battlefield to the War Department in 1895. Three thousand dollars were allocated for the battleground portions around the Union lines. The GBMA did not look to purchase land again until 1866 with the help of the Pennsylvania Legislature.[34] The same amount was again allocated in 1868 to expand GMBA holdings through the battlefield.

As 1869 ended, the GBMA had purchased several tracts of land that comprised the Union line at Gettysburg. Purchases included land near lower Culp's Hill where the Army of the Potomac had built breastworks, Union artillery positions on East Cemetery Hill, and the area leading up to the summit of Little Round Top.[35] These purchases of land were supplemented by the personal purchases made by David McConaughy and the purchase of the battle lines around Steven's Knoll (later known as Barlow's Knoll) north of the town. However, the GBMA did not build monuments on purchased land. One of the reasons for this was the plan then in place for the battlefield. David McConaughy intended the battlefield itself to be the monument, with its natural and artificial defenses preserved, and left in the same form and condition as during the fighting.[36]

As part of its stewardship, the GBMA created a place where Union veterans could come and visit where they fought. The association also created rules and regulations for battlefield preservation that would set the standard for later sites:

> [T]he president and directors of the said Gettysburg Battle-field Memorial Association shall have power and authority, by themselves, committees, engineer, surveyor, superintendent, or agents, by them to be appointed, to survey, locate, and lay out roads and avenues from any public road or roads in the vicinity of Gettysburg, or of the said battle-grounds, to and upon, and also in and through, any portion or portions of said battlegrounds, not, however, passing through any dwelling-house, or any burying-ground, or any place of public worship, and to open and fence, or otherwise enclose, such roads and avenues, the latter of a width not exceeding three hundred feet; and the same may be laid out so as to embrace any breastworks, or lines of defences, or positions of the forces engaged in the battle of Gettysburg, and with power to plant rows or colonnades of trees upon said roads and avenues.[37]

However, the association's goal was not to build monuments but to preserve the land as if soldiers were still fighting in the fields. As Union veterans began to get involved in the GBMA and other memorial associations after the war, the GBMA changed its policies on how Gettysburg would be memorialized.

The GBMA's first attempt at memorialization was through planning a reunion in August 1869, and Union commanders from the battle were sent invitations. One of the goals of the reunion was to help the GBMA identify essential events of the battle and unit locations so that granite markers could identify them on the field. By placing these markers, the battlefield would become its own tour guide. In a surprise move, the GBMA invited Robert E. Lee, commander of the Confederate army at Gettysburg. However, Lee declined his invitation, stating that he had nothing to add to what was already in the Official Reports, and so as "not to keep open the sores of war but to follow the examples of those nations who endeavored to obliterate the marks of civil strife."[38]

Although several Union commanders declined to attend due to scheduling conflicts, the reunion took place on August 23, 1869, and included dozens of former Union officers. Over the last week of August 1869, participants walked the battlefield, identifying unit locations and points of engagement with the enemy. The reunion helped the GBMA to determine where battle lines had been formed and to map out unit locations. The information compiled at the reunion, as well as discussions with battle participants via correspondence, would become the foundation of the monumentation period at Gettysburg.

The August 1869 meeting would also trigger strong feelings among Union veterans. Many veterans felt they had too short a time with their old comrades, but all agreed that marking their accomplishments should be a priority at Gettysburg.[39] Even though veterans wanted more reunions, there would not be another gathering until the 1880s. The organization's charter focused on preserving battlefield land for future generations, including marking battle lines. It would be up to veterans to organize and run reunions that would be large in scope, usually meaning inviting everyone who was known to be alive at the time.

One reason for the initial lack of markers and infrastructure on the Gettysburg battlefield was the lack of funding. Nearly all the funds for the GBMA came from local citizens buying shares in the association or donating money. The GBMA membership voted to solicit contributions from other states to increase its national appeal.[40]

However, interest in the battlefield waned considerably during the 1870s. The GBMA's plan to sell shares of the association to other states did not gain the traction needed to maintain the battlefield. The public's lack of interest in Gettysburg and other Civil War battlefields was common during the era.

One reason was the difficulty of traveling to Gettysburg, which required changing trains several times and passing along unimproved roads. Coupled with most of the country recovering economically from the Civil War and moving forward with Reconstruction, battlefield visits and remembrances were not as important then as the United States recovered economically from the war. As in the modern day, events, however tragic, lose their importance as future generations move forward with their lives. Helping the South rebuild and grow economically was of greater importance than visiting battlefields. However, Union veterans still made a point to discuss the importance of the Civil War and Gettysburg. Conflicting views from civilians and veterans on contextualizing what the Civil War did to the country would be debated during the 1870s and 1880s.

Civilians wanted to return to normalcy after the Civil War ended. The country's cultural, social, and economic fabric had changed during Reconstruction. Many veterans also faced the challenge of reacclimating themselves to the civilian world, facing the same issues that plague veterans of today's wars. They had learned different skills and seen things that most civilians had not, changing their outlook on the world and its priorities. Union veterans' combat experiences also resulted in different opinions on dealing with conflict and the consequences of violence. These conflicting views would play a part in national politics and how veterans would see Gettysburg once they decided they wanted to memorialize their experiences on the battlefield.

CHAPTER 2

Politics and Early Attempts at Monumentation, 1878–86

The end of the 1870s changed how the Gettysburg Battlefield Memorial Association would define monumentation on the battlefield. While the association still focused on preservation, restrictions were loosened for the placement of individual unit monuments. This change allowed regimental associations to place monuments where they fought on the field. While the reason for building monuments would vary among units, including individual unit monuments during this period at Gettysburg would be a first for any Civil War battlefield in the country.

One of the chief complaints during Reconstruction from Union veterans concerned the quality of medical treatment they received. When elections were held, Republicans used the sacrifices of veterans during the war for political gain. However, these same Republicans dragged their feet in providing aid to wounded and homeless Union veterans. On the other hand, Democrats, based largely in the South, would not address Union veterans' medical issues because the party believed they needed to move past the Civil War and its effect on the country. In the modern era, multiple private organizations, in addition to the Department of Veterans Affairs at the federal level, provide aid for veterans' needs. However, during the Civil War, infrastructure for assistance was barely passable and hardly existed after the war ended. One of the groups that assisted wounded Northern veterans during the Civil War was the United States Sanitary Commission.[1] The organization operated on private funds, but its orders came from the War Department. However, the work provided by the commission was not intended to assist with care indefinitely. The government abandoned the commission in May 1866,[2] leaving many veterans in limbo for support and care. The feeling of abandonment by Union veterans was exacerbated by the public's growing willingness to leave the war in the past and embrace the future.

Location of monuments 1878–86. (Created using ArcGIS Pro by Esri)

During Reconstruction, civilians were already moving past the emotional effects of what four years of war had done to their daily lives. The most brutally affected were veterans who were wounded to the extent that they could not work or care for themselves or their families. Many of these veterans were cast aside by society. Veterans who came home from front-line duty found their prewar jobs filled by others. They had low employment prospects, and experienced difficulties learning how to reassimilate into civilian life. Nevertheless, veterans could apply for pensions from the federal government to ease their financial hardships. Nearly 85 percent of all Union veterans or their families applied for pensions after the war ended. The process was arduous, however, and required a vote by Congress on a case-by-case basis. By the 1870s, if approved, a Union veteran could receive $20 to $32 monthly from the federal government.[3] However, veterans had to wait and hope their pensions would be approved. At the peak of pension approval in the early 1900s, almost one million Union veterans or their families had received some sort of assistance from the government.

The destructive nature of the Civil War touched the entire country, and after so many years of conflict, moving on seemed to be the best medicine for healing wounds. Remembrance parades and building monuments to honor the sacrifices of veterans during the war would only keep the tensions alive. However, this forgetting came at a cost. Over time, the alienation of veterans, especially in the North, inspired a new movement to organize and advance the interests of veterans. One such organization took the lead in shaping the monumentation era at Gettysburg.

The largest Union veteran organization that would form during Reconstruction and be a driving force for veteran issues in the United States was the Grand Army of the Republic (GAR). The GAR was founded in April 1866 in Springfield, Illinois, by Dr. Benjamin Stephenson, a former Union army surgeon assigned to the 14th Illinois Infantry. The organization's goal was to provide Union veterans with a place to share their wartime experiences and to provide a voice for veteran affairs.[4] The GAR rallied veteran voters in the presidential election of 1868 to help carry Ulysses S. Grant to the presidency. The GAR also contributed financial support to Grant's campaign. Many GAR members who were active politically found support from fellow members, and this ability to support campaigns solidified the GAR's position as a power broker in local and national politics.

The first requirement of membership in the GAR was service in the Union army or navy during the Civil War. Anyone who served faithfully and secured an honorable discharge could apply for membership.[5] The GAR was organized on different geographical levels throughout the United States. At the local level, meetings of members occurred at posts. Typically, posts were assigned a number named after a Union soldier who died in battle and who the post members wanted to memorialize. Forming a new post required a minimum of ten veterans who would conduct business and pay dues.[6] The next highest level of organization was a department with at least ten local posts, and, finally, the national encampment, or headquarters. Each level of the organization provided support for the next. GAR members looked out for one another and supported families who had lost loved ones during the war or who passed after the war ended. While the national headquarters lobbied for the political interests of its members, local posts and departments focused on the immediate needs of veterans in their communities. Due to steady movement of the population west, the GAR spread across the United States, most of its posts were based east of the Mississippi River. States with higher population densities of Union veterans naturally tended to have more posts.

Pennsylvania and New York were the two states with the highest number of GAR posts. Members throughout both states focused on supporting local charities and helping veterans. GAR posts brought attention to their organization by hosting parades and remembrances on important dates related to the Civil War. Due to its proximity, Gettysburg was a frequent location for Pennsylvania GAR posts to visit and reminisce. However, the discussion of Gettysburg was also a national topic because it was the only major battle of the Civil War fought on Northern soil, and the Union victory there had saved Harrisburg and Philadelphia from possible destruction. It was also the first time the Army of the Potomac had soundly defeated the Army of Northern Virginia. The individual GAR post visits to the battlefield reminded veterans of the good times that they had with their fellow soldiers during the war. Eventually, several posts would want to come together on the battlefield. These visits built camaraderie between other local and state departments. When GAR posts came together, the visits were called an "encampment." Encampments were open to any GAR member in the United States, providing a venue for Union veterans to fraternize and reminisce. One of the first encampments occurred at Gettysburg in July of 1878.[7] This would provide the setting for dedicating the first two monuments on the battlefield outside the National Cemetery.

The oldest Union monument on the battlefield at Gettysburg was not to honor a unit but a fallen commander. Colonel Strong Vincent, a resident of Erie, Pennsylvania, commanded a brigade in the 1st Division of the V Corps of the

Colonel Strong Vincent. (Library of Congress)

Army of the Potomac at Gettysburg.[8] On July 2, 1863, Vincent, with his brigade, was moving toward the Union front line at Gettysburg when a staff officer passed looking for troops to rush to the far-left flank where Confederate soldiers were approaching. On his own initiative, Vincent asked the staff officer where his men needed to deploy and moved his brigade into position on Little Round Top just minutes before Rebels from General John Bell Hood's division began attacking up the hill.[9] One of the regiments under Vincent's command was the 20th Maine, which would receive tremendous distinction for its job on July 2. During the ferocious fight to hold the hill, Vincent received a mortal wound.[10] The fallen brigade commander remained on the field with his men until the evening of July 2, when he was moved to a field hospital.

By the evening of July 2, 1863, Vincent's brigade had stopped the Confederate advance on the left flank of the Army of the Potomac. The brigade, which included the 83rd Pennsylvania Infantry, 16th Michigan Infantry, 44th New York Infantry, and 20th Maine Infantry, went into battle with around 1,300 men ready for combat. The casualty count for the brigade (killed, wounded, and missing) was 336.[11] Vincent lingered for several days until July 7, 1863, when he died from his wounds at the age of 26. General George Meade, commander of the Army of the Potomac, promoted Vincent from Colonel to Brigadier General for his action on Little Round Top. Shortly after the battle, a general order to commemorate the passing of Vincent circulated through the brigade. The written order described him as "a soldier, a scholar, and a friend who is an example of fidelity and patriotism."[12] Vincent's sacrifice on Little Round Top would lead to his official memorialization by survivors of his command in 1878, but, mysteriously, it wasn't the first dedicated to Vincent.

In the fall of 1864, a newspaper writer from Erie, Pennsylvania, Issac Moorhead, visited the battlefield. While visiting Little Round Top, Moorhead

Vincent's Rock on Little Round Top, Gettysburg National Military Park.

found a stone etched with an inscription that supposedly marked the spot where Strong Vincent was wounded. The rock, now known as Vincent's Rock, is inscribed with "Col. Strong Vincent fell here/Com 3rd Brig. 1st Div. 5th Corps/July 2nd, 1863."[13] The inscription is unique because the letter "s" in both the division and corps identification are etched backward.

Moorhead's guide during his visit to Gettysburg was local farmer John Frey. The guide surmised that a sharpshooter could have killed Vincent, firing from around a clump of rocks near the bottom of Little Round Top called Devil's Den. Frey went so far as to show Moorhead a shallow grave of a dead Confederate soldier in the spot where a firing position was.[14] However, none of the official accounts or personal recollections of soldiers verify John Frey's account. The placement of the rock inscription is also in dispute because there is no record of someone taking credit for making the inscription. When the local Erie, Pennsylvania GAR Post visited Little Round Top to decide where they would place the tablet for Vincent, they found the inscribed stone already present near Vincent's wounding site. All in attendance from the GAR post could not recollect who inscribed the stone.

As GAR members gathered in Gettysburg for the 1878 encampment, they stayed near the Union lines during the battle. The encampment occurred between July 20 and July 27, 1878, with most official festivities near the National Cemetery and East Cemetery Hill.[15] Most accounts attest to several thousand veterans and their families attending the encampment. Most of

Vincent Wound Site Marker near the saddle of Little Round Top, Gettysburg National Military Park.

the time was spent reminiscing with old comrades and visiting sites on the battlefield. Leisure activities and "camp sports" were also provided for the veterans to pass the time. Due to their proximity to Gettysburg, veterans visited other battlefields like Antietam and Harpers Ferry.

In the middle of the 1878 encampment, members of the Strong Vincent GAR Post No. 67 dedicated a monument to their namesake, on ground the GBMA controlled and selected. The organization approved the monument, even though the organization at the time did not have a formal monument policy. The ceremony included details of the fight on Little Round Top provided by Captain John Graham of the 83rd Pennsylvania and songs sung by George Arbuckle, another Union veteran.[16] The GAR post placed the monument where Vincent had rested behind his brigade's front line after being wounded. While some men in attendance felt that the monument's placement identified Vincent's wound site, more veterans agreed that the spot was where he received medical attention.[17] The monument provides an example of how future dedications of Union monuments would happen at Gettysburg, and how personal recollections often differed from official accounts.

The monument was dedicated on July 25, 1878, and is a funerary type. The marble slab includes a V Corps Maltese Cross with the inscription "Third Brigade, First Division, Fifth Corps/General Strong Vincent/Wounded July 2. Died July 7, 1863." The importance of where the monument was dedicated would continue to be contentious among veterans. Many 83rd Pennsylvania veterans would be the most vocal about the proper placement of the monument. Veterans of the 83rd felt reverence for Vincent because he was their commander before taking command of the brigade. Many veterans, after the dedication, felt that the monument should have been near Vincent's Rock. Veterans felt that this location would show future visitors where their commander was taking fire, fixing the brigade's lines during the Confederate attack.[18] Veterans conflicting with one another about where an event happened during battle would be a continual problem during the monumentation period at Gettysburg.

The distance between the two markers is about four hundred feet. While by today's standards, it may not seem to be an issue, for the men who served under Vincent and watched him get mortally wounded, marking the exact spot where it happened was very important for all involved. While age and fogging memories may not have pinpointed the exact location, it is poignant that the effort was made. Walking between both points on Little Round Top is not as daunting today as on July 2, 1863. Recently updated paths installed by the National Park Service provide a clear trail between these areas of the hill.

Having visited both sites before these trails were updated, I found that walking to Vincent's Rock was not very hard. However, finding the nondescript rock was another matter. It is located amongst the many various rocks at Little Round Top. Sometimes, individuals fill in the inscription with dirt or chalk, making it easier for passersby to find and read. However, if no one has filled in the inscription or precipitation has washed over it, the weathered rock blends in with the rest, making it hard to find. Visiting the Vincent wound marker required walking behind the trees of the 83rd Pennsylvania Regiment. While these markers provide two locations where Colonel Vincent was mortally wounded, what cannot be disputed was Vincent's achievement in placing his troops just in time to avert a severe threat to the Union line.

The conflict between veterans about where events occurred on the battlefield plagued another monument placed during the 1878 GAR Encampment at Gettysburg, and this time the scrutiny resulted in a monument's relocation. Similar to the Vincent GAR Post, the Colonel Taylor Post No. 19 dedicated a tablet to its namesake, Colonel Charles F. Taylor, who commanded the 13th Pennsylvania Reserve Infantry at the battle. The 13th Pennsylvania was assigned to the 1st Brigade, Pennsylvania Reserve Division, of the V Corps and was nicknamed the "Bucktails" due to the tail of a male deer that the men wore in their caps. Taylor was promoted from captain to colonel in March 1863, at age 23. He had seen combat prior to Gettysburg, including being wounded at Fredericksburg and paroled as a prisoner of war in 1862.

The Pennsylvania Reserves were assigned near Washington before the Gettysburg campaign. The Rebel invasion of the North prompted Taylor's unit and the rest of the division to shift away from the capital's defense and move into Maryland to join the V Corps and the Army of the Potomac. Taylor wrote to his sister before the march, stating, "We have at last orders to prepare to move at a moment's notice … I presume we will have a stirring campaign."[19] The regiment arrived at Gettysburg on July 2 and moved to support the left flank of the Union line near the Round Tops. Taylor and the 13th Pennsylvania were positioned off Little Round Top, toward the area called the Valley of Death. The valley is between the Round Tops and Houck's Ridge, which connected to the Wheatfield. Late in the afternoon of July 2, Taylor's regiment and the rest of the brigade were ordered forward into battle.

Fighting for Rose's Wheatfield, or simply "the Wheatfield" at Gettysburg on July 2 led to the change of possession between both armies throughout the day. Taylor, the 13th Pennsylvania Reserves, and the rest of their brigade moved forward to support the Union artillery batteries in the Wheatfield. At first contact, the attack was going well for the Northern units. The Pennsylvania Reserves gained "the enemies flank, dashed upon the enemy, who, endeavoring for a moment to make a stand, finally broke across the field."[20] When the Confederates turned to fight again, the 13th Pennsylvania lost its commander. A family friend, Corporal Aaron Barker, wrote an account to Taylor's family, stating, "… he was urging his men forward, and the last words he spoke before he fell was to a Rebel regiment not fifty yards in front of us. He called on them to halt and surrender …"[21] The Rebel units did not surrender; they opened fire, killing several men instantly, including Colonel Charles Taylor.

After the Confederate counterattack, the 13th Pennsylvania regained its composure and continued to fight. The regiment's total casualties at Gettysburg were 48 out of 301 engaged.[22] Fifteen years later, the regiment's survivors wanted to place a tablet where they thought Colonel Taylor had died. There is no evidence to show if the Taylor GAR Post obtained permission from the GBMA to place the monument. While this would be a large issue in later years with the GBMA, it was not in this case. Going over records within the park archives, the placement of this monument falls within the realm of asking for forgiveness later if the veterans association did something wrong. A major contributing factor as to why the GBMA did not block the placement of the monument was because it was within the original battle line of the regiment.

The tablet dedicated at Gettysburg contained a single inscription that looked more like a headstone. The inscription was straightforward and said, "Here fell Colonel Fred. Taylor/Commanding First Pennsylvania Reserves."[23] The tablet's placement is in the line of march of the 13th Reserves as they approached the Wheatfield. However, the tablet's placement occurred where the march started near Houck's Ridge and not where Taylor died on July 2. Contemporary accounts of the unit's actions and other eyewitness accounts placed Taylor's death site closer to the Wheatfield on the edge of Rose's Woods. There were also two other errors in the tablet. The first is that the stone stated Taylor's first name was Fred when his first name was Charles. The second error is that Taylor was in command of the 13th Regiment, not the entire 1st Brigade of the Pennsylvania Reserves. While the importance of Taylor's death is evident in veterans wanting to mark their commander's death, accuracy in properly identifying his name and which unit he commanded is lacking. Placing the tablet with the wrong information and location would not be addressed for nearly thirty years.

In 1905, a group from the 13th Pennsylvania Reserves Veterans Association created a new monument for Colonel Taylor. The monument would be a funerary monument that included Taylor's personal information and details about his command at Gettysburg. The new monument would reside near the 13th Pennsylvania's monument dedicated by the state of Pennsylvania in 1890. The "new" Colonel Taylor monument dedication occurred on October 6, 1905, with 26 survivors of the regiment and other family members in attendance.[24] The monument is made of granite and engraved on one side is a hat with a bucktail sticking out the side. The primary text inscription on the

Colonel Charles Frederick Taylor's death monument at the Wheatfield, Gettysburg National Military Park.

tablet reads, "Here fell/Charles Frederick Taylor/July 2, 1863/Age 23 Years 4 Months 26 Days/Colonel of the 'Bucktails.'"

The 1905 dedication speech was by Colonel Edward Irwin, a friend of Taylor's during the Civil War. Irwin ended his dedication by stating, "This stone is but a slight testimonial from his surviving comrades … and will tell those of after years the whole story of a young life given for his country and its flag."[25] With the new monument, the Veterans Association had to decide what to do with the old memorial tablet. The association decided to remove the flawed original marker from 1878.[26] The Colonel Taylor monument is another example of Union veterans coming to Gettysburg and using their collective recollections to place a monument to their fallen leader.

The dedication speech for Taylor's monument exemplifies what Union veterans wanted from their monuments. They wished for later generations to understand why they fought and the importance of their sacrifice on the battlefield. Another theme of the early monuments describes personal sacrifice for the United States. All speeches and remembrances for General Vincent and Colonel Taylor focused on their personal beliefs and what they were willing to give for their country. In these monuments on the battlefield, Union veterans focused on commemorating the fallen by marking where they were wounded. Raising money for a monument to single out an individual over the group was a sign of respect during the era. The focus was on the sacrifice of the individual and not the group.

Today, Taylor's monument is barely visible from the road that winds through the Wheatfield. Due to the complexities of the fight for the area, monuments are scattered throughout the landscape. While these monuments depict where a regiment fought, they do not necessarily mean that all the regiments fought there simultaneously. Taylor's death monument is surrounded by all of this but near some grass overgrowth that can almost make the monument disappear at times. While this may not have been the exact condition of the land when survivors of the regiment dedicated the monument, it does bring peacefulness and tranquility to the spot. The land almost acts like a shade for the fallen commander.

What I find interesting about this monument is that, like the few we have discussed in the last two chapters, it is yet it does plenty to captivate you with its information. The marker feels more like a tombstone than a monument. The reason for this is the language on the memorial. It captures Taylor's death and some biographical information, like most tombstones. The monument is set to not only capture death but also memorialize the location. As we will see, regimental monuments or other monuments dedicated to people have multiple reasons for existence.

For example, a monument may commemorate both the living and the dead. In this case, however, the monument is there for the simple purpose of marking a death. It is also fitting that monuments first dedicated at Gettysburg were focused on the dead. The reason is that since they were built and dedicated so close to the battle, the focus on lost comrades was much higher than wanting to dedicate a monument to veterans' accomplishments. One of the more straightforward explanations is that surviving veterans had yet to become old enough for their legacy to be the issue.

The first monument dedicated to a regiment, rather than an individual, on the Gettysburg battlefield was in 1879. While the Memorial Urn to the 1st Minnesota was dedicated in 1867, the memorial did not meet the criteria for a regimental monument. The urn was not considered a regimental monument because it was only dedicated to the dead as a memorial urn in the National Cemetery. The veterans who placed it there had no plans to create a regimental monument because none existed in 1867. However, the monument built by the 2nd Massachusetts Infantry Association was built to remember the living and the dead.

Members of the 2nd Massachusetts Infantry Association visited Gettysburg in the summer of 1879 to tour the battlefield and select ground for a monument. The visit and subsequent monument dedication of the 2nd Massachusetts would change how Union veterans memorialized their experiences at Gettysburg.[27] Instead of remembering the dead exclusively, monuments would begin being placed to remember what survivors of the battle endured. The 2nd Massachusetts Infantry engaged on the far-right flank of the Army of the Potomac on Culp's Hill on July 2–3, 1863. The exploits of the regiment on Culp's Hill are a poignant reminder of the human cost of Civil War battles and what effect combat had on veterans. By the time of Gettysburg, the 2nd Massachusetts was already a veteran regiment. One of the unit's previous officers, Colonel Robert Gould Shaw, left after the battle of Antietam to command the 54th Massachusetts Infantry (immortalized by the 1989 movie *Glory*).

During the battle of Gettysburg, the 2nd Massachusetts was with Colonel Silas Colgrove's 3rd Brigade, 1st Division of the XII Corps, commanded by General Henry Slocum. The fighting on Culp's Hill on July 2 was intense. By the end of the day, Confederate units had secured defenses built by Union soldiers on the lower section of the hill, stretching the Union XII Corps lines thin.[28] The 2nd Massachusetts spent most of July 2 detached to help support Union operations on Cemetery Ridge while the III Corps fell back.[29] When the regiment returned to its position on Culp's Hill on the night of July 2, plans were put in motion to dislodge the Confederate units that occupied the lower section of works first thing in the morning.

On the morning of July 3, division commander Major General Thomas Ruger, seeing that there were not as many Confederates in the breastworks as previously, ordered an advance on the position. General Ruger ordered Colonel Colgrove to advance skirmishers to see if a full assault was possible. However, Colgrove misinterpreted the order, provided verbally through an aide. Colgrove believed Ruger wanted him to launch a direct attack on the Confederate position and selected the 27th Indiana Infantry and 2nd Massachusetts Infantry for the job.[30] Both regiments would be attacking a fortified line where they were outnumbered and moving through open ground of about 100 yards.

Once both units received orders, they moved into position. Having received the order, the commander of the 2nd Massachusetts, Lieutenant Colonel Charles Mudge, stated, "It is murder, but it is the order. Up, men,

2nd Massachusetts Infantry Monument on Culp's Hill, Gettysburg National Military Park.

over the works! Forward, double-quick!"[31] Mudge led 316 men from the 2nd Massachusetts toward the enemy. Once the regiments moved out, they immediately came under heavy fire from the Confederates. By the time the unit returned to its line a few minutes later, it had sustained 136 casualties, along with the death of Lieutenant Colonel Mudge.[32] Furthermore, the attack ordered by Colonel Colgrove was unsuccessful and a needless waste of lives. Though the 2nd Massachusetts suffered heavy losses during the attack at Culp's Hill, they stayed in the fight after Gettysburg. When the XII Corps moved to the Western Theater, the 2nd Massachusetts Infantry followed suit. However, though the 2nd Massachusetts fought in both theaters and in several critical battles of the Civil War, its Officers' Association chose Gettysburg as the place for their monument.

Procuring land from private owners to build the 2nd Massachusetts monument was the first step in the process. Committees then had to decide about the design and shape of the monument, as well as the text. In the fall of 1879, a final design was agreed upon and created by the sculptor John Fox.[33] The monument, made of granite, is a funerary type and stands on a boulder that made up part of the line of battle for the unit. The monument's inscription includes, "… to perpetuate the honored memories of that hour of the survivors of the regiment have raised this stone." On the backside of the monument is a list of the regiment's members killed during the battle. The monument would be dedicated at Gettysburg in December 1879 near

Spangler's Spring by Charles Morse. Morse took charge of the regiment on July 3, 1863, after Lieutenant Colonel Mudge's death.[34]

There are many things to unpack about the 2nd Massachusetts monument at Gettysburg. The two most significant aspects are that this was the first regimental monument built on the battlefield, and the second to use aspects of the existing terrain in its construction. Being the first to do something is a common thread with most soldiers and veterans in almost any conflict, including the Civil War. There are many accounts to stake the claim of doing something first, either in a diary, letter, or even an official report. While in many of these cases on the battlefield, there could be dispute over who had done something first (this will play into a monument discussed in a later chapter), the 2nd Massachusetts can lay claim to raising the first regimental monument on the battlefield.

Another unique feature of the monument is its use of the large rock that was part of the 2nd Massachusetts' position during the battle. Instead of removing the rock or building next to it, the monument committee decided it was best to place the monument right on top of it. Doing so gave the monument an elevation over the landscape that would not be available on the ground. Using existing terrain as a feature of the monument, a precedent would be set that would be repeated at Gettysburg. Instead of altering or destroying the terrain to place a monument, working with the land helped make a monument distinctive. Veterans building these monuments within the landscape was, in effect, no different from what they did in battle—using the terrain to their advantage.

The first three monuments on the Gettysburg battlefield shared a common theme that would become a trend for future Union monuments. The focus of these was on the loss of men who died and the effect of those losses on the living members of the regiment. These first monuments did not have the same type of dedication speeches that later ones would have. During this early period of monumentation, the focus was on remembering who the unit lost during the battle. With the Civil War having ended only 14 years previously, many veterans who dedicated their efforts to the early monuments did not need a reminder as to why they fought during the conflict.

The 1880s would see a shift in national sentiment about the Civil War and its effect on society in the United States. The change mirrored shifts in feelings about the Civil War after Reconstruction, including the involvement of Union veterans and the role they played in national affairs. Following the end of the war in 1865, the United States underwent massive social and economic shifts. The first change was devoting massive resources to rebuild the South.

The loss of Southern population due to war casualties, the emancipation of its enslaved labor force, and the destruction of infrastructure due to four years of war had left the region in ruin. The second change was in the societal norms of the entire country due to the abolition of slavery with the passage of the Thirteenth Amendment. Formerly enslaved people could begin a life outside the farms and plantations where they worked. All these factors contributed to how the United States worked through Reconstruction.

Sectional tension and division in the North and South remained high in the years immediately after the Civil War. There was a faction of Northern politicians that wanted punitive measures levied against the South for causing the war. These politicians would become known as Radical Republicans and would be responsible for dividing the South into military districts after the war. They also demanded that Southern states pass the 14th Amendment before being allowed back into the Union.

However, other Northern politicians wanted to follow the words of President Lincoln's second inaugural address and provide "charity for all" after the war ended. This would allow the South to come back into the Union in a dignified manner, However, with the assassination of President Lincoln on April 15, 1865, most feelings of charity toward the South were marginalized. Beyond Radical Republicans, another movement to punish the South took shape. This movement came to be known as "Wave the Bloody Shirt" to emphasize the bloodshed the North endured as the result of the South's treason.

After more than a decade of division, tension, and calls for punishment, most Americans were ready to move on from the war. To maintain voters' support, Republicans had to turn from the project of Reconstruction to embrace policies aimed toward growing the economy, westward expansion, and reuniting the nation. While the most significant casualties of the abandonment of Reconstruction were four million previously enslaved people; initiatives to improve the condition of Union veterans were also left behind in the race toward reunion.

Citizens began looking for common ground to seal the breach between North and South. Both sides began to agree that the Civil War occurred because each side had noble ideas about the country's direction.[35] The prospect of acknowledging the South's presence at Gettysburg through reconciliation monuments met with mixed opinions from Union veterans. Some were accepting of acknowledging how the Confederate army fought, while others did not want Confederates mentioned at all in the battlefield's monumentation or memorialization. This difference of opinion came to a head with the planning and dedication of General Gregg's Cavalry Shaft in 1884.

On July 3, 1863, the Confederate cavalry circled around the Union center, three miles behind the Union lines, to what is now called East Cavalry Field. The goal of the Confederate cavalry assault was to support the grand infantry assault on Cemetery Ridge. Confederate General Robert E. Lee ordered cavalry under General Jeb Stuart to attack the Union line from the rear while the divisions of General George Pickett, General James Pettigrew, and General Issac Trimble attacked it in front.[36] While Confederate cavalry usually succeeded against Union cavalry, their fortunes changed at Gettysburg. Stuart planned to move south and east around the Union flank, pass through the Rommel farm, and set up an ambush for Union cavalry working there.[37] However, a division of Union cavalry under the command of General David Gregg stood in Stuart's way. The cavalry battle that ensued east of Gettysburg would stop the Confederate cavalry's advance to the rear of the main Union line.

Gregg's division used tactics different from those of the Confederates during the fight. Several Union cavalry regiments fought dismounted and used cover against the enemy. Fighting dismounted also allowed the Union to use their breech-loading weapons effectively to slow the Confederate advance. General George Custer's brigade of cavalry supported Gregg's division, allowing the Union to field some 3,200 men against Stuart's 3,500 men. However, many of Stuart's men lacked the ammunition for a prolonged engagement and could not break through Union lines. Most of Stuart's men carried only 10 to 15 rounds per trooper. The troopers could also not be given more ammunition since the supply wagons were too far away to be helpful during the battle.[38] At the height of the fighting, Gregg ordered a mounted counterattack that pushed the Confederate cavalry back, securing the Union rear at Gettysburg. The significance of the cavalry battle brought members of Gregg's division back 20 years later to dedicate a monument to their actions.

In 1880, the 3rd Pennsylvania Cavalry Association members met for their third organized reunion, and discussion centered on how best to memorialize their accomplishments and their division commander, General David Gregg. However, Gregg requested that if a monument was to be placed, it would not honor just himself. A compromise between the committee determined that the monument be "representative of the various brigades and batteries engaged in the cavalry on the right flank."[39] The memorial association asked for subscriptions, also known as pledges, to raise funds for the monument. The campaign was so successful that the association would have enough money to take care of the monument well into the 20th century.[40] With funding secured, the association then had to decide the best way to commemorate the event.

General Gregg Cavalry Shaft on East Cavalry Field, Gettysburg National Military Park.

With General Gregg's direct involvement, the monument association meticulously planned its construction, ensuring that the inscription would accurately reflect the historical significance of the event. The committee's decision to create a simple yet powerful granite shaft with clear inscriptions was a testament to their dedication. The winning bid for the granite shaft, awarded to sculptor Penrose Eisenbrown and the Eagle Marble and Granite Works, further underscored the meticulous planning and execution of the project.[41] The monument would not be thrown together haphazardly because the association wanted a reputable company that could create a work of art. The monument's location, strategically placed where the heaviest fighting of the cavalry battle occurred, is a unique aspect that draws attention. Each side of the shaft identifies the units and commands involved with both armies, including Confederate names and units, making it the first of the Gettysburg monuments to do so. This unique feature, while sparking modern-day scrutiny, provides a fascinating insight into the historical context and the reconciliation efforts that influenced the monument's construction.

The General Gregg Cavalry Shaft dedication occurred on October 15, 1884. Local papers described attendance at the dedication: "The party numbered around 150 people, and the monument is the most imposing of the battlefield to date."[42] Several Union veteran associations noted the work done by Eisenbrown on the monument. Over the coming years, Eisenbrown would be called upon to create several more Union monuments that would be dedicated at Gettysburg. The dedication ceremony itself included opening prayers and hymnals played by local bands.[43] William Rawle, a former officer in the 3rd Pennsylvania Cavalry, gave the dedication address. Rawle asked the veterans to "go back to that eventful time when we first met on the historical field, and sanctified it with blood then shed, the trials endured, and sacrifices made in defense of the nation's cause."[44] Rawle provided an overview of the cavalry battle and ended with remarks about what the monument should mean to Union veterans.

Rawle discussed how Union veterans should move forward and remember their time at the battle of Gettysburg. The surviving veterans should pay tribute to the fallen and point to the monument as a place to give future generations an example of how Union soldiers fought and what they accomplished. Rowle closed his dedication by reflecting on the battle at East Cavalry Field. The old Union veteran stated, "Fortunately for us, fortunately for the Army of the Potomac, fortunately for our country and the cause of human liberty, the Confederates failed."[45] While the Gregg Cavalry Shaft lists Confederate names and units, it is not for commemoration; it simply identifies the enemies the Union cavalry faced on that field.

The dedication speeches highlighted this critical point on who the monument was built for. The monument was built to "pay a reverent tribute to the memory of those brave men, our companions-in-arms, who here poured forth the full measure of their lives' devotion for the Cause they love."[46] An extension of the intent of the monument was the news coverage of the monument in the South. For example, *The Marion Times-Standard* in Alabama reported that there would be a "reunion to dedicate a monumental shaft erected on the field of cavalry operations during the battle on the right flank."[47]

Visitors wanting to see the Gregg Cavalry Shaft must first find East Cavalry Field. Unfortunately, it is not an area of the modern Gettysburg National Military Park visited regularly. There are a couple of reasons for this, the first and most common being that the location is off the beaten path and separated from the rest of the battlefield. Visitors who are trying to do the battle in a day or following the auto tour route are not directed out to the field. Visitors may also find it does not fit with a two- or three-hour tour. The second reason is that there is not much space to get out and visit the tablets and monuments that dot the small field. Lastly, the road has no prominent markers to find the shaft itself.

The shaft is off the road behind trees, modestly surrounded by a wrought iron fence. What I find ironic about this monument is that it is much smaller than the Michigan monument across the road. While the Michigan regiments at Gregg's disposal during the third day's battle were not his entire command (they were Custer's troops), a casual observer would not realize this by comparing the monuments. This is one of the reasons it is essential to read what is on monuments, not just at Gettysburg but at any historic site that one visits. The information and intent of the monument are usually plainly written and help explain the monument's purpose. The monument, at its core, is a reminder of a battle between two forces that had been playing a chess match in the saddle since 1862 that would continue until the war's end. If this monument did not exist, it would be hard for visitors to identify who was fighting who unless a previous study was made before coming to the battlefield.

Reconciliation efforts between the North and South in the United States in the 1880s influenced the monuments at Gettysburg. The GBMA did not have protocols by the early 1880s regarding monument placement and what inscriptions were permitted. The lack of official rules allowed a border state unit that fought with the Confederacy to place a monument at Gettysburg that would trigger a chain reaction among Union veterans and the GBMA to change the rules. The 1st Maryland Battalion, later designated the 2nd Maryland Infantry Regiment (CSA), would cause controversy regarding monument placement at Gettysburg.[48] At the time of the 2nd Maryland's monument dedication, the discussion of reconciliation was sweeping through the United States. The country was rebuilding economically, and commerce was open throughout the nation due to expanding infrastructure for people to thrive if they worked together.[49] However, Union veterans were opposed to Confederate monuments at Gettysburg. The battle between remembering the recent past and national healing in the form of progress would face off at Gettysburg.

The 1st Maryland Battalion had deployed in the Culp's Hill area of Gettysburg on July 2, 1863. After a series of costly charges, the battalion helped capture part of lower Culp's Hill and, with the 3rd North Carolina Infantry, took the brunt of the Union counterattack on their position the next morning.[50] Eventually, the 1st Maryland Battalion left Gettysburg with the rest of the Confederate army on July 4, 1863. The battalion went into Gettysburg with 400 able-bodied men and left with nearly half as casualties. During the fall the unit received new volunteers, and at the beginning of 1864, the 1st Maryland Battalion was redesignated the 2nd Maryland Regiment.[51]

When 2nd Maryland Infantry veterans approached the GBMA for permission to build a monument near the line they had held at Gettysburg, the board members resisted. Until the Confederate Maryland association's request, only monuments and tablets dedicated to the Union were present on the battlefield. The GBMA debated allowing the monument on August 11, 1885.[52] Several board members felt that simply marking Confederate positions was acceptable, but monuments were an entirely different matter. Board member General Henry Barnum, a Medal of Honor recipient during the Civil War, proposed a safeguard to appease both sides. The proposition stated, "Locating any monument at a point other than the position occupied by a regiment or command in battle, the memorial association, in addition to the historical inscriptions already required by its rules, reserve the right to remove any monument so located to its correct position."[53] The board approved the stipulation, and the 2nd Maryland Association verbally agreed. However, the monument and dedication speeches for the 2nd Maryland Monument would be met with anger by several Union veteran groups because they were thought to glorify the Confederate cause. The arguments against the monument would initially occur within the GBMA. Union veterans associations would not attempt action until several years later when they came to Gettysburg to dedicate their own monuments.[54]

The 2nd Maryland Association took over a year to design and build its monument. Placing the monument was of critical importance to Confederate veterans in view of all the Union veterans who were in talks to place monuments

2nd Maryland Infantry (CSA) Main Monument on Culp's Hill, Gettysburg National Military Park.

at Gettysburg. If a Confederate monument could be placed on the battlefield before a formal monumentation process was in place, there was a chance to set a precedent to include more Confederate monuments. However, as we will see in a subsequent section, this did not come to fruition. Many Confederates felt that since Maryland was a border state during the Civil War, the 2nd Maryland Association pushed the issue of allowing the monument to be a test case. The monument is a memorial that provides the unit's position during the battle, its strengths and losses, and the command to which the unit was assigned at Gettysburg. However, a marker that the 2nd Maryland Veterans Association added without consent caused controversy at the time that continues today. The inscription is a forward unit marker added after the dedication of the primary monument. While the primary monument is on the Confederate line of battle, as the GBMA prescribed, another marker positioned near the Union line states, "Point reached by 1st Maryland Battalion CSA July 3rd, 1863." Union veterans would question the addition of the second marker and how the monument was dedicated.

The dedication of the 2nd Maryland (CSA) monument occurred on November 19, 1886, which coincided with the 23rd anniversary of President Lincoln's Gettysburg address. A crowd of nearly 2,000 people, including Confederate veterans, family, and friends, attended the dedication.[55] The large crowd for the first Confederate monument did not surprise the Confederate veterans. Several days before the ceremony, General Bradley Johnson had pleaded with other Confederate veterans to join them at Gettysburg for the dedication. The purpose of having more people at the dedication was to show that "we have the power, and power always compels respect; I hope that our demonstration for Friday to Gettysburg will be impressive."[56] Johnson was ardent about Southern rights even after the Civil War ended. Like many Confederate veterans, he believed reconciliation would occur through mutual respect for both North and South. In his address, Johnson also stated that Union and Confederate veterans should have "a common heritage of glory and respect between both sides and in future generations."[57] They could find common ground if the Union and Confederates could see why the other side fought for their beliefs. This type of reconciliation would be evident during the dedication speech for the monument at Gettysburg.

The regiment's adjutant, Captain George Thomas, gave the monument's dedication speech at Gettysburg. Thomas, like Johnson, dedicated the monument with reconciliation in mind. The former adjutant stated that the monument would be "an added page to the great record which belongs to no one section and to no time, the joint heritage of the North and of the

2nd Maryland Infantry (CSA) Advance Marker on Culp's Hill, Gettysburg National Military Park.

South, and of right to be trans-mitted in all its fullness to the ages yet to come."[58] The idea of reconciliation and moving forward from the past was a theme for most Confederate veterans during the 1880s. It was essential to find a path where Southerners could move on and keep their dignity during the era. For most veterans, this meant acknowledging the war and explaining their reason for fighting. Many, like General Bradley Johnson, felt like they were fighting for the existence of the Confederacy and civil liberty.[59] However, many Union veterans did not accept the Confederates' explanation of the monument's importance and what it symbolized. This approach by the Confederate veterans association spurred more Union veterans groups to build monuments at Gettysburg.

How the 2nd Maryland Infantry (CSA) built its monument at Gettysburg heightened the fear of many GBMA board members. In a letter to Colonel John Bachelder, board member David Buehler voiced his concerns about the Confederate monument. Buehler believed "the erection of their monument was not so much to mark their position, as to glorify their achievements on the field."[60] Over time, Union veterans would also voice their displeasure since they would see the Confederate monument when they came to Gettysburg to dedicate their own monuments. When giving a dedication speech for the 84th Pennsylvania Infantry in 1889, Thomas Merchant clarified what should happen to the Confederate monument on Culp's Hill. Merchant proclaimed, "The government should have swept from its soil the first monument to rebellion, with the warning that placing a second would be treason."[61] However, the Union veterans' displeasure with the Maryland Confederate monument would not change the GBMA's stance on allowing it.

The rancor and disdain that Union veterans felt for the Rebel monument being so close to their own make perfect sense considering the timing of the monument. Visiting the Confederate Maryland monument today is a surreal experience due to its proximity to Union monuments on Culp's Hill, and the forward marker on the route sits even farther up the hill. Official accounts and histories of the battle indicate that the fighting on Culp's Hill was intense, and at times the lines were very close. However, the Rebel monument sticks out as a sore thumb amongst the other monuments.

When you approach the monument, it looks like any of the others close to it and would seem to be a Union monument just ahead of everyone else. When reading the monument, it is evident that it is not a Union monument since it has "CSA" emblazoned across it. Another way this monument is not like all the others is that small Rebel flags usually dot the ground near it. While the GBMA could have removed the monument at any time, they did not. The same could be said for later administrators of the park. However, veterans who ran later park administrations would not allow another Rebel monument on park grounds. Confederate monuments would eventually be allowed on park property, but not until Union veterans were no longer in a position of power to stop them. The monument is important because the GBMA accepted its placement but would not allow it to deter them from their overall mission of Union monumentation on the battlefield.

While many Union veterans hoped the government would intervene, it could not. The United States government did not have the authority to remove monuments from private property. Another reason it stayed in place was the Southern influence in the United States at the time of the monument's dedication. The 1880s saw the official return of all Southern states back into the Union and within the Congress. Squabbling over monument placement and the prospect of offending Southerners was the last thing many in the government wanted. Instead, the GBMA doubled down on its monument placement policy and scrutinized every monument proposed for GBMA land at Gettysburg. This policy would also affect future Union monuments placed on the battlefield.

The early monuments built at Gettysburg followed two themes in their construction and dedication. The first theme was commemoration of the dead. The need to remember fallen comrades was strong among many veterans. The GAR reunions that came to Gettysburg gave Union veterans a chance to visit and commemorate the men they lost during the battle. Another theme of early Gettysburg monuments was commemorating the deeds of men who fought on the battlefield. However, the reasons for the Civil War were not commemorated or mentioned in dedication speeches or made visible on the monuments themselves.

By the middle of the 1880s, dozens of Union veteran organizations began to look closely at how they could dedicate monuments at Gettysburg. While changes in GBMA policy would dictate where monuments were allowed, applications began arriving exponentially to place monuments on the field. The increase in applications was triggered by veterans wanting to build monuments where they fought, not just in their hometowns. In communities across the United States, veterans groups sponsored monuments dedicated to local men who fought in the Civil War. Now the increase in local monuments would help drive interest in Gettysburg. However, only one of the two armies that fought at Gettysburg would be represented for the time being. Even though the GBMA stated they would look at Union and Confederate monument proposals equally, this was not the case. The GBMA would not entertain an application for another Confederate monument during its battlefield administration. Meantime, between 1885 and 1887, the number of Union monuments dedicated at Gettysburg nearly doubled as state veterans organizations received monument funding.

CHAPTER 3

Early "State Days" Monumentation, 1885–87

The mid-1880s saw a shift in Civil War memorialization and monumentation in the United States. In the North, communities wanted to build monuments to memorialize their local veterans, which provided an incentive for veterans organizations to look at battlefields as places to memorialize their experiences during the war. An example of an early community Civil War monument was dedicated in September 1885 in Grand Rapids, Michigan. This sentinel-type monument stands approximately 30 feet tall, topped with a Civil War-era soldier standing at parade rest. The front of it contains an inscription stating, "To the memory of the soldiers of Kent Co. 1861–1865."[1] Memorials such as this, dedicated to the service of local community members in the Civil War, continued to sprout up across the North. The interest in building local monuments sparked efforts by Union veterans to seek more funding.

Increased interest in local monuments also spread to building monuments at Gettysburg. Union veterans wanted to build monuments where they fought, not just where they lived. Since the battlefield at Gettysburg had land already preserved by the Gettysburg Battlefield Memorial Association, Union veterans organizations wanted to build monuments there first. Unlike on other battlefields, Union veterans only needed authorization from the GBMA to construct a monument. Other battlefields would require regimental associations to buy land from private citizens to place the monument as well as raise funds to build it. The attractiveness of needing less money to build monuments at Gettysburg, plus its location in the North, and the very magnitude of the battle, drove Union veterans to memorialize their actions there.

The interest in building monuments coincided with political elections in Northern legislatures. Increasingly during the postwar years, elections placed Union veterans throughout the country into positions that allowed them to control spending and allocate funds for building monuments. In 1885,

Location of monuments 1886–87. (Created using ArcGIS Pro by Esri)

New Jersey's Monument Bill "authorized $2,500 to erect monuments at Gettysburg to mark positions of New Jersey units."[2] Several more Northern states soon followed this example with appropriations. Gettysburg was the focus because veterans knew the GBMA had secured the battlefield for monument placement.[3] Union veterans began petitioning state legislatures and the GBMA to build regimental monuments at Gettysburg. However, due to the different sizes of state legislatures, some states could pass legislation for funding faster than others. As money was provided to regimental associations, and monuments were constructed, state organizers began coordinating when monument dedications at Gettysburg would occur. These coordinated events would be known as "state days," when a state would dedicate all its monuments simultaneously.

One of the first monuments dedicated at Gettysburg during this period was that of the 9th Massachusetts Infantry. While the regiment played a role in defending a relatively quiet point of the Union line on the night of July 2, 1863, veterans attempted to attach more prominence to their role in the battle. The 9th Massachusetts Infantry was formed in Boston in 1861. After a brief tour securing Washington, the regiment joined the Army of the Potomac and participated in every one of its campaigns until the summer of 1864.[4] Veterans of the 9th, however, disagreed with official records about their actions at Gettysburg.

During the Gettysburg campaign, the 9th Massachusetts was assigned to Colonel Jacob Sweitzer's brigade of the V Corps of the Army of the Potomac. It arrived at Gettysburg in the early morning of July 2, 1863[5] and was detached from the brigade to perform skirmish duty for the army's left flank. Skirmish duty involved deploying men in a line before the main force. The job was to make first contact with the enemy and identify where the enemy was positioned. The skirmish assignment at first went to the 32nd Massachusetts, an inexperienced regiment; however, the command staff decided instead to put forward the veteran 9th Massachusetts. The change in assignments placed the 9th Massachusetts on Burkhoff's Ridge and eventually Big Round Top on the night of July 2, 1863. Thus, while most of Sweitzer's Brigade was in constant contact with the enemy during the second day of fighting, the 9th Massachusetts was detached on skirmish duty, protecting the army's flank.

The result was that, while the rest of the brigade sustained heavy losses in the second day's fighting, the 9th Massachusetts only suffered 15 casualties. However, the regiment's records greatly embellished the role played by the 9th Massachusetts. The official history of the regiment stated that it held

9th Massachusetts Infantry Monument, Big Round Top, Gettysburg National Military Park.

"Big Round Top all day against the determined assault of [General] Hood's skirmishers."[6] If this statement were true, the 9th Massachusetts would have held the extreme left of the Army of the Potomac, not the units positioned on Little Round Top, against whom the Confederates concentrated their attacks.

Accounts of the 9th playing a pivotal role on Big Round Top surfaced after the monument dedication when it became clear to veterans that Gettysburg would be "the great memorial battlefield of the world."[7] Union veterans wanted their regiments' contributions to matter on an important battlefield like Gettysburg. For some veterans, this could mean stretching what happened in their combat experiences to match everyone else's. This often contradicted what happened and what was recorded to tell a more dramatic and significant tale.

The 9th Massachusetts Infantry monument dedication occurred on June 9, 1885, on Big Round Top. The monument is made of granite, stands approximately 15 feet tall, and is inscribed with text on three sides. The front side states that the "Ninth Regiment was detached from the 2nd Brigade and held this position on the Round Top." On the rear of the monument is a list of the battles in which the regiment fought during its three years of service. The regiment's monument at Gettysburg would mark where the regiment fought in battle and become a testament to its service during the entire Civil War.

The cost of the monument totaled $700. However, the 9th Massachusetts Regimental Association did not have to worry about raising all the funds for their monument. The Massachusetts State Legislature authorized $500 for each regimental monument built at Gettysburg. The stance of applying state funds to building veteran monuments was not a luxury earlier veteran groups had building monuments at Gettysburg. While most Massachusetts regiments would have their monuments placed on the battlefield in October 1885, the 9th Massachusetts preceded them with its placement in June. The regiment wanted its contribution memorialized by the written word and by stone in its battle line position. However, recollections of aging veterans and official reports did not always align, creating conflicting stories. Balancing official reports with veterans' memories would become a common struggle surrounding many Gettysburg monuments in the years to follow.

July 1885 marked the 22nd anniversary of the battle of Gettysburg. While several Northern states passed legislation to build monuments for the 25th anniversary in 1888, several regiments wanted to place them sooner. Like those in the late 1870s, these monuments would provide a blueprint for future designs and dedication speeches. There would not be a rush to get monuments built during every battle anniversary. Almost all the monuments at Gettysburg were dedicated either during the week of the battle's anniversary or in October. The reason why October was selected was due to the summer weather of Pennsylvania—full of heat and humidity, followed by the usual storm in the afternoon, the summer did not provide the best time to dedicate monuments outside. For this reason, pushing dedications to October provided cooler temperatures and steadier weather patterns.

In the 1880s, monument dedications received a significant amount of news coverage. The first early dedications were usually covered by local or regional newspapers in Pennsylvania. Occasionally, the hometown of the regiment or person being memorialized at the battlefield would also cover the ceremony. However, by the 1880s, monumentation caught the attention of Union veterans living across the country, and people wanted to know what veterans said at the dedications. The increased interest in ceremonies at Gettysburg led to national press coverage when the ceremonies occurred.

The monument placement and dedication speeches of the 9th Massachusetts was one of the first examples of monumentation at Gettysburg shifting to a national audience. Previous dedications were small and considered a local affair. However, when the issues of what the 9th Massachusetts did during the battle were called into question, this dedication was followed closely by a larger group of people. No one doubted that the regiment was engaged in the battle and that it contributed to the Union army's efforts during the campaign. What was called into question was where and who they engaged around both Round Tops on the left of the line in July 1863.

I visited the 9th Massachusetts at the bottom of Big Round Top before heading toward Little Round Top, a quiet wooded battlefield section. Flanked on either side by other flank markers and monuments of other regiments, the 9th's monument does stand out. The monument is slightly higher and taller than the others because it is more of a column than a headstone. The monument visually dominates those on its left and right. The feelings and statements of the 9th Massachusetts veterans who told their stories to help inspire the monument are essential because they must be taken from their perspective. While the historical record may have showed that the exploits were not the same as how the veterans remembered it, these stories and recollections help direct the way the historical record is sent to find truth. By taking a veteran's story, a historian can use the recollection as a guidepost to look for more information and more sources to set the record straight.

The common soldier generally has a view of a battle from what is right in front of them, especially during the Civil War. Veterans of the war did not have social media to discuss what others were doing during the battle. As such, veterans' stories and memories exist based on what they experienced. While some memories may have changed due to age and by hearing other accounts, their main stories are theirs from what they went through and observed. The advent of spreading regional stories to the national media would affect how veteran accounts were shared in the late 1800s. The shift in media coverage of monument dedications at Gettysburg started with the coverage of the 20th Connecticut Infantry's dedication in July 1885.

The 20th Connecticut was formed in August 1862 in New Haven, Connecticut, though the regiment's first battle was not until Chancellorsville in May 1863. The regiment was attached to the 1st Brigade, 1st Division of the XII Corps. At the start of the campaign, it was commanded by Lieutenant Colonel William Wooster and arrived at Gettysburg on the night of July 1, 1863. To shore up Union defenses, the 20th Connecticut, with the rest of the XII Corps, was placed on Culp's Hill to help anchor the right flank of the Union army. The 20th Connecticut spent the second and third days of the battle supporting other units on the battlefield.

On July 2, 1863, the 1st Division of the XII Corps was pulled off the line on Culp's Hill to stand in reserve. That afternoon, after the collapse of the Union III Corps, the 20th Connecticut, as part of the division, was sent to fill a gap next to the II Corps on Cemetery Ridge.[8] With the division in motion, new orders arrived before they reached the position, sending them back to Culp's Hill. During the march and subsequent countermarch back to their original position, Confederates attacked along sections of Culp's Hill and occupied the line once held by the 20th Connecticut.

Early in the morning of July 3, the 20th Connecticut received orders to scout the Confederate position on Culp's Hill. To support their mission, several artillery batteries supported the regiment as it advanced. The artillery support was important since the enemy position was behind a stone wall. Despite maintaining constant communication with the 20th Connecticut, the artillery gunners mistakenly fired into the regiment. Lieutenant Colonel Wooster was angry about halting the regiment's advance. He sent a courier to the Union batteries, stating he would pull the 20th out of position, turn them around, and charge the batteries himself if they did not stop firing.[9]

However, the 20th Connecticut held its advance together and pushed the Confederates back. Later on July 3, during Pickett's Charge, the 20th Connecticut moved to support the Union units on Cemetery Ridge. The regiment took position behind the Union center to help shore up the line against "an attack then being made with great determination on the part of the enemy."[10] Eventually, the unit returned to Culp's Hill and followed the Army of the Potomac away from Gettysburg on July 5, 1863. The regiment went into Gettysburg with 321 men and 28 became casualties. Most of these came from the friendly fire incident from the Union cannonade on July 3. The regiment would later be transferred to the Western Theater for the duration of the Civil War. Like many of the XII Corps regiments, the 20th Connecticut chose Gettysburg, not one of the western battlefields, to build and dedicate monuments to their exploits on the field.

Planning for the 20th Connecticut Infantry monument began in 1884. To veterans of the unit, Gettysburg was the obvious choice for the location of their monument. On July 19, 1884, Colonel Wooster wrote a circular letter to survivors of the regiment. The letter stated, "All recognize Gettysburg as one of the great battles of the world. It was the great decisive battle of our late war."[11] Wooster would continue in his reasons for placing a monument at Gettysburg by saying, "Every soldier will desire once more to look upon that bloody field … a tablet to the memory of those engaged in that great battle will in future years be looked upon as a credit to their state."[12] The resulting membership drive raised the appropriate funds for the monument, which the Curtis & Hughes Company of Stratford, Connecticut completed.[13] The monument was completed in less than a year, and the regiment's survivors met on July 3, 1885, for its dedication.

On the dedication day, veterans and onlookers headed to Culp's Hill for two Union monuments. Members of the 29th Pennsylvania were on hand to dedicate a monument to their regiment.[14] The 20th Connecticut monument is located on the regiment's original position on July 1, 1863. It is a memorial type of monument placed on a rock that was part of the regiment's battle line. The monument is made of granite and adorned with small pillars. Each side of the monument includes all the casualties and significant engagements in which the regiment participated throughout the entire Civil War.

During the dedication ceremony, poems and speeches honored the 20th Connecticut. George Warner, a veteran of the unit, unveiled the monument. Warner had lost both arms at Gettysburg and used a rope around his waist to pull the cover off the monument. Chaplain Henry Stevens of the 14th Connecticut Infantry gave the oration. In his address, Stevens discussed what the Union victory meant to the veterans. He stated, "The hosts of treasonous armed force were the mightiest and where that force received a baffling and a shock, the most humiliating and hurtful."[15] The regiment's

20th Connecticut Infantry Monument, Culp's Hill, Gettysburg National Military Park.

dedication focused on the greatness of the Union victory and the defeat of treasonous Southerners.

The dedication speeches of the 20th Connecticut do not pull punches about why its veterans joined to fight in the war. The Rebels needed to be punished for breaking away from the Union. The statement made in the dedication speech is also in plain language. Regardless of what period someone reads the transcript of the speech, it is obvious what the feelings were of veterans dedicating the monument. This can also be perceived in their choice of a disabled veteran tying the drop rope to himself to uncover the monument.

Walking up to the monument today, it is clear that the 20th Connecticut used a terrain feature to increase the height of its monument. The granite rock on which the monument rests provides an elevated position for anyone coming to pay their respects to view the monument. Another type of headstone-looking monument joins the gaggle of granite tributes on Culp's Hill. Walking through these monuments can give you a pretty good picture of how the hill was defended during the battle. While looking at monuments today, there is a visual reason for why the veterans of the regiment were so plain with their vitriol toward the Rebels. The Confederate 2nd Maryland Regiment monument is within shouting distance of the 20th Connecticut's. (I know this because I tried it on a recent visit to the site.) At the time of this writing, it is unknown if the veterans giving dedication speeches for the

20th Connecticut knew ahead of time that there was a Rebel monument within eyesight of theirs. However, considering the contents of the speeches, it was either known ahead of time, or there was some last-minute editing of the speeches before the dedication, which could also explain one of the reasons why the dedication ceremony drew interest from national publications like the *New York Times*. Beyond press coverage, other changes were coming for Union monuments to be dedicated at Gettysburg, as compared to the earlier ones.

Union regimental associations' interpretation of the GBMA battle line rule for monuments changed in the mid-1880s. Some associations interpreted the battle line as an opportunity to place multiple monuments on the field to show the various positions they occupied throughout the three days of battle. One of the first regiments to do this was the 12th Massachusetts Infantry. By July 1863, the 12th Massachusetts went by the moniker, "Webster's Regiment." The nickname was given to the regiment due to Colonel Fletcher Webster being the son of the American orator and statesman Daniel Webster. However, the younger Webster was killed at Second Manassas.[16] The regiment was considered a veteran unit, having served under Banks in the Shenandoah, Pope in northern Virginia, Antietam, Fredericksburg, and Chancellorsville. At the battle of Gettysburg, the 12th Massachusetts was assigned to the I Corps of the Army of the Potomac.

On July 1, 1863, the I Corps moved into the fields west and north of Gettysburg to meet the oncoming Confederate army. The 12th Massachusetts found a position on the right flank of the I Corps near Oak Ridge. The regiment and much of the brigade suffered heavy casualties and ran out of ammunition in the face of a massive assault by General Richard Ewell's Corps. During the assault, the regiment's commander, Colonel James Bates, was wounded twice, turning control over to Lieutenant Colonel David Allen.[17] With the surviving members of the I Corps, the regiment retreated south of Gettysburg to Cemetery Hill. The regiment then spent the next two days of the battle supporting batteries on Cemetery Hill.

The 12th Massachusetts helped repel the final Confederate assault against the Union center on July 3. Moving from Cemetery Hill to Cemetery Ridge to support the II Corps, the 12th Massachusetts and other regiments in their brigade came under fire from Confederate sharpshooters stationed at the Bliss farm to their front. General Baxter, the brigade commander, ordered the "12th Massachusetts and 90th Pennsylvania forward to drive the enemy back, which was done promptly and with deserved credit to those engaged, moving steadily forward though not without considerable loss."[18] The 12th Massachusetts suffered heavy losses during its involvement at Gettysburg. Before the battle, 261 men filled the regiment's ranks. By the time the regiment left Gettysburg, 119 were casualties. The regiment's loss of life would result in monuments at several battlefield locations.

During a legislative session of the Massachusetts legislature, a resolution was passed for funds to build regimental monuments at Gettysburg. On March 24, 1884, each regiment was granted $500 for construction.[19] Most of the regimental associations in the state agreed on several dates in October 1885 for monument dedications. The date of October 8, 1885, was selected for several monuments for the 12th Massachusetts. On receipt of the appropriation, the regimental veterans association took a little more than a year to construct its monuments.[20] On the day selected, the 12th Massachusetts dedicated three monuments to its actions at Gettysburg, each placed at a different location where the regiment saw action.

The main monument was erected near Oak Ridge, north of the town, where the regiment suffered most of its casualties. It is a conical granite shaft with an image of Daniel Webster etched on the front. A notable line from one of Daniel Webster's speeches engraved on the monument is his famous 1830 response to the threat of secession: "Liberty and union, now and forever, one and inseparable."[21] This memorial-type monument stands 10 feet, 9 inches tall, with a carved flag draped around the back. It also features an empty cartridge box and a bayonet scabbard, a nod to when the regiment ran out of ammunition on July 1 and held its ground by wielding bayonets. The other two monuments to the unit are simple stone inscriptions on their July 2 and 3 battle lines. The dedication speeches for all three monuments occurred at the large monument near Oak Ridge.

Corporal George Kimbrell, a veteran of the regiment wounded at Gettysburg, was the keynote speaker. Kimbrell focused on what the battle of Gettysburg achieved for the Army of the Potomac and the North during the Civil War. Kimbrell noted, "The direct hand of Providence made Gettysburg a turning point in the war."[22] He also believed that the regiment's dead and the rest of the Union dead at Gettysburg fell for a worthy cause. Kimbrell surmised, "The Union has proven itself worthy of the great sacrifice here offered."[23] Placing monument markers at different locations at Gettysburg would become commonplace for Union regiments that fought hard in multiple locations on the battlefield. The 12th Massachusetts marked its actions at Gettysburg so people would understand what the regiment sacrificed during the battle.

12th Massachusetts Infantry Main Monument, Oak Ridge, Gettysburg National Military Park.

12th Massachusetts Infantry, July 2, 1863 Marker, Cemetery Ridge, Gettysburg National Military Park.

12th Massachusetts Infantry, July 3, 1863 Marker, Ziegler's Grove, Gettysburg National Military Park.

The 12th Massachusetts Infantry was one of the first regiments to dedicate a monument at each position it held during the battle. This would be standard practice for many units that fought on the first and subsequent days of the battle. Due to the change in position of the Union army after its retreat on the first day, units were positioned and repositioned as needed. This shuffle of units provided by regimental associations in later years caused the landscape to be dotted with the different locations of their units. The 12th Massachusetts, like several of the other initial units deployed in the battle, was engaged in all three days of fighting.

Visiting all three monuments on the battlefield today will take visitors to the north and the south side of town. The main monument is historically significant since it includes an impression of Daniel Webster. Monuments can provide a snapshot of a unit's history for visitors as well as provide insight into what the unit believed in. For example, using the Webster relief and designating itself the Webster Regiment meant it had deep ties to early Republican ideas. Webster had been a strong proponent of a strong federal government that should keep states together. During the early stages of issues regarding states' rights and slavery, Webster spoke out against the dissolution of the Union from the 1820s until his death. Webster held various positions in the government, including being elected to the House of Representatives and the Senate in different stints. Webster also served as Secretary of State for two different presidents. While identifying Webster and what he believed may have been common knowledge in the 1800s, this may not be the case today. Visitors with a good understanding of American history must identify who Webster was to understand the significance of his face being placed on the monument.

During the 1880s, funding for Union monuments shifted from private subscriptions to state appropriations. Private donations initially funded most Union regimental monuments, and regiments later returned and added monuments in multiple locations with state money. The 27th Connecticut Regiment Association used state and private funds to place five monuments at Gettysburg. The ratio of men to monuments constructed makes the total number of monuments for the regiment noteworthy. At the time of the battle, the 27th Connecticut deployed only 75 men.

The 27th Connecticut was formed in 1862 from men living around New Haven, Connecticut. The regiment initially consisted of 829 men who signed on to fight in the Union army for nine months.[24] Fighting at Fredericksburg in December 1862 and Chancellorsville in May 1863 crippled the effectiveness of the regiment in battle. During the battle of Chancellorsville, eight out of the regiment's ten companies were captured. This left a small band of two understrength companies to fight at Gettysburg. At the beginning of the Gettysburg campaign, the 27th Connecticut's assignment was to the 4th Brigade in General Caldwell's Division of the II Corps of the Army of the Potomac. Like most Union regiments, the 27th did not receive replacement troops when needed on the eve of battle. The model used by the Union army was to raise new regiments of men rather than replenishing older formations, thus leaving the 27th the size of an undersized company.

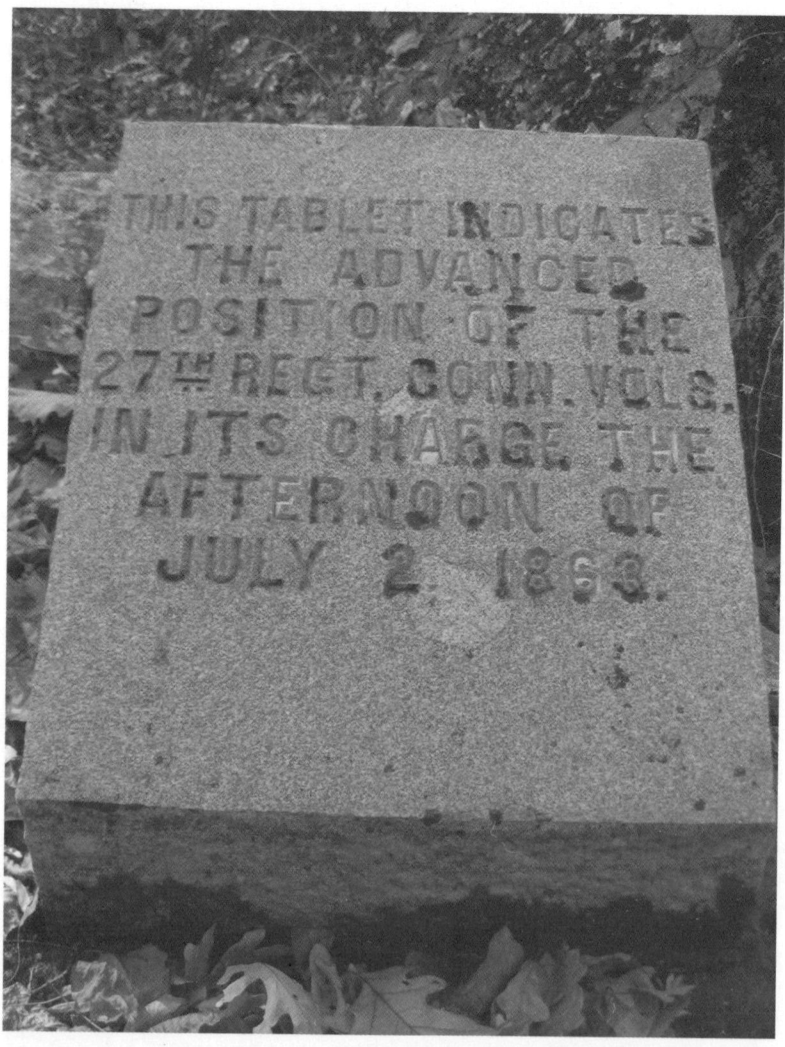

27th Connecticut Infantry Advance Marker, Wheatfield, Gettysburg National Military Park.

The 27th Connecticut arrived at Gettysburg late on the first day and on July 2 was heavily engaged, assisting in securing the II Corps' left flank. Deployed from Cemetery Ridge, the 27th Connecticut was ordered into Rose's Wheatfield to hold back the Confederate advance at the notorious Sickles salient. The regiment charged through the Wheatfield to flush out Confederate troops under General Paul Semmes. The ensuing fight would claim the regiment's commander, Lieutenant Colonel Henry Merwin. Of the 75 men that made up the regiment going into the battle, 37 became casualties. The back-and-forth fight between Union and Confederate forces in the Wheatfield destroyed the already depleted 27th Connecticut.

Catching on to the monument building that exploded at Gettysburg in the mid-1880s, the 27th Connecticut Regiment Association began collecting money for a monument to honor their fallen commander and the sacrifices of the regiment. The association raised enough money for two monuments. The first, an advance marker, marked the forward progress of the regiment in the Wheatfield. The second main monument stands where its commander, Colonel Henry Merwin, was killed. The monument is approximately 25 feet tall, with a granite shaft adorned with an eagle on top of artillery tubes. The monument includes the II Corps trefoil emblem and unit identification information. The regiment also included the unit's operational history before and after Gettysburg. Both monuments, constructed by the St. Johnsbury Granite Company in Vermont, cost the 27th Connecticut Association $1,200.[25] Once the completion date of the monuments neared, the association planned to dedicate them at Gettysburg in October 1885.

The 27th Connecticut Association members left for Gettysburg on October 20, 1885. Nearly sixty survivors, including many of those captured at Chancellorsville in May 1863, made the trip from New Haven to Gettysburg.[26] The dedication ceremony was held on October 22, 1885. The themes of both dedication speeches that day focused on the importance of preserving the Union and the heroic deeds of the unit. Corporal Simeon Fox stated that the monuments "stand on Gettysburg's memorable and historical battlefield to commemorate the valor and bravery of that little band of men who stood against the Rebel invasion."[27] In another speech, Governor Henry Harrison stated, "The slain fell fighting under the starry flag of the Union and upholding high that older flag … the Union was made indivisible and whose freedom perpetual by the great victory."[28] Interestingly, there is no mention of freeing enslaved people in the speeches from a region of the country that was known for an abolitionist stance. Instead, both speakers focused on preserving the country and remembering the fallen.

27th Connecticut Infantry Wheatfield Monument, Gettysburg National Military Park.

Colonel Henry Merwin Death Site, Wheatfield, Gettysburg National Military Park.

The 27th Connecticut would also add two more monuments for their fallen leaders, leaving five total monuments at Gettysburg. Both tombstone-like monuments mark where Colonel Merwin and Captain Jedidiah Chapman fell on July 2. It was important for veterans of the 27th to keep the memory of their fallen commanders alive in public consciousness. For these veterans, such markers symbolized that both men were willing to die for their beliefs in preserving the Union. Evidence of these beliefs was mentioned during the 1885 dedication ceremony of the regimental association president, Simeon Fox.

Fox stated in his dedication speech, "The names of Merwin and Chapman, and those whose lives went out in glory on this dreaded field but shall be a lasting memorial to those brave men who lived to enjoy the delights of peace once more and to witness a nation saved."[29] These markers also helped veterans trace their steps during the battle when they returned to visit. All the 27th Connecticut monuments lead a path to follow, allowing these men to stand again on the ground that was so hallowed to them. Veterans' dedication to multiple monuments, like the 27th Connecticut's on one part of the battlefield, was not standard procedure at Gettysburg. Most regiments selected one location and dedicated one monument.

Captain Jedidiah Chapman Death Site, Wheatfield, Gettysburg National Military Park.

The 27th Connecticut fought around the Rose property at Gettysburg where the Wheatfield and Rose's Woods saw some of the heaviest fighting of the entire battle. The effects of Gettysburg on the veterans of the 27th were strong since the survivors would erect five different monuments to its exploits on the field. Even more telling is that the survivors ensured their fallen commanders were also included in the memorialization. There is something special about regiments that make sure their officers are commemorated on the battlefield. Loss of officers in any Civil War regiment was commonplace during the war. Officers were expected to lead from the front and be in the center of the action with their men. As such, their casualty rate during the Civil War was high. However, not all regiments erected monuments to their fallen officers, and the 27th dedicated two.

Tracing all five of the 27th Connecticut's monuments can be an adventure at Gettysburg. This depends on the time of year and whether the three smaller monuments are grass-covered. During the summer, it would not be unheard of for the advance marker, Lieutenant Colonel Merwin, and Captain Smith monuments to be completely covered in grass. However, walking the same ground as these men who fought here in 1863 is a small price. Walking in their shoes, especially during the same time of year that they did, allows someone to experience briefly what soldiers had to go through while on the field.

At the end of October 1885, Indiana held its own "state day" for its monuments. The themes presented during dedication ceremonies varied from unit to unit. North of the town of Gettysburg lay the fields of the first day's fighting. One of the critical features of the north end of the battlefield was an unfinished railroad cut that acted as a ravine during the battle. One of the Union units that fought in this section of the battlefield was the 3rd Indiana Cavalry. The regiment's commander was Colonel George Chapman, a lawyer from Indianapolis. The 3rd Indiana Cavalry was attached to General John Buford's division and combined with the 12th Illinois Cavalry in Colonel William Gamble's brigade. Both regiments were understrength due to battle losses and disease and together fielded 893 troopers.[30] Buford's division engaged in a delaying action with lead elements of the Confederate army under General Harry Heth on July 1, 1863. The 3rd Indiana's position was along McPherson's Ridge just south of the unfinished railroad line.[31] The Union cavalry was vastly outnumbered but recognized the importance of holding the ridgelines north and west of town until their infantry could arrive from the south.

After holding its positions until relieved by infantry, the 3rd Indiana Cavalry was called upon to hold a different part of the line. The I Corps and XI Corps could not hold back the Confederate troops converging on Gettysburg. The decision was made for both corps to fall back through the town. Deciding to fight dismounted like infantry instead of on horseback, and using breech-loading carbines, the 3rd Indiana pushed back flanking enemy forces, providing more time for retreating Union forces to regroup south of the town. Like most of Buford's division, the troopers using breech-loading rifles could get off several shots in the time it took a muzzle-loading infantryman to shoot and reload once. This helped level the odds from a numerical standpoint. The following two days for the 3rd Indiana included reconnaissance and flank protection for the rest of the Army of the Potomac. After the battle, when the cavalry pursued the Confederate army south, the 3rd Indiana suffered 32 casualties out of 313 engaged. The regiment served until the war's end and was mustered out in June 1865.

The state of Indiana provided funds for monument-building at various Civil War battlefields in the early 1880s; following previous "state days" held by Massachusetts and Connecticut, Indiana officials decided to dedicate all seven of their monuments on the same day. Indiana followed the same template as other states for its ceremonies at Gettysburg. A special train would arrive a day or two before dignitaries dedicated the monuments. Local GAR Posts would host veterans and include different activities for everyone who made the trip.[32] The Indiana regiments, including the 3rd Indiana Cavalry, dedicated their monument on October 28, 1885. The dedication day included walking the battlefield and visiting where the survivors fought. Bands played at the monument site, and speakers gave dedication speeches.

The 3rd Indiana Cavalry monument was placed where its first fighting position was on July 1, 1863, by the railroad cut. The memorial-type monument is an obelisk made from Vermont granite, approximately 18 feet high. On each side of the monument is historical information about the regiment during the war. In his dedication remarks, Major George Spahr focused on what Gettysburg meant to the men of the 3rd Indiana Cavalry and their wartime experience. Spahr stated that the victory at Gettysburg "brought assurance that the Government still lived, and our cause would be triumphant."[33] Even though Spahr focused on the Union victory at Gettysburg, he was gracious to the Rebels they had faced in battle. Spahr acknowledged their enemy as "the chivalric sons from the sunny south."[34] However, the victory for the Union was the writing on the wall for the Confederacy.

While his dedication speech did not focus on one theme, Spahr's remarks are telling. He does not mention slavery or emancipation in his address. This is in part due to the timing of the dedication speech. Slavery and emancipation

3rd Indiana Cavalry Monument, Railroad Cut, Gettysburg National Military Park.

would not become prevalent in dedication speeches until the end of the 1880s. The focus continued to be on remembering the dead and how the Union victory at Gettysburg started the downward spiral of the Confederacy. Another reason for the lack of discussion about slavery in the dedication speeches for the 3rd Indiana Cavalry was Indiana's proximity to Southern states. Recent scholarship has shown that states north and south of the Ohio River before the Civil War had more in common than just the argument over slavery.[35] Many communities in southern Indiana and northern Kentucky came from the same families and worked together. During the Civil War, while political decisions and sectional tension divided the region, a bond remained between the two sides.

After the Civil War, Indiana became a location where Southern goods were distributed to the North.[36] Spahr wanted to address the victory over the Confederacy but acknowledged Southerners' ability to fight. While the 3rd Indiana Cavalry's dedication speech had reconciliation overtures, the primary purpose was to establish the great Union victory at Gettysburg. The battle between what Gettysburg and the Civil War meant to the Union veterans became contested throughout the entire period in which Union veterans were responsible for building monuments. States like Indiana, which shared a border with former Southern states, tended not to speak ill of the South. However, Northern states that did not share a border with Southern states tended to focus their dedication speeches on the treason that Rebels committed.

The railroad cut is an interesting area of the Gettysburg battlefield. Several regiments have their monuments located along the cut; however, not all of them were fighting in the area at the same time. The use of the obelisk is always an interesting choice in monumentation because it is vastly different from most other monuments in the field, which are usually square or rectangular. A glaring issue that can be observed by anyone passing through is the proximity of some of the monuments to the current road through the park. While most monuments have been able to keep their original spot in the battle, some have had to move for the improvement of roads for vehicles and buses.

While the 3rd Indiana Cavalry did fight in the area where their monument is located, it is not where the veterans dedicated it. Like several other markers on the battlefield, it had to be moved to allow for roads to be built for automobile tours. The 3rd has the distinction of having its obelisk moved twice since its dedication to allow for modern conveniences. It was first moved to allow the current Reynolds Avenue to be built and was moved for a second time so a bridge could be constructed over the railroad. Even with these changes, the monument is as close to its battle line as currently allowed.

As discussed in Chapter 2, Maryland, a border state, contributed men to both the North and South during the Civil War. Delaware, also a border state, only contributed regiments to the Union war effort.[37] The reason for this was the careful political stance of the state government. Delaware put the issue of secession to a vote on January 3, 1861, and voted against joining the Confederacy.[38] However, Southern sympathies remained high in farming areas of Delaware, where the slave population was highest. The result was a pro-Union, slave owning state that would remain split between two sides.

Despite this split, however, Union sentiment remained high and was better organized to support the Northern war effort. Pro-Union factions were able to organize full regiments while the Confederacy was not able to recruit a full regiment from Delaware. One of the reasons for this pull towards the Union while still being a slave state was that the government allowed Delaware to keep their enslaved people. Since Delaware pledged allegiance to the Union, it did not fall under the Emancipation Proclamation or any other contraband of war law used against the South during the Civil War. This, in large part, had to do with President Abraham Lincoln's original pledge when he was elected president that he would not disturb slavery where it currently existed. Two of the pro-Union regiments, the 1st and 2nd Delaware, fought at Gettysburg. The 1st Delaware Infantry was a veteran regiment when it arrived at the battle. In fact, members of the 1st Delaware had fought in every major battle of the Army of the Potomac since 1862. During the Gettysburg campaign, the 1st Delaware was part of the 2nd Brigade, 3rd Division of the II Corps.

After arriving on the night of July 1, after the first day's fighting was complete, the 1st Delaware advanced from its position on Cemetery Ridge. It occupied the Bliss farm in front of the Confederate main line on the morning of July 2. Heavy fighting at the Bliss farm exhausted the regiment's ammunition, so Colonel Edward Harris ordered a partial withdrawal back to Cemetery Ridge. The corps commander, General Winfield Scott Hancock, had not approved the withdrawal and removed Colonel Harris from command, placing him under arrest.[39] Eventually, orders were received from II Corps headquarters, sending the regiment back to the main line on Cemetery Ridge.

On July 3, with the rest of Brigadier General Alexander Hays's 3rd Division, the 1st Delaware faced the main Confederate assault on Cemetery Ridge. The regiment's position placed them in the path of lead elements of General George Pickett's and General Isaac Trimble's divisions. The 1st Delaware held its ground and even joined in a brief counterattack, capturing several stands of Confederate regimental colors.[40] For their actions during the battle, three members of the 1st Delaware received the Medal of Honor. During the battle of Gettysburg, casualties for the regiment numbered 77 out of 280 men.[41] Following other states in the mid-1880s, Delaware's House of Representatives debated how best to memorialize its Union veterans' deeds at Gettysburg.

On June 9, 1885, the Delaware legislature passed a resolution to locate and mark the position of the Delaware troops at Gettysburg. The legislature also appropriated $2,000 to build monuments in the marked locations.[42] The 1st Delaware monument was placed on the regiment's main battle line on Cemetery Ridge. The design was a seven-foot-tall monument with polished faces with the unit's name, corps badge, and a diamond representing the "diamond state" nickname for Delaware.[43] A second marker, placed near the remains of the Bliss farm, identifies the regiment's forward location. While the monument was placed at Gettysburg in 1885, dedication ceremonies did not occur until June 1886. The theme of the 1st Delaware's dedication speech mirrored the state's position during the Civil War when loyalties were divided.

Lieutenant John Dunn spoke on behalf of the 1st Delaware Regiment Association. Dunn described the battle of Gettysburg from the regiment's perspective: "This consecrated soil pitted the chivalry of the South in hand-to-hand conflict with the more stubborn brethren of the North."[44] Dunn, a veteran of the regiment, oversaw the flag detail during the battle. Some of the themes Dunn discussed included what the regiment's fallen members accomplished during the battle. The monument exemplifies what the surviving veterans and dead soldiers stood for at Gettysburg. Dunn explained that the monument "has enduring qualities like your own, will bid defiance to the storms of time, and in the breast of future generations, it will serve to kindle the fires of liberty."[45] Dunn also gave a context for what the Union victory did for morale. Dunn explained, "The spirit and morale of our army was increased and theirs was correspondingly depressed, to say nothing of the fearful loss in men from which they suffered and never recovered."[46] The speech did not mention why men from Delaware fought for the Union instead of the Confederacy. Since Dunn may not have wanted to offend anyone who kept Southern ties, his speech focused on remembering the dead.

Newspapers in Delaware acknowledged the monument dedication as a nod to a bygone era. The reason for the dedication ceremonies was described to the reader as "another generation of Americans remembering why some fought for civil liberty, and others fought for republican institutions."[47] The discussion of one side fighting for "civil liberty" and the other for "republican

1st Delaware Infantry Monument, Cemetery Ridge, Gettysburg National Military Park.

institutions" became a common explanation for the Civil War. Southerners wanted their reasons for fighting not to reflect their preference for slavery. Eventually, phrases describing the conflict would develop into Southerners fighting for states' rights and the ability to do what they wanted and the North fighting to preserve the Union.

The inclination to let go of the past by the citizens of Delaware can be seen in the designs of their battlefield monuments. The monuments to both Union Delaware regiments are nondescript and completely blend into the scenery. While the monuments give proper inscriptions to identify the units, they are very similar and can be mistaken for one another. However, Union veterans from Delaware understood that they needed the opportunity to dedicate a monument to their unit to show that they were willing to fight to keep the Union whole. Since there were no Rebel units from Delaware at the battle, there was very little in the way of fighting for funds at the state legislature level, which was a different issue in Maryland. Due to a Confederate Maryland regiment having a monument at Gettysburg, before the Union monuments were established, tensions occurred among Union veterans when asking for money. Union Maryland monument dedication speeches would directly aim at the lone Rebel monument on the battlefield.

Not everyone during this era thought that monument dedications at Gettysburg were solely for remembering surviving Union veterans and the dead. Some press members found the region of southern Pennsylvania uninspiring and thought that it owed its prosperity to the battlefield. A visitor from Delaware stated that Gettysburg, "has nothing of which to boast save the rich farmland and the groups of hills and mountains on every side."[48] Younger generations had already wanted to distance themselves from the era they did not remember before they were born. However, this did not mean strong Union veteran feelings were not reflected in media coverage. Union veterans were able to use the media to cover their monument ceremonies. Two examples of this are monuments dedicated by Rhode Island and New Hampshire.

New Hampshire dedicated five monuments to its veterans at Gettysburg during the battle anniversary week of 1886. One of the commemorated regiments was the 2nd New Hampshire Infantry. The unit was attached to the 3rd Brigade, 2nd Division of the III Corps of the Army of the Potomac. On the second day of battle, without orders, the III Corps commander, General Daniel Sickles, advanced his corps west from its position on Cemetery Ridge.

He intended to secure higher ground in front of the main Union line.[49] However, the movement put his command in a bad defensive position. They were separated from the main line and both flanks were exposed to enemy attack, a position known as being "in the air." This movement, creating a forward salient, also created a massive gap in the main Union line along Cemetery Ridge. The advancing Confederate forces under General James Longstreet took advantage of the Union's position to attack the exposed flanks. The 2nd New Hampshire was caught in this pincer attack as it attempted to support artillery batteries on a rise called the Peach Orchard. The 2nd New Hampshire fought a delaying action to allow for the withdrawal of Sickles's forces back to the main Union line.

The resistance of the 2nd New Hampshire slowed the enemy's advance. However, with enemy brigades advancing on both sides of their position, the regiment's commander, Colonel Edward Bailey, "ordered a rapid yet cool retreat of his men back to Cemetery Ridge."[50] The cost for the regiment to delay the enemy was steep, with over half of the men falling as casualties. By the time of the 2nd New Hampshire's monument dedication, the number of men left to visit the site was small. Martin Haynes, a U.S. Congressman, who was a private in the 2nd New Hampshire at Gettysburg, gave the dedication speech on July 2, 1886. In it, he focused on one central theme: remembering the sacrifices of the dead.

The end of Haynes's speech summarizes what he and other New Hampshire veterans felt about what happened to them at Gettysburg. Haynes had time to reflect on the bloodletting that befell the regiment that he served. He would observe that at Gettysburg, "One hundred and ninety-three men stricken not from a division, not from a brigade, but one single skeleton regiment of 355 men."[51] Haynes finished the speech with a view of the battle from a survivor's perspective. Haynes explained, "This monument is a memorial to our comrades, our brothers, who here gave up their lives."[52] The monument stands near the 2nd New Hampshire's battle line in the Peach Orchard. Each side shows a relief of a musket and the diamond badge of the III Corps. On the base of the monument is historical data of the regiment. From base to tip, this memorial type of monument is 13 feet tall and is constructed like a pyramid.

The fighting in the Peach Orchard and the Sickles salient are among the most debated actions during the battle. Why would a corps commander move his entire command forward, causing a gap in the line between adjoining units on both flanks? To understand what the III Corps saw on July 2, 1863,

2nd New Hampshire Infantry Monument, Peach Orchard, Gettysburg National Military Park.

visitors must look at its position from the Trostle farm. Looking west, the area of the Peach Orchard is at a higher elevation than the downslope of Cemetery Ridge and the flatland before heading back up toward the Round Tops. Sickles moved his men up to the higher ground, thinking it would provide him with an advantageous spot to engage the enemy, but this was not the case. Once the Rebel attack converged on his lines, the corps had no choice but to fall back or risk incurring heavier losses.

The three-dimensional look of the 2nd New Hampshire monument is fascinating. The unique shape falls in line with other markers from the state. For example, the one dedicated to the 5th New Hampshire is also shaped differently, with its base being built of granite rocks and another set of granite rocks sitting on top of it. Looking across the field in which the 2nd New Hampshire was attacked, it is easy to understand the plight they faced. With the Rebel attack coming from both sides up into the Peach Orchard, the regiment had to hold on as long as possible to give the artillery and other units time to fall back.

While the theme of sacrifice is common in dedication speeches, it is much more dominant in those monuments honoring small units that suffered high casualties. Another theme that gained traction in the mid-1880s among Union veterans was recalling not their actions but rather the scenes they witnessed in combat, suggesting their lasting effects on the individual soldiers. The 2nd Rhode Island Infantry Regiment saw little action with the VI Corps at Gettysburg. However, the regiment's men witnessed the desperate fighting on Little Round Top and Cemetery Ridge during Confederate assaults on both locations and provided eyewitness testimonies to the carnage. In the dedication speech for the unit's monument, a veteran stated, "The regiment witnessed the sealing of Little Round Top and the gallant but fatal charge of Pickett's division."[53]

The 2nd Rhode Island suffered few casualties in two days of combat. The unit started with 409 men and left Gettysburg with seven casualties.[54] Its monument, dedicated on October 12, 1886, stands approximately nine feet tall with bronze depictions of a drum, canteen, bayonet, and cartridge box. Before pulling out of town, the regiment placed another marker west of Cemetery Ridge to identify its location on July 4, 1863. As more states and their regimental associations added monuments to the Gettysburg landscape, a more resounding theme of remembrance began to form. Veterans of Gettysburg, with life expectancies of white men in their late forties, were beginning to age rapidly in the late 1880s. Preserving the memory of this tremendous event became essential to them.

2nd Rhode Island Infantry Monument, north of Little Round Top, Gettysburg National Military Park.

While the loss of life at Gettysburg was high on both sides, not every Union unit was engaged. Many of the VI Corps units saw limited action during the battle. However, their veterans' recollections and battle descriptions are just as important. Having a front-row seat to a battle allows others to get an overview of the fighting when letters and recollections are shared. This, however, does not mean that the 2nd Rhode Island did not have a storied history in the Army of the Potomac. The regiment had been engaged in battles before Gettysburg and would see more combat afterward. However, in the case of this battle, they did not face the brunt of the fighting.

The detail of the 2nd Rhode Island primary monument is quite ornate. Walking up to today's monument, one notices usable items stacked on the granite base. While regimental associations were required to keep their monuments on the battle line, the monument's uniqueness was at the association's discretion. Great care was taken with the 2nd Rhode Island monument to show an infantry soldier's detailed accoutrements (hat, bayonet, drum, and cartridge box), topped with the laurel of victory. The 2nd Rhode Island Infantry monument is an example of how symbolism in a monument can show the feelings of veterans who helped design and dedicate it.

2nd Rhode Island Infantry Advance Marker, west of Cemetery Ridge, Gettysburg National Military Park.

Not all regiments that fought at Gettysburg were fortunate enough to have light casualties like the 2nd Rhode Island. While this can be considered the luck of the draw and how the order of march can dictate the order of battle, a vast majority of the Union regiments at Gettysburg saw heavy combat. Modern visitors to the top of Culp's Hill are greeted with one of the park's many observation towers that give stunning battlefield views. Just a short walk from the Culp's tower is the primary monument of a regiment from Ohio. The 66th Ohio Infantry Regiment mustered into service in December 1861 at Camp McArthur. The regiment mainly consisted of men from Champaign County and left the state with 850 men.[55] A veteran regiment by the time of Gettysburg, the 66th Ohio had already fought in several major battles in the Eastern Theater.

The regiment was assigned to the XII Corps at the battle of Gettysburg. On July 2 and July 3, it helped push back a series of Confederate attacks against the Union right flank on Culp's Hill. At one point on July 3, the 66th Ohio moved forward from the main line on Culp's Hill and counterattacked the enemy toward the lower end of the hill, driving them back. Following this success, the regiment was recalled to the main line by late morning.[56] Several regiment members received commendations, including the Medal of Honor, for their actions during these attacks. The 66th Ohio began the battle of Gettysburg with 299 men and left the field with 17 casualties.[57]

Major Joshua Palmer was mortally wounded and would die a week after the battle concluded. However, the monument to the 66th Ohio was not placed according to the battle line cited in official reports. Furthermore, the monument placement was not where veterans remembered their position in the battle. Instead, the 66th's monument was placed to fit in with existing monuments on Culp's Hill.

The Ohio legislature began planning regimental monuments at Gettysburg in 1885. A resolution passed by the legislature promised $35,000 to "identify sites and obtain ground to memorialize and build monuments for all Ohio units that fought at Gettysburg."[58] Due to transportation problems, the 66th Ohio monument's placement on Culp's Hill was delayed until after the "Ohio Day" dedication on September 14, 1887.[59] However, the dedication for all 19 Ohio monuments continued on "Ohio Day" without the 66th Infantry's monument. Two different monuments on Culp's Hill are for the 66th Ohio Regiment. The main monument's location is on a granite boulder. It is approximately 14 feet tall, with the XII Corps star and a pair of Springfield rifles crossing on the monument's front.[60]

66th Ohio Infantry Monument, Culp's Hill, Gettysburg National Military Park.

Major Joshua Palmer Wound Site Marker, Culp's Hill, Gettysburg National Military Park.

Another marker designates where Major Palmer was mortally wounded and where the 66th Ohio advanced from Union lines to counterattack the Confederates on July 3. However, regimental veterans wanted the monument and marker placed differently. The account of where Major Palmer was wounded is where the left flank marker now sits, and the main monument should have been placed at the current location of the Major Palmer marker.[61] However, to this point, the GBMA would not make an exception to the battle line rule. The 66th's main monument had to be with the other XII Corps Units on Culp's Hill. One possible explanation for the unwillingness to allow the monument to be farther down the hill is the size of the monument itself. The monument needed better support than what was provided where the veterans wanted it. The current location of the 66th's monument features a solid granite rock in which the monument is anchored. The position farther down the hill is steep and the ground is loose, which could cause structural support issues.

The general address given by Governor Joseph Foraker summed up what the men of Ohio fought for at Gettysburg and throughout the Civil War. Foraker stated, "Ohio men were willing to sacrifice their lives to defeat the heresy of secession and allow our government to live."[62] Governor Foraker also tasked the GBMA to protect the Union monuments that dotted the landscape. Ending the address, Foraker asked the GBMA to "jealously defend the monuments as long as loyalty is appreciated, and treason despised."[63] While the governor

66th Ohio Infantry Left Flank Marker, Culp's Hill, Gettysburg National Military Park.

made it clear that men fought during the Civil War to defeat treason, the governor assigned no more significant meaning to the war. Within a week of Governor Foraker's address, the 66th Ohio's monument arrived at Gettysburg for placement on Culp's Hill.

The placement of the 66th Ohio Infantry monuments posed a host of challenges for the regiment's veterans association and provides an enjoyable trek around Culp's Hill for anyone wanting to visit all three locations. The main monument sits just off the edge of a path that takes you around the top of the hill. The path is steep and uneven sometimes, even with recent efforts to clear trails and underbrush from the area. Visitors to the area then have a short but steep walk down to the current site of the Colonel Palmer wounding marker. Even with modern technology and building practices, placing a sizeable primary monument in this location as the veterans wanted would require an example of creative engineering.

The Colonel Palmer marker is on a downwards slope of Culp's Hill with little room or flat surface for a large monument. The placement of the 66th Ohio monument is an example of how veterans stayed within the parameters of the GBMA of the battle line rule but also adjusting to make use of the terrain for a stable monument. The 66th Ohio moved its main monument to the top of the hill so that there was a better position to build the monument they wanted. If they had kept with the exact battle line rule, the size of the monument would be smaller. The workaround was placing a marker for Colonel Palmer's wounding in the spot where the line was held against the Rebels. While the location of the actual site where veterans stated Colonel Palmer was wounded was easy to get to during the battle and the monument dedication, this is not so in modern times. The left flank marker is covered in heavy brush and trees that have taken over the area between the main monument and its location. Added to the difficulty that what was once a path is now completely covered, it can feel like a wilderness adventure to find the left flank marker, depending on what time of year the marker is visited.

The 27th Connecticut added a third regimental monument to the Gettysburg landscape after its state legislature passed resolutions on March 16, 1887, to provide money for Connecticut units that fought at Gettysburg to build monuments.[64] The 27th Connecticut Association planned a monument on the battle line with the rest of their brigade at Gettysburg. Their memorial-type monument was made of granite and included reliefs of sabers, the II Corps badge, and rifles. The dedication of the third monument occurred on

27th Connecticut Infantry Rose's Woods Monument, Gettysburg National Military Park.

October 21, 1889, nearly five years from the day of the first one. Governor Harrison's speech built upon the earlier dedication speech in 1884 to describe why the men of the 27th Connecticut fought. Harrison told the crowd, "The war for the Union stands out in the history of mankind, among all those modern times, because it stood for the emancipation of a race, as well as the solidification of a nation.... Gettysburg broke forever the ambitious hopes of those who sought to destroy the Union."[65]

Harrison's speech was one of the first recorded dedication speeches that mentioned emancipation as a cause of the war. As the 1880s were ending, the messages surrounding Union monumentation began to incorporate emancipation into the war's meaning. One of the factors for including the topic of emancipation in dedication speeches was the date a regiment was formed. Regimental units were more likely to include emancipation in their dedication speeches if they were formed after the release of the Emancipation Proclamation.

By the end of 1887, the landscape around Gettysburg was becoming known as the "forest of monuments."[66] Union veterans pushed to remember comrades they had lost and to explain why they fought during the Civil War. The reasons cited during the mid-1880s varied from defeating treason to abolishing slavery. As the country moved farther away from the fighting, a new generation of Americans began to lose sight of why the North and South had fought one another. Coupled with more veterans dying from their wounds and old age, surviving veterans began to focus on explaining why they fought in their dedication speeches.

As the 1880s closed, larger states with bigger budgets began to allocate funds for their regimental monuments, which allowed for more significant ideas in monumentation. Two states, New York and Pennsylvania, would begin a race to see who could add the most to the number of monuments at Gettysburg. Both states would add monuments continuously from the late 1880s through the 1890s. Veterans from both states would also declare different reasons for fighting the Civil War. New York and Pennsylvania would help start the golden era of monumentation at Gettysburg as well as drive legislation to preserve other Civil War battlefields.

CHAPTER 4

The Empire and Keystone States, 1887–97

As discussed in previous chapters, Union veterans moved quickly in small states like Rhode Island, New Hampshire, and Connecticut to convince state legislatures to fund monuments at Gettysburg. While this represented the early period of monuments constructed at least in part with state funding, the years 1887–97 saw exponential growth due to the participation of larger states like Pennsylvania and New York. Larger states like Massachusetts had also approved funding, allowing veteran associations to design and dedicate regimental monuments as they saw fit. However, states that contributed most heavily to the Union war effort had just begun to get monument-funding legislation approved in the mid-1880s. Eventually, states like Pennsylvania and New York would contribute public funding to most of the monuments built by Union veterans at Gettysburg. One of the biggest reasons for building so many monuments was state pride—Pennsylvania and New York contributed a great deal to the war effort on behalf of the Union. At the outbreak of the Civil War, they were the two largest Union states, assuming a comparable burden for both manpower and money. It was thus natural that both states wanted to ensure that their volunteer regiments were recognized on the battlefield. A common theme for monuments from both states would be a focus on fighting for the other men in their regiment and not wanting to let their friends down. Both states would also be responsible for the two most imposing Union monuments on the battlefield, testifying to what Pennsylvanians and New Yorkers sacrificed for their country. As the 1880s gave way to the 1890s, people traveling to Gettysburg could see that the landscape was newly filled with monuments from New York and Pennsylvania.

One reason for the influx of monumentation at Gettysburg during this period was the economics of the era. Between 1870 and 1900, the United States experienced significant industrial growth. Industries such as railroads,

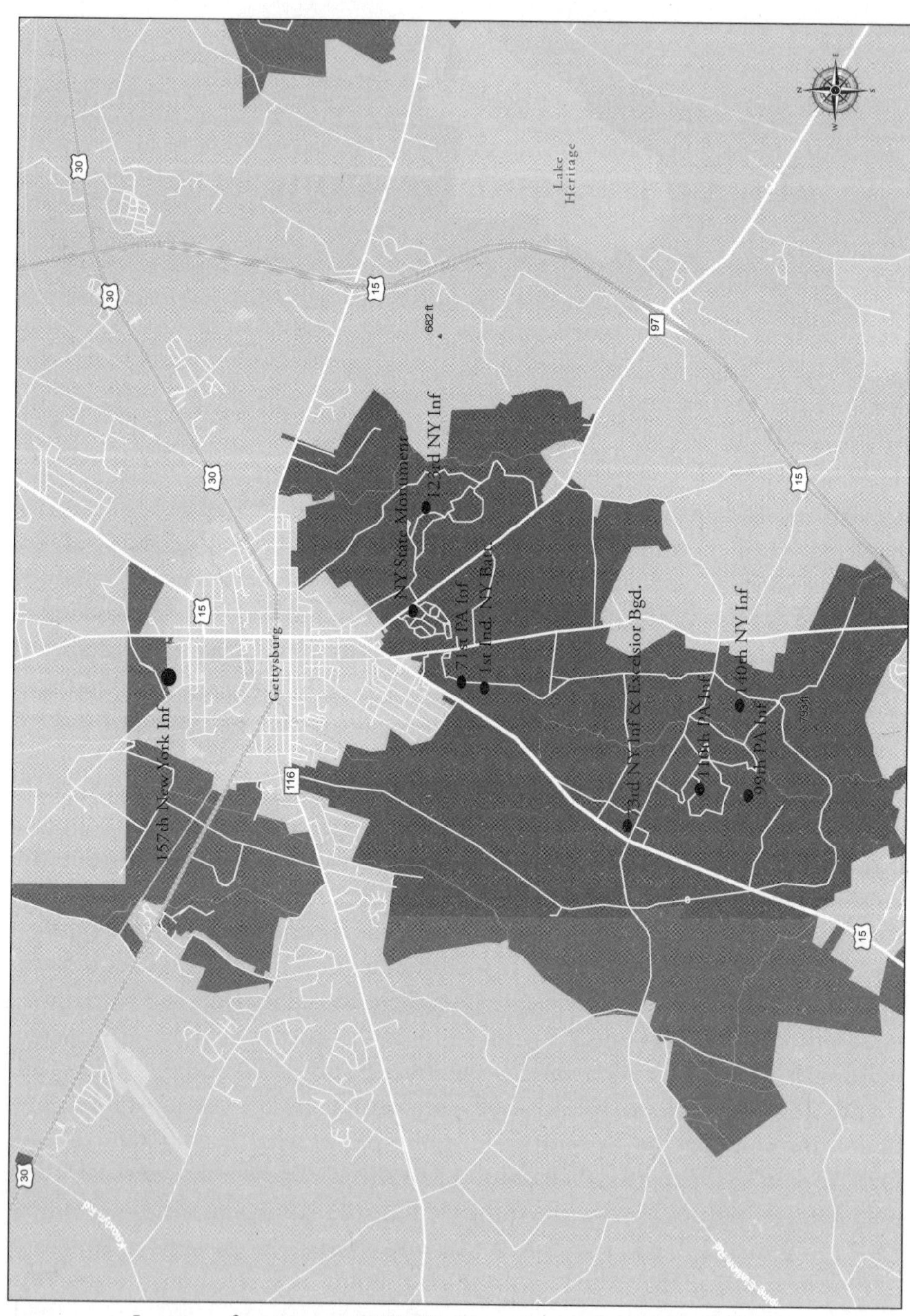

Location of monuments 1887–97. (Created using ArcGIS Pro by Esri)

oil, and banking exploded and contributed significantly to the burgeoning economy. This era in American history became known as the Gilded Age. With economic growth came an influx of wealth among the middle and upper classes, as well as increased tax revenue for state governments. State legislatures were willing to allocate funds for projects that their constituents desired.

At Gettysburg, Pennsylvania and New York supplied nearly half of the 93,000 men in the Army of the Potomac. Both states also suffered the highest number of casualties. New York and Pennsylvania ranked first and second, respectively. Union veterans from both states used these numbers as evidence for why their state legislators should provide funding for monuments on the battlefield.

The first legislature to act between the two states was New York's. In Albany, discussions over the best course for monument funding began on May 11, 1886, with the passage of the Raines Gettysburg Monument Commission Bill.[1] The bill aimed to select a commission of individuals to identify New York unit locations at Gettysburg and provide recommendations for costs associated with building monuments.[2]

The New York Monuments Commission included two former Union generals who commanded troops at Gettysburg. Daniel Sickles, commander of the III Corps during the battle, would head the commission. General Henry Slocum, commander of the XII Corps at Gettysburg, would assist. Both men were paid $5,000 to defray costs. On May 3, 1887, the New York legislature passed a bill providing veteran associations "$1500 to each regiment and batteries of the state of New York to build monuments at Gettysburg."[3] The bill also required each regiment to verify the proper location of its monument on the battlefield with the commission and the GBMA.[4] The commission worked closely with the GBMA to verify troop positions through official records. However, the bill passed in New York did not require changes to the placements of New York monuments that had already been dedicated, such as the one for the 157th Infantry, dedicated during the flurry of regimental commemorations in 1886.

The 157th New York Infantry Regiment served in the Union army from September 1862 until the end of the Civil War. The regiment's commander, Colonel Phillip Brown, had been its commander since the regiment's first day of service. Men from the 157th were recruited from the northern area of the state.[5] During the Gettysburg campaign, the regiment served in the 1st Brigade, 3rd Division, XI Corps. The 157th New York arrived at Gettysburg on July 1, 1863, deploying north of the town with 409 men.[6] The fighting on the first day of battle would and make the 157th combat ineffective for the rest of the battle due to the loss of men, like many of the other I Corps and XI Corps regiments.

The 157th New York came onto the field north of Gettysburg in the late morning, to the right of the I Corps, as the fight was already raging. While both Union corps initially held against the enemy approaching from the west, they could not long resist new Confederate units attacking from the north. As Union units began to pull back, the 157th New York, like the rest of the 3rd Division, was flanked from the left, and its line began to crumble. In the retreat from north of Gettysburg to its final position south of town, the 157th lost most of its men as casualties, mainly prisoners. The 157th shifted positions between Cemetery Hill and Culp's Hill as a reserve unit for the following two days. Of the 409 men that went into battle on July 1, 1863, only 102 men left Gettysburg with the Army of the Potomac. After Gettysburg, the 157th New York operated in the Carolinas and Georgia. However, when veterans began planning memorialization for their regiment, they resolved to build a monument at Gettysburg.

A unit veteran, Albert Barlow, wrote a memoir after the war, describing the importance of building a monument at Gettysburg. Barlow wrote that Gettysburg was where "glory was in the air; one could fairly taste it when Lee turned back for Virginia with his heart heavy. The cause of secession and human slavery had started down to destruction, and the people of the North rejoiced."[7] Barlow continued that Gettysburg also marked the location where "the 157th should have never been sent forward to fight two regiments alone, unaided."[8] While Barlow believed that his unit was sent alone to stop the Confederate advance, this was inaccurate since two full Union corps were forced to retreat on Gettysburg's first day, and instead of facing "two regiments," the Union troops faced four divisions from two Confederate corps. Like many veterans, Barlow spoke about personal feelings and experiences of the battle from his singular point of view. Nevertheless, the need to memorialize where the regiment lost so many at Gettysburg was on the minds of the veterans following the battle.

Planning for the 157th's first monument started in 1885 within the regiment's veterans association. After several other states and individual regiments began building monuments at Gettysburg, the 157th veterans did not want to wait for the state to pass a bill for funding; nor did they want to wait for the state to decide where such a monument should go. In order to hasten the process and ensure their opinions about placement remained at the forefront, the veterans collected enough money from private donations and subscriptions to build and ship the monument to Gettysburg. Although the 157th New York veterans decided not to wait for state funding to come

157th New York Infantry Regiment Monument. Built by the Regimental Association, North of Gettysburg, Gettysburg National Military Park.

through, they did reserve the right to use that eventual distribution to build a second monument in due course. The regimental association dedicated its first, privately funded monument on September 8, 1886.[9] The construction material is marble and granite, and on one side, the inscription reads, "Erected by the survivors of the 157th Reg't New York Vol's in memory of their gallant comrades who fell here, July 1, 1863." The monument is placed where the unit suffered most of its casualties.

One of the regiment's commanders, Colonel James Carmichael, gave the first dedication speech for the monument. In his address, Carmichael explored the theme of remembrance of the fallen. Carmichael explained, "Today we unveil our tribute to our fallen comrades. Let the everlasting granite stand, and may its words tell to coming generations through all ages the story of soldiers' love for soldiers. May it be a record of their appreciation for the sacrifices of their comrades."[10] The focus on the loss of men coincides with many regiments that lost most of their commands at Gettysburg. Interestingly, the 157th Veterans Association requested that some of the Confederate soldiers they faced on the battlefield on July 1, 1863, be invited to the dedication ceremony. Some former members of the 44th Georgia made the trip to participate. It was an opportunity for past adversaries to discuss their experiences from another era.

157th New York Infantry Regiment Monument. Built by the State of New York, north of Gettysburg, Gettysburg National Military Park.

157th New York Infantry Skirmish Marker, north of Gettysburg, Gettysburg National Military Park.

Eventually, New York also funded a monument to the 157th in the battle line with the rest of the brigade. The state monument to the 157th New York is an obelisk with the regiment's historical data and campaign history written on each side. The state also added a forward position marker where the regiment first engaged Confederate skirmishers on July 1, 1863. The Monument Commission for the state of New York would go to great lengths to ensure that New York regiments were well documented on the field at Gettysburg. The care taken to ensure monuments were in correct positions for each regiment would be apparent throughout New York's monumentation journey.

Walking to the three different 157th New York monuments, one notes that they are almost within eyeshot of one another. The committee could not make up its mind about where the monuments should go. However, their placement makes sense after looking at them from the lens of a veteran in the 157th. The regiment's veterans placed the first monument to mark where they took the most casualties. The state-sponsored monument followed the GBMA rules for battle line placements and also honored the 157th's initiative in battle by placing the forward marker. Not to be outdone by the 157th, another New York unit would describe their battle reminiscences in greater detail, and whereas the 157th invited Confederate soldiers to its dedication, the 1st Independent Battery of New York Artillery would actually include Confederate regalia on its monument.

Historians have extensively discussed the Confederate attack on the center of the Union line on July 3, 1863. The attack has been called many things, including "Pickett's Charge," "Longstreet's Assault," and the "Pickett, Pettigrew, and Trimble Attack."[11] The attack on the Union center was the Confederates' attempt to split the entire Union army. The feelings of the Rebel command staff were that attacks on the right and left flanks the previous two days had weakened the center of the line, allowing for an attack that would cause the Union army to retreat. However, the attack failed.

Union units that held the center during the attack marked their positions stating they were a part of the defense of the assault with inscriptions on their monuments since many felt the attack was the reason for the Confederate defeat. One of these units was the 1st Independent Battery of New York Artillery. During the Gettysburg Campaign, the battery was assigned to the Artillery Brigade of the VI Corps, Army of the Potomac. The unit had mustered into service in December 1861, and prior to Gettysburg served in every engagement involving the Army of the Potomac.

The battery arrived at Gettysburg on the night of July 2, 1863, and consisted of 103 men and six guns.[12] Its original orders were to support infantry on the left of Cemetery Ridge on July 3, 1863. Due to the presence of numerous Union batteries in the area, the 1st New York Independent Battery moved to the center of the line. The position held by the battery was near a clump of trees supporting General Webb's brigade.[13] That afternoon, the New York battery and General Webb's brigade would find themselves at the center of the Confederate assault.

During the Confederates' pre-attack bombardment, the 1st New York Independent Battery conducted counterfire. However, as Confederate infantry began to move across the field, the Union cannons focused on the approaching threat. Batteries used canister rounds at close range (less than 200 yards), consisting of dozens of projectiles in a cased shell, with an effect similar to a giant shotgun round.[14] The canister's effect on the approaching troops was immediate. Captain Andrew Cowan, the battery commander, explained that it "literally swept the enemy from my front, being fired at less than 20 yards."[15] The battery would continue firing until the Confederate survivors pulled back to their lines. By the end of the day, the 1st New York Independent Battery had suffered 12 casualties. The devastation they inflicted on the enemy would have a lasting effect on the unit's veterans and inspire the incorporation of the Confederacy into their monument.

Unlike the 157th New York, the 1st New York Independent Battery did not construct a monument until state funds became available. The artillerists placed their monument adjacent to their position on Cemetery Ridge, near the

1st Independent New York Battery Monument, Cemetery Ridge, Gettysburg National Military Park.

"Copse of Trees," which marked the rallying point for attacking Confederate troops. Their memorial-type monument is built of granite and bronze, featuring a bas-relief of the battery firing on Confederate troops. A bas-relief is a sculpture lightly carved into a surface; in the case of this monument, it was carved into a bronze plate. The inscriptions around the monument describe the battery's actions on July 3, 1863, and a breakdown of their casualties by type. On the relief is a Confederate flag flown by troops attacking the Union position. This was the first time a Confederate flag was featured on a Union monument at Gettysburg. Like the earlier Gregg Cavalry Shaft, including Confederate themes warranted explanation.

The 1st New York Independent Battery dedicated its monument on July 3, 1887, 24 years after its involvement at Gettysburg.[16] The dedication speech by Congressman Sereno Payne spoke of forgetting the past and moving forward as a united country. However, the veterans assembled for the dedication took part in other ceremonies that reminded them of days past. The speeches, dances, and reminiscences reminded the veterans of what it was like to be around their comrades again, albeit a little bit older. Payne's speech addressed how the country had changed since the end of the Civil War:

> Better that the captured emblems of that memorable struggle be hidden away until the slow tooth of Time shall have eaten away the last shred than that they are brought into the light of day to awaken the dying enthusiasm of other days or to enkindle old animosities. Let our anger slumber with these embattled flags. One bright, glorious, significant flag—the Stars and Stripes—is enough for us.[17]

Payne concluded with a nod to the growing tension of Southerners who did not like the country's direction after the Civil War: "The war is now over, and the feeble groans of discontented souls are lost in the flood tide of voices in the new south."[18] While Payne hoped that time would fix the past problems and the country could move forward, Union veterans still supported their Confederate counterparts.

During the dedication ceremony, Andrew Cowan brought and displayed a sword captured on the field at Gettysburg. His goal was to reunite the sword with the family of the fallen Confederate. Also, during this time, Cowan and members of the 71st Pennsylvania (whose monument will be discussed later) wanted the GBMA to allow a monument to be built for a fallen Confederate commander, General Lewis Armistead.[19] Armistead led one of the Virginia brigades that briefly pierced the Union line on July 3, 1863. Colonel John Bachelder of the GBMA stated that since the marker's placement would be where Armistead was mortally wounded, the marker would not break GBMA rules.[20] While the GBMA's shift would have allowed for more Confederate monuments at Gettysburg, the organization still exercised considerable scrutiny on who could place monuments on the battlefield.

While focusing on a Rebel commander during a Union unit's memorial dedication speech seems different than previous ceremonies, this was an exception and not the rule. There are several reasons why there was a focus on Armistead during the dedication from the perspective of the New Yorkers, Pennsylvanians, and the GBMA. Among the veterans associations of both states, the thinking reflected the times in the United States. During this period of monumentation, reconciliation between the North and South was commonplace. Veterans on both sides wanted to look past the motives for fighting the Civil War and simply acknowledge the bravery of the individuals they fought. From the perspective of Cowan, the other members of the 1st New York Battery, and the 71st Pennsylvania veterans, acknowledging the bravery of an individual seemed respectable, regardless of what side that person fought on.

The GBMA did not have an issue with the marker for Armistead's wounding site. While Bachelder himself said the marker broke no rules, it was by a technicality. The GBMA at that time distinguished between markers for individuals and unit monuments. Since the marker was to signify the site for one individual, regardless of what side they fought on, there was no issue. What was not allowed was a monument built for the brigade that Armistead led during the assault on July 3. Another reason why the GBMA accepted the marker was that it would provide a focal point for both sides to come visit. Bachelder himself focused on the Union center and the attack that happened there on July 3 when he discussed the battle. Having a marker that incorporated both sides of the fight was acceptable since it would bring both sides together. The marker itself is simple and only states that "General Lewis Armistead, C.S.A. fell here July 3, 1863." Providing a place where both the North and South could talk about a shared experience was important to the GBMA.

With the ideas of balancing a dedication to the dead and the survivors of the battery with reconciliation, the 1st Independent New York Battery designed their monument. Casualty rates among artillery crews, especially on the second and third days of the battle, were high. However, the New York Battery decided to go beyond a monument dedicated to the fallen. The battery would be one of the first to openly acknowledge the enemy they were facing. One of the interesting aspects of Union monumentation at Gettysburg is the faceless enemy on most monuments. While their dedication speeches spoke of a great victory, who did they face? It is tough to win laurels for a battle and not be able to acknowledge who the enemy was.

General Lewis Armistead Wound Marker, Cemetery Ridge, Gettysburg National Military Park.

Close-up of the bas-relief on the 1st Independent New York Battery Monument, Cemetery Ridge, Gettysburg National Military Park.

Due to the battery's location and the assault on the Union center, veterans felt that they needed to memorialize the attack from the vantage point of both sides.

The monument captures this in the relief tablet on its side. The tablet is very detailed, as can be seen today, almost like a picture. An observer can feel the intensity of the scene being captured. But as you look closer, you can see the Rebel battle flag flying as it approached the Union line. While today that may not seem exceptional, when the monument was constructed it was a huge deal. By creating the monument the way they did, the unit's veterans incorporated the enemy in a way that would memorialize them forever on the monument. The 1st New York Independent Battery stands as an example that if people are willing to take time to study and read the monuments on the battlefield, an interesting story will be shared.

The 1st Independent New York Battery was open to acknowledging Confederate veterans at their monument dedication, not all New York veterans associations felt the same way. The 123rd New York Infantry fought in two Union armies, the Army of the Potomac and the Army of the Cumberland. Even though the regiment fought in both the Eastern and Western theaters, veterans came to Gettysburg to dedicate their monument. During the Gettysburg campaign, the 123rd New York was attached to the 1st Brigade, 1st Division, XII Corps of the Army of the Potomac. The regiment came to Gettysburg with 495 men, mainly from Washington County near Lake George.[21] The New Yorkers helped to construct defensive works on Culp's Hill and supported the III Corps on the battle's second day. The regiment was assigned to the same brigade as the 20th Connecticut Infantry, whose monument was discussed in chapter three.

While the regiment would spend most of the battle supporting other units, the 123rd New York was part of the skirmish line that attempted to dislodge Confederates from the defensive works on lower Culp's Hill on the morning of July 3. Unfortunately, the 123rd would suffer the same friendly fire attack from artillery that plagued its sister regiment, the 20th Connecticut. Union shelling attempting to dislodge the Confederates also landed amongst the 123rd New York. Fortunately, the damage was not as bad as among the 20th Connecticut. The New Yorkers suffered one killed and another wounded. Overall, the 123rd New York suffered comparatively less than most regiments at Gettysburg, only 14 casualties. The regiment saw heavier fighting in the West and lost more in that theater than in the East. However, the veteran regiment wanted its monument in Pennsylvania because there was a deeper connection among the veterans to their losses and the battles that they fought in the Eastern Theater, especially at Gettysburg.

After applying for and receiving funds from the New York legislature, the 123rd New York designed its monument. The monument is approximately 20 feet high with a pedestal and a sculpture of Clio, the Greek muse of history. Clio is writing on a scroll, which is to convey that she is writing about what the regiment did during the Civil War. A smaller advance marker indicates the regiment's left flank and skirmish line against Confederates. This memorial-type monument also includes the battles fought by the regiment, casualty stats, and a brief history of the unit. The monument's dedication occurred along with three other New York monuments on September 4, 1888.[22]

The opening remarks for the monument dedication came from the regiment's adjutant during the battle, Seth Cary, and the focus of his address was remembering the dead. Cary stated, "We meet here on this sacred spot, on this twenty-sixth anniversary of our muster into the United States service, to dedicate this beautiful monument as a memorial of our comrades living and dead."[23] Cary wanted to show that the living still remembered their dead comrades and that the monument was for them as much as it was for the living.

The primary dedication speech for the 123rd New York monument came from Chaplain Henry Gordon. Gordon explained that "the war clearly proved the fact that the strength of government is in the intelligent attachment of the people to the principles on which it is based." The speech emphasized what the unit helped accomplish in a national sense: "The response to the call for men to defend the flag and maintain the integrity of the Union, considering everything, was the finest exhibition of patriotism ever given by any nation."[24]

123rd New York Infantry Monument, Culp's Hill, Gettysburg National Military Park.

123rd New York Infantry Skirmish Marker, Culp's Hill, Gettysburg National Military Park.

Gordon focused on fighting for the good of the government and the nation; however, nowhere in the dedication speech was there mention of fighting for abolition or freeing enslaved people. The focus on defending the nation and government in dedication speeches was also evident in that only Union veterans could attend. The men of the 123rd did not want Confederate veterans in attendance.

The monument for the 123rd New York stands out amongst a cluster of monuments leading to the top of Culp's Hill. Including Clio at the top of the monument allows visitors to locate it without much difficulty. As Clio writes deeds on her scroll, it is like she is looking out over the battlefield. The focus on the 123rd's dedication speeches on preserving the Union and the government is also quite fitting, considering the monument's location. The 2nd Maryland (CSA) is in the field of view of the 123rd. As discussed previously, the positioning of a Rebel monument so close to Union ones caused quite a stir once more Union veterans found out about the enemy marker. While there is no direct mention of the Rebel monument in the dedication speech of the 123rd New York, the closing remark of Cary's speech is telling. He ended his dedication with, "Here, in the presence of scenes so familiar to these comrades, and with this magnificent monument to perpetuate what they and the dead accomplished, we all, comrades, and citizens of this good county of Washington, dedicate this memorial and ourselves to Truth, Liberty, and Righteousness!"[25] Cary made sure to end his speech with a comment on what side of history he felt his unit was on—the side that was fighting for righteousness.

These issues during this period illustrate that even though the war had ended, there were still raw feelings about what happened 20 years earlier, while also trying to reconcile those feelings. Each veteran and veterans organization had different responses to these types of issues. For example, New York and Maryland veterans did not appreciate the Rebel monument on Culp's Hill. However, on Cemetery Ridge, New York and Pennsylvania veterans pushed for placing a wound site marker for a Rebel brigade commander. The individuality of each regiment was worked into what was said during dedication speeches and how the monuments were designed. An argument can be made that since a Rebel monument could be placed so close to the Union line, it was only fitting that a Union regiment could return the favor by placing a forward skirmish marker farther down into Rebel lines. The individuality of the Union monuments at Gettysburg continued with the 140th New York Infantry.

The 140th New York's role at Gettysburg has nearly been lost in the historical record. The regiment was formed in September 1862 by men around Rochester. At Gettysburg, the regiment was attached to the 3rd Brigade, 2nd Division, V Corps of the Army of the Potomac and deployed 453 men. Commanding the 140th from its inception through the Gettysburg campaign, Colonel Patrick "Paddy" O'Rorke had graduated first in his class at West Point in 1861. On July 2, 1863, the 140th was ordered to march to the Wheatfield but then was suddenly rerouted to Little Round Top.

The need for the 140th New York on Little Round Top was urgent on July 2, 1863. Colonel Strong Vincent's brigade was the only Union command on the hill, attempting to hold back part of a division of Confederates under General John Hood. The army's chief engineer, General Gouverneur K. Warren, helped identify the importance of the hill to the Union defense, stopped the 140th

New York, and ordered them up the hill to help secure the line. By the time the 140th arrived, parts of the 16th Michigan had broken and pulled to the rear. Fresh troops were needed as the Confederates were beginning to pour through the line, threatening to unhinge the entire Union position on the hill.[26] Leading from the front, Colonel O'Rorke ordered his men forward, straight for the gap in the Union line. As he charged at the head of his men, O'Rorke was shot and killed instantly by enemy fire, but the 140th continued forward, pushing the lead Confederate elements off their section of Little Round Top.

Eventually, more units and an artillery battery would follow the 140th up the hill and secure the northern slope. During the July 2 fight, the regiment suffered 133 casualties.[27] Since the end of the battle, the exploits of Colonel Vincent's brigade has dominated the scholarship of Little Round Top. However, attention and credit should also be extended to the 140th New York for its rescue of the floundering Union line. There is no official report in primary source material for the 140th New York. Brigade and division-level commanders mention that the unit was on Little Round Top, and the death of its commander is the extent of their mention in official reports.[28] However, the creation of the 140th New York monument on Little Round Top and the subsequent dedication speech give insight into what the regiment's veterans thought of their experiences at Gettysburg.

At Little Round Top, the 140th New York dedicated its monument on September 17, 1889. The spot selected was where Colonel O'Rorke was shot and killed.[29] The monument is a funerary type made of granite and bronze. The monument includes the seal of New York and historical data of the unit. On the side facing out and looking down toward the Wheatfield, Colonel O'Rorke's bas-relief finishes the monument. Forgoing private donations, the regiment association used state funds only for their monument.

Veterans of the 140th New York gave three speeches on dedication day. In Robert Lester's speech, the former Union officer discussed the state of veteran care by the government. Lester stated, "Less than 25 percent of the amount paid by the national treasury for pensions is paid to the survivors of the war. Over 75 percent is paid to the widows, orphaned children, or dependent parents of those who lost their lives because of service in the field."[30] The former Union officer continued in his speech that it was the duty of veterans to remember their fallen comrades' "virtues, and emulate their patience and patriotism, their courage and self-sacrifice. Let it be our part to conserve and maintain what they secured at such a cost."[31] The speeches following Lester's would extend the theme of how veterans should remember the sacrifices of the fallen.

140th New York Infantry Monument, Little Round Top, Gettysburg National Military Park.

Lieutenant Colonel Louis Ernest, another of the regiment's officers, continued with a speech at the dedication of the 140th New York monument. In his brief address, Ernest wanted the monument dedicated to the memory of the fallen and their fallen commander. Ernest said, "Many good men were lost on that day, and we are here to unite in a tribute to their memory. Among them all, our young Colonel O'Rorke, who was here cut off in the flower of his youth, stands foremost in our minds."[32] Ernest's sentiments aligned with those of Captain Porter Farley, who gave the main dedication speech.

The former Union officer was a company commander during the battle and witnessed the death of Paddy O'Rorke. Farley explained, "O'Rorke was among the dead. Shot through the neck, he had fallen without a groan, and we may hope without a pang. The supreme effort of his life was consummated by a death heroic in its surroundings and undisturbed by pain."[33] The attention the 140th New York brought to civic duty in their dedication speech is not unique to the unit. The men felt a reverence for their fallen commander and wanted all to know what he meant to them. Unfortunately, the regiment's actions did not receive as much acclaim as their counterparts on the flank at Little Round Top. Some of this can be attributed to those who survived the battle and who did not. O'Rorke died on Little Round Top, and so did his brigade commander, Brigadier General Stephen Weed. Strong Vincent was mortally wounded, and artillery commander First Lieutenant Charles Hazlett was killed outright. In the vacuum, subordinates and other commanders drafted what happened to the 140th New York, not giving them proper credit. Survivors of the battle could continue to write about their own regiments' exploits into old age, cementing their legacy without discussing the 140th New York. The 20th Maine's commander, Colonel Joshua Chamberlain, would survive the war and rise to prominence by writing about his experience in the battle, securing glory for himself and his regiment.

There is an adage: if you don't write it down, it didn't happen. This saying can be easily applied to the 140th New York and its commander. The 140th went headlong into the battle to push back the Rebel attack down Little Round Top. However, since O'Rorke did not survive the battle and the armies were on the move after the battle's conclusion, it was months before a hearsay account emerged of what happened to the 140th New York on Little Round Top. However, if the 140th had not rushed into battle, the security of the hill would not have been assured.

Visiting the monument today, I saw a tremendous view of the battlefield from its location. While most of the monument is a standard square with bronze accents, its surprising feature is on the front, where the fallen commanders' faces are relieved, giving the monument depth. Another interesting feature of the monument, specifically O'Rorke's face, is that his nose is shiny. The shininess did not come from a design flaw in the monument. It comes from the practice of people rubbing the nose of the commander, causing wear on the monument. From the time after the monument's dedication to the current day, rubbing the nose of Paddy O'Rorke is considered a good luck charm. While this can conjure up ideas of the luck of the Irish, there could be another reason the ritual happens. Instead of being for luck (O'Rorke did die, after all), rubbing his nose may draw on some of the strength and courage shown by the unit and by himself on Little Round Top. While one monument can be visited for luck, another New York regiment, the 73rd New York, made civic duty the center of its monument.

A unique attribute of the 73rd New York Infantry is the background of the men who enlisted with the regiment. Most of the regiment was recruited from New York Volunteer Fire Department firehouses, and they were nicknamed the "2nd Fire Zouaves."[34] During the Civil War, the regiment saw extensive service with the Army of the Potomac, participating in all major engagements in the Eastern Theater. During the Gettysburg campaign, the regiment was attached to the 2nd Brigade, 2nd Division, III Corps of the Army of the Potomac. The regiment arrived at Gettysburg on July 1, 1863, with 349 men.[35] The next day, the regiment was part of the III Corps deployment forward of the main Union line. It took a position in a field near the Peach Orchard, supporting Union batteries.

Oncoming Confederates would push the III Corps back toward Cemetery Ridge and threaten a breakthrough of the entire Union line. Captain John Downey, a company commander in the 73rd, gave an account of the Confederate attack. Downey wrote a friend, "My regiment fought the Mississippi Brigade, composed of the 17th, 19th, and 21st Regiments, led by Gen. Barksdale, who was killed. My regiment lost 160, as near as possible, in killed and wounded."[36] Another company commander, Captain Frank Moran, also discussed what happened to the regiment. Moran said, "Our little regiment was melting away fast in the deadly crossfire, but stood to its work unflinchingly, and closed at last in a semi-circle around its riddled flag. Our color-bearer was struck dead."[37] The remaining men retired from the Peach Orchard in a fighting withdrawal to Cemetery Ridge. The regiment suffered 162 casualties at Gettysburg and would continue fighting with the Army of the Potomac until the war's end. The surviving New Yorkers of the regiment would return 34 years later to honor their dead.

The 73rd New York Infantry has two monuments and a stone marker dedicated to its veterans. The first monument and the marker were dedicated on July 2, 1893.[38] The entire brigade, known as the "Excelsior Brigade," dedicated a monument to all its regiments since they were from New York and were raised by General Dan Sickles, who was their first brigade commander. The monument is a memorial type made of granite pillars and bronze inscriptions, adorned with an eagle and the New York state seal. Included near the monument are stone markers that acknowledge the battle line of each regiment.

While each regiment in the brigade was given the option to build their monument with state funds, they decided to pool their money together to create a single brigade monument. The regimental associations decided to create a single monument together because of how they identified themselves. In the dedication speech, General Henry Tremain explained, "As our five regiments were always united in service and sentiment, it was fitting that their survivors should unite in consolidating their interests in this enduring monument. May it help to perpetuate the memory of the Excelsior Brigade."[39] However, the 73rd returned to Gettysburg and placed a monument of their own four years later, in 1897.

The addition of the regimental monument represents the distinctive heritage of the 73rd. While the regiment considered themselves "Excelsiors" like the rest of the brigade, they were also New York Firefighters. A nod to their sense of fraternity can be seen in the monument itself. This sentinel-type monument consists of two bronze figures: a Union soldier with a rifle standing next to a firefighter with a firehose. The monument includes the other campaigns the regiment fought during the Civil War and other historical data. It was dedicated on September 6, 1897.[40]

The dedication again fell to General Tremain, who had delivered the brigade monument's speech. The central theme during his dedication was the origin of the regiment. Tremain stated, "The volunteer fireman never failed to risk life to save life or the country. That men associated with civic life for such exigencies should make good soldiers does not seem strange."[41] The monument emphasizes the regiment's heritage by including bronze inscriptions detailing the historical data of the New York Volunteer Fire Department. During the Civil War, the department moved from a volunteer department to a professional one. The New York Firefighter Association supported the memorialization of these veteran firefighters by raising most of the $15,000 needed to build the monument.

New York Excelsior Brigade Monument, Peach Orchard, Gettysburg National Military Park.

73rd New York Marker near Excelsior Brigade Monument, Peach Orchard, Gettysburg National Military Park.

73rd New York Infantry Monument, Peach Orchard, Gettysburg National Military Park.

New York Firefighters Association (NYFA) Plaque, Peach Orchard, Gettysburg National Military Park.

Today, the 73rd New York Infantry monument seems out of place due to its location. The monument stands out in a field all by itself. This is not because it is misplaced but because the other regiments in the brigade did not build a monument dedicated to themselves. If you were to draw a line from the 73rd's monument to the Excelsior Brigade monument, there would be the battle line that the GBMA expected. Many monuments on the battlefield pay homage to the geographic location a regiment was formed, often through symbolism on the monument. For example, the monument to the 42nd New York Infantry is adorned with Chief Tammany, the Delaware chief who assisted American colonists in adapting to the new world they inhabited and who became a symbol of the Tammany Society of New York. Most people would now recognize the Tammany Society as the political machine in New York called Tammany Hall. The society was the reason for the existence of the 42nd New York, as it provided funds to create the regiment.

In the same vein the 73rd New York was also formed, except instead of a political machine creating a regiment, emergency responders from the city came together to form one. Adding a firefighter standing slightly behind the soldier on the 73rd's monument gives an impression of where the regiment's men came from before they were soldiers. The monument is a testament to the importance of federal service to the New York Fire Department. In almost every major conflict that the United States has fought since the inception of the New York Fire Department, firemen either formed volunteer regiments, such as the 73rd, or provided direct assistance in other ways through the department. The monument is a great one to visit because it connects the past to the present, highlighting the importance of the sacrifices made by these volunteer soldiers before they enlisted to fight in the war.

A significant piece of New York's monumentation at Gettysburg is the monument dedicated to the men who died during the battle. Soldiers from New York constituted the highest number of men buried at the National Cemetery at Gettysburg. While allocating funds for regimental monuments, the New York Monument Commission also suggested allocating funds for a monument that would honor all the New York dead buried at Gettysburg.[42] The legislature agreed, and the commission began searching for a sculptor and builder. Commissioners from New York wanted a monument made of granite and bronze to commemorate the fallen New Yorkers, and they went through several designs.

Eventually, the Commission settled on the design of sculptor Casper Buberl. The monument, designed and built by Buberl, stands 93 feet tall and

New York State Monument, Gettysburg National Cemetery, Gettysburg National Military Park.

is primarily granite with bronze reliefs surrounding the victory-style shaft. Although the monument's design is in a Roman victory style, it is considered a funerary monument due to the inscriptions commemorating the New York dead. At the top of the monument is a bronze statue of a woman holding flowers and a staff, gazing toward the New York section of the cemetery. Construction of the monument began in 1891 and was completed before the "New York Day" ceremonies at Gettysburg in July 1893. It cost the state of New York $59,095.30 to build. The principal ceremonies of New York during the 30th anniversary of the battle of Gettysburg would center around the state monument.

The dedication speech of the New York State Monument focused on state pride and the loss of life at the battle of Gettysburg. General Daniel Sickles's oration opened with, "New York may always remember with satisfaction the distinguished part borne by her soldiers on this memorable field."[43] Sickles continued his speech by comparing the importance of Gettysburg in the Civil War to the battle of Waterloo during the Napoleonic Wars. Sickles stated:

> Waterloo terminated France's military supremacy in Europe. Gettysburg assured the perpetuity of the American republic. Waterloo was the triumph of the reigning monarchs over the French Revolution. Gettysburg prevented European intervention in our Civil War. Waterloo restored France to the Bourbons. Gettysburg broke the chains that fettered millions of enslaved people, giving force and effect to Lincoln's Proclamation of Emancipation, which before was only an edict.[44]

Sickles covered all the reasons why New Yorkers fought during the Civil War and lost so many men at Gettysburg, while acknowledging that the men of New York fought for different reasons. By comparing Gettysburg to Waterloo, Sickles was also able to examine multiple reasons for the importance of the battles in relation to their participants' perspective, and what victory meant for the winning side in both conflicts.

The monument to all New York veterans is one of the tallest on the battlefield today. Considering that most people view New York as a large state with a large, bustling city, this would make sense. However, another reason for the monument's size is the state's contribution in the Civil War. New York was rivaled only by Pennsylvania in its sacrifice for the Union during the Civil War, especially during the battle of Gettysburg. Both states would dedicate significant monuments to their dead since they lost the most.

What makes the case unique for New York is that they placed their monument as close as possible to the spot where their dead were buried in the National Cemetery. The monument's placement within the cemetery's main entrance means that anyone visiting the site would have to walk by the New York monument. Like the Soldiers' Monument at the center of the cemetery, visitors can use the top as a point of reference when walking around the cemetery and parts of Cemetery Hill. The addition of state monuments would become a common practice throughout Civil War battlefield monumentation. While not every state would pay for monuments at every battlefield, there was a strong likelihood that a state would build a state monument at a battle where its casualty rate was higher than most. The New York monument would remain the tallest monument at Gettysburg until Pennsylvania decided to build its own state monument. Until then, New York's monument would testify to what their veterans fought and died for at Gettysburg.

Two New Yorkers departed from the common themes of sacrifice and remembrance to address the issue of slavery by attacking a speech given by the Confederate States of America Vice President Alexander Stephens. In an address on March 21, 1861, Stephens had stated that the Confederate government "… is founded upon exactly the opposite ideas; its foundations are laid, its cornerstone rests, upon the great truth that the negro is not equal to the white man; that slavery, subordination to the superior race, is his natural and moral condition."[45] Twenty-seven years after Stephens made these remarks, two different New York monuments directly confronted the ideas behind this speech that some say precipitated the war. The first was the 134th New York Infantry, which placed its monument on Cemetery Hill, on the battle line protecting Union batteries. In his dedication speech, the Honorable Thomas Barhydt, a politician from the same region where the 134th's enlisted men originated, explained that they fought against the Rebels because the enemy was trying to "establish a new confederacy of states in which cotton would have been king and traffic in human beings of no less prominence."[46] Another example of attacking slavery in dedication speeches came during the dedication of the General Gouverneur Warren monument on Little Round Top.

Reverend Charles Hull, who served with the 5th New York Infantry during the Civil War, provided the oration for the General Warren monument. Hull stated, "We glance backward to the outbreak of the war … [the] fair structure of our Temple of Liberty could no longer be sustained on the cornerstone of slavery."[47] In the case of the 134th's and Gouverneur Warren's dedication speeches, fighting against slavery added another layer of complexity to the issues that Union veterans fought for during the Civil War.

Pennsylvania is second only to New York in the number of its monuments at Gettysburg. The state's approach to monumentation at Gettysburg was strict and methodical, and rules were closely adhered to. However, the state's dedication speeches covered multiple themes. Like in New York, the Pennsylvania legislature directly funded monuments honoring its regiments. On June 15, 1887, Act 272 of the 1887 Session of the Pennsylvania State Legislature provided money to regimental associations. The act proclaimed, "The sum of fifteen hundred dollars for the payment of the monument for each Pennsylvania command or organization participating in said battle."[48] However, the legislature was strict on when regimental associations could apply for the funds and how the monuments could be designed. The bill further stated that if the associations could not forward plans for how the funds would be employed to erect their monuments within a year, the commission would assume control and create a monument for the regiment.[49] This stipulation would put a time constraint on some Pennsylvania veterans. Most of the Pennsylvania regimental monuments were dedicated on "Pennsylvania Day" (which was extended to two days due to inclement weather), September 11–12, 1889. However, some Pennsylvania regiments dedicated their monuments before the state passed funding, using their own resources.

An example of these early Pennsylvania monuments is that of the 71st Pennsylvania Infantry. The regiment was formed in 1861 with men primarily from Philadelphia. However, the unit designation was not the 71st Pennsylvania but the "California Regiment." The reason was that the state of California provided money for the regiment's mobilization, and some of the men had moved back to Pennsylvania from California to serve in the East. Senator Edward Baker of Oregon, who organized the regiment requested that it be allowed to have the California designation so that all states of the Union were represented in the Army.[50] However, by 1862, after the death of Baker, the regiment was renamed the 71st Pennsylvania Infantry in keeping with the rest of its parent unit, nicknamed the Philadelphia Brigade.

During the Gettysburg campaign, the 71st Pennsylvania and its brigade was attached to the 2nd Division, II Corps of the Army of the Potomac. When the regiment moved into position on Cemetery Ridge on the night of July 1, it brought 261 men into line.[51] While the regiment assisted with the defense of Cemetery Ridge on July 2, 1863, most of its fighting took place the next day, during Pickett's Charge. During the massive Confederate assault, men of the 71st assisted in handling understaffed Union batteries. At one point the regiment fell back when the Confederate tide threatened to overrun the position, but it rallied and returned to the line. Once the Rebel attack crested, the regiment would be responsible for "taking some 500 prisoners, as many arms, and three stands of rebel colors."[52] However, the regiment was badly damaged after two days of fighting at Gettysburg. In its defense of Cemetery Ridge, the regiment suffered 98 casualties.

The regiment did not wait for the state of Pennsylvania to provide funding to build a monument at Gettysburg. Like the rest of its brigade, the 71st dedicated its monument on July 3, 1887. As mentioned in the chapter, Confederate veterans were invited to the dedication.[53] The 71st monument is a granite memorial-type monument with historical data on the regiment from all its campaigns during the Civil War. On one side is a description of the regiment's actions at Gettysburg, including the II Corps trefoil symbol and a nod to its "California" ties. To assist with quota rules from each state of the Union for military service, the rules were changed to rename some of the Philadelphia units to a California designation. The theme of the regiment's dedication speeches spoke to the mix of Union and Confederate veterans present at the dedication.

Acknowledging the bravery of both sides during the Confederate assault on July 3, 1863, was a common theme during the dedication of the 71st Pennsylvania. General William Burns, a former brigade commander, said in his address that "the Philadelphia Brigade fraternizes with Pickett's Division.

71st Pennsylvania Infantry Monument, Cemetery Ridge, Gettysburg National Military Park.

They recognize each other's bravery and respect each other's fame. The world will applaud both, and history will record their deeds together. This memorial of a regiment's deeds is a memento-mori of those who fell on both sides."[54] The theme of reconciliation also resonated in the dedication speech by a former regiment commander, Colonel Issac Wistar. Wistar asked the veterans standing before him, "While life remains for this small remnant, may every one of us, till our last breath, continue to cherish for our friends and comrades, affection, love, and personal friendship, and to share with our gallant enemies of long ago—enemies, thank God, no longer—peace, concord, and fellowship under one common flag forever more."[55] These speeches focused on peace and the idea that Union veterans should get along with their Southern counterparts.

While seeing the state of California as part of an inscription is not something most would expect to find at Gettysburg, it had ties to the conflict due to the desire by some to split the state in half, with one part being free and the other part being a slave state. However, California was admitted to the union in 1850 as a free state and was home to most of the known gold in the United States. The gold had to be shipped east through the Isthmus of Panama and to eastern ports. However, despite the state's desire for strong Union ties, it did not send infantry troops to the east. One battalion of cavalry was shipped from California to fight with the Second Massachusetts Cavalry. The majority of Californians enlisting in the Union Army were used to block rebel attacks from Texas and deal with Native American incursions from Mexico. Another unique attribute of the 71st Pennsylvania monument is not what is on it, but the acceptance of who the regiment fought against during the battle of Gettysburg. The fighting on the third day was intense in the 71st's sector of the line—the famous "Angle" of Cemetery Ridge. When it was time to dedicate their monument, the veterans wanted to pay tribute to the men they had fought against and simultaneously return war trophies. Even though reconciliation had not yet gained momentum when the monument was placed, events like this helped shape the conciliatory view of the war for generations later. While the 71st Pennsylvania focused on healing old wounds, some Pennsylvania regiments only wanted to remember the fallen.

Standing in a less traveled part of the Wheatfield at Gettysburg is the monument to the 110th Pennsylvania Infantry. This regiment formed in December 1861, with most of its enlistments coming from Bedford, Blair, Centre, Clearfield, and Huntingdon counties.[56] The 110th was a veteran unit that fought in most of the Army of the Potomac's engagements. During the Gettysburg campaign it was assigned to the 3rd Brigade, 1st Division, III Corps, though it brought only six companies to the battle, totaling 152 men.[57] Due to the III Corps' position, forward of the main Union line, the brigade had to spread itself thin, covering ground between the Wheatfield and Peach Orchard. A member of the 110th stated that "scarcely had we got into a position when we heard the fearful rebel yell. On they came like an avalanche."[58]

During the initial Confederate assault through the Wheatfield, the 110th Pennsylvania and the 5th Michigan found they could flank the enemy attack. The focus of both Union regiments was the flank of the 9th Georgia Infantry. The 110th Pennsylvania's fire forced the 9th Georgia to fall back, disrupting the Confederate assault.[59] However, the 110th Pennsylvania and 5th Michigan were not strong enough to stop the full enemy assault. Union regiments were supposed to be on the stony hill to their rear, not below on flat marshy land. As the regrouped enemy regiments shifted their fire toward the 110th's position, the Union troops suffered heavy casualties.

A company commander later surmised that losses would have been lighter had the regiments been placed on the hill.[60] Eventually, more reinforcements moved from Cemetery Ridge to help shore up a defensive line in the Wheatfield. The additional reinforcements allowed the 110th Pennsylvania to assist with the final charge that would push the Confederates out of the Wheatfield. As dusk fell over the field, the remnants of the 110th Pennsylvania and the rest of Regis de Trobriand's 3rd Brigade pulled back from the main line and went into reserve near the headquarters of the III Corps. The regiment would support batteries on Cemetery Hill on July 3, watching the final Confederate assault on the Union center.

The 110th Pennsylvania's battle in the Wheatfield cost the unit 53 casualties. Based on contemporary reports, half of the unit's officers were killed or wounded.[61] When the survivors returned to dedicate the regiment's monument on September 11, 1889, they did not forget that fact. The regiment used the state funds to create a sentinel monument in line with the rest of the brigade line in the Wheatfield. The monument is of a Union soldier standing guard facing the direction in which the enemy attack came on July 2, 1863. The theme of the dedication speech was remembering what the country needed from the men in the regiment. Sergeant Major Edmund Shaw, a unit veteran, gave the dedication speech. Shaw summed up the makeup of the men who fought in the 110th Pennsylvania as "beardless boys of 1861 whose rollicking manhood and patriotic courage urged them to put on the habiliments of war in response to their country's call in a time of need for courageous men."[62] Shaw would end the address by explaining what the regiment felt about their fallen comrades. Shaw stated they "were the sons of the sturdy, industrious

110th Pennsylvania Infantry Monument, Wheatfield, Gettysburg National Military Park.

and patriotic people of those localities, who had no silver or gold with which to employ substitutes or to pay exemption from the military service, but who tendered their flesh and blood in the performance of a public duty."[63]

The area known as the Wheatfield is an area of land that was once tilled and worked over, allowing wheat to grow and be harvested. This battlefield section is confusing because, like Culp's Hill, units from different corps fought there at different times. The area where the 110th Pennsylvania fought sits off DeTrobriand Avenue, named after the regiment's brigade commander. The monument is one of the classic designs of a sentential monument type. It depicts a soldier standing at parade rest, hands crossed in front of his body, holding his rifle. The toll of the battle on the regiment—over a third of the men casualties— is representative of many of the Union regiments that fought in the Wheatfield. The 110th was thrown into a battle line to stop the advance of the Rebels; being an understrength regiment did not stop the men from standing their ground and fighting until they were relieved by another unit, not long before their ammunition was expended.

What makes the stand of the 110th notable is that they were an understrength regiment that held against two Rebel regiments. Even though the monument is out of the way, it establishes that monuments can be placed anywhere on the battlefield, depending on where the fighting happened. The dedication speeches for the regiment also pointed out that the 110th was a working-class regiment, not worried about roughing it out in the field. This working-class image of themselves also pushed many to do their duty and not take credit for their accomplishments at first.

An example of Pennsylvanians contextualizing what Gettysburg could mean for future generations is the dedication speech of the second monument of the 99th Pennsylvania Infantry. The unit had initially built a monument in 1886, but when state funds became available, it built a more prominent one to take its place. The unit was attached to the 2nd Brigade, 1st Division, III Corps of the Army of the Potomac. The regiment had seen several battles and fielded 277 men at the time of the battle.[64] The regiment did most of its fighting in the center of Devil's Den, a boulder field near the base of Little Round Top.

The Confederate assault through this part of the III Corps line was an extension of the assault in the Wheatfield. The commander of the 99th Pennsylvania, Major John Moore, recalled, "The fighting was fierce. We held the position for over thirty minutes until the brigade began to retire on the right when I ordered the regiment to fall back slowly, covering the rear."[65] The regiment would eventually make it back to Cemetery Ridge on the night

99th Pennsylvania Infantry Monument, Devil's Den, Gettysburg National Military Park.

of July 2. During its fighting retreat through Devil's Den, the 99th suffered 110 casualties.[66]

The dedication ceremony occurred on September 11, 1889. The monument is a granite pillar with the unit's name and the III Corps' diamond symbol. Each side of the funerary monument displays historical data of the regiment, focusing on the loss of men at Gettysburg and other battles that the unit engaged in. Due to the regiment's defense of the area, the GBMA allowed the monument to be placed at the top of Devil's Den. The dedication speech by Captain Albert Magnin, a unit veteran, explained the battle's meaning to the regiment's veterans and what Gettysburg should mean to the rest of the country. Magnin explained that Gettysburg "shall be the 'Mecca,' and this monument one of those shrines at which patriotism shall come to offer her devotions. Here, our children and our children's children and the children of unborn generations shall come to pay tribute to undying valor and heroism."[67]

Magnin would also address the sacrifices of the fallen by stating why they fought. Magnin explained that, "Confirmation of the Republic was the object of their efforts, and we know that the Republic can be maintained only on the eternal pillars of public intelligence, virtue, and religion."[68] In his dedication

99th Pennsylvania Infantry Monument, Cemetery Ridge, Gettysburg National Military Park.

speech, Magnin wanted people to know what the regiment stood for and that veterans were still willing to fight. State funds allowed the 99th to replace their original monument, dedicated by the regimental association in 1886. The original was a memorial monument on Cemetery Ridge, where the regiment was ordered on July 3, 1863.

The 99th Pennsylvania has two distinct and different monument types and locations. When visiting Devil's Den today, the 99th's monument sits on top of a knoll that overlooks the entire area. The monument is so prominent that it is visible from Little Round Top when looking at Devil's Den. Another reason to gravitate to the Devil's Den location is the monument's shape. The tall column and stone on top draw the eyes upward. The monument is also an example of what money can buy if available. When the veterans association designed the second monument, they had the funds to build what they wanted.

The 99th Pennsylvania Infantry did not undertake a second monument just because they disliked the first one they had built; they fought in different areas of the battlefield and on different days, so they chose to build and dedicate monuments for both locations. The speeches given during the initial dedication day do not mention having a "bad" or "ugly" looking monument. On the contrary, the money the association gathered to make their first monument included all the information they wanted and was made to the standards of the GBMA. However, given the opportunity to have two significant monuments in both locations where the regiment fought during the battle, they would take that option. Veterans who built monuments later in the monumentation era at Gettysburg had plenty of examples to make them stand out. With the battlefield filling up with monuments, regimental associations understood that, to be seen, their monuments had to have a different type of inscription or shape to make them distinct from all the rest. Union veterans also understood that their time was short, and getting their story told in granite and bronze was important.

Two Pennsylvania regiments further demonstrate the emphasis on slavery embraced in monument dedications during this period. The 98th Pennsylvania fought on the north slope of Little Round Top on July 2, 1863. The regiment dedicated a monument in 1885 and used state funds to dedicate a more substantial one on September 11, 1889. In his 1889 dedication speech, Corporal Fredrick Leobling, a unit veteran, attacked the Confederacy for its defense of slavery. Leobling explained that one of the reasons for enlisting to fight for the Union was to go "face-to-face with the most wicked, uncalled for and unscrupulous attempt of traitors and rebels, to overthrow the government and establish slavery on a firm and everlasting foundation."[69]

Another Pennsylvania infantry unit, the 105th, would also center its dedication speech on attacking the institution of slavery. The 105th fought in the Peach Orchard on July 2 with the III Corps and suffered over fifty percent casualties.[70] The regiment dedicated its monument on September 11, 1889, with Reverend John Truesdale, the regiment's chaplain, giving the speech. Explaining the reasons for fighting the war from the Union perspective, Truesdale said:

> This four-year fratricidal war was a dreadful thing, but for this Nation, there was something worse than this war. The dissolution of the Union was worse; slavery was worse, and so when the gauge of battle was thrown down by those who were determined to have a government with slavery for its cornerstone, we said rather than these things, let us have war.[71]

Even though fighting in their backyard was a theme in both speeches, both speakers focused on defeating slavery and treason as the reason for fighting for the Union.

New York and Pennsylvania contributed significantly to Union monumentation at Gettysburg. Both states provided money for their state regimental associations to build monuments but required rules to be followed in their completion. By 1889, the combined total of regimental monuments built by both states was 170. The guidelines set forth by Pennsylvania and New York would be a blueprint for other states that had not yet built regimental monuments at Gettysburg. The uniqueness of monument dedication speeches was as varied as the units from both states. There was not a central theme for all monuments; both states dedicated monuments for different reasons. While most dedicated monuments for remembrance purposes, several included the importance of fighting for the abolition of slavery. Gettysburg monumentation, moving into the mid-1890s, would soon reach its stride and help solidify how other battlefields would model their preservation efforts.

CHAPTER 5

The "Golden Age" of Monumentation at Gettysburg, 1888–94

The addition of New York and Pennsylvania monuments marked the beginning of a trend in which state legislatures began to control the funding and construction of regimental monuments at Gettysburg. From 1888 to 1894, the remaining seven states without monuments on the battlefield followed the blueprint set by New York and Pennsylvania. The period would be considered the "Golden Age" of monumentation at Gettysburg. Using state money and following templates from other states allowed veterans to create monuments quickly. Interest in Union monumentation also triggered conversations about battlefield conservation in newspapers. National papers, such as *The New York Times*, wrote editorial pieces questioning whether enough was being done to protect the battlefield. The article read, "To the soldiers who fought on this field, to the whole country almost, this ground is sacred. Yet of 16,000 acres, all but 540 acres is private property."[1] The editorial opined that the federal government should be involved in preserving battlefields in the United States.

While this discussion was in its infancy in the late 1880s, debates over federal funds to protect battlefields began. Due to the slow bureaucracy in Washington, however, state legislatures passed funding to place more monuments on land the GBMA had already purchased. This is why many monuments at Gettysburg are so close together—most regimental associations did not want to buy land from private owners to place a monument. Regimental associations preferred to place their monuments on GBMA land, as this would eliminate the need for them to incur additional costs to purchase private property for their monuments. The increase of Union monumentation at Gettysburg is also explained by the growing battle between newspapers and veterans over the true history of the battle. Regiments wanted to place monuments to mark where they fought in order to silence news articles questioning their role in the battle. Writing for the *Weekly News-Democrat*, George Kilmer described

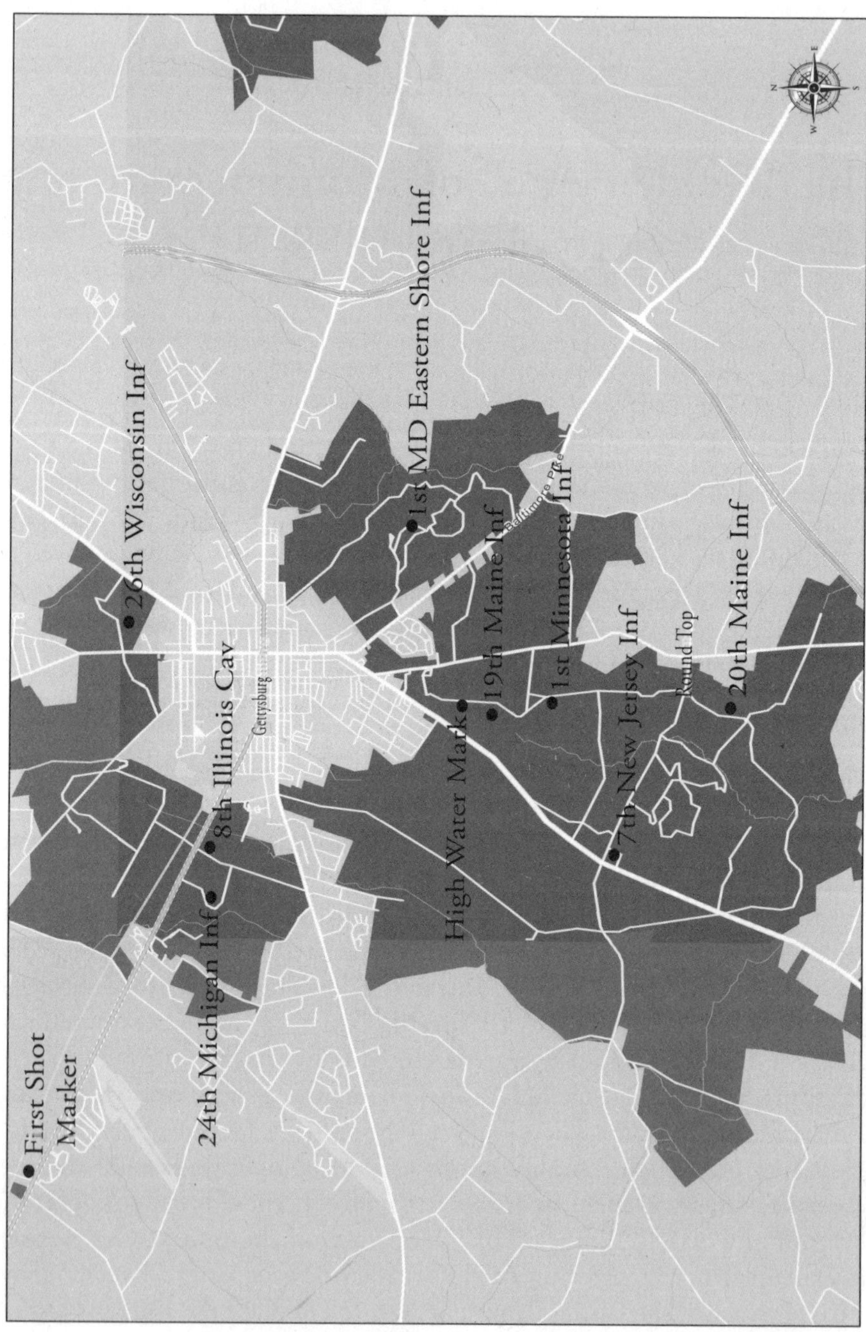

Location of monuments 1888–94. (Created using ArcGIS Pro by Esri)

the battle as "a campaign of mishaps all around and explanations that do not explain have been in order ever since the battle took place."[2] Excerpts from contemporary articles reveal writers questioning the tactics and actions of units during the battle. Civilians' questioning of soldiers further motivated Union veterans to commemorate their actions at Gettysburg.

Wisconsin was one of the first states to place regimental monuments during this era. Although Wisconsin dedicated monuments at Gettysburg in 1888, planning by the state legislature began a year earlier. On March 16, 1887, the Wisconsin legislature passed a bill to provide funds for the GBMA and Wisconsin regimental associations to build monuments at Gettysburg. Section One of the bill provided the GBMA "$1,500 to be expended by the said association in the purchase of lands of especial interest, on that field."[3] In need of funds toward the end of the 1880s and early 1890s, the GBMA requested money from states to manage the land they already owned at Gettysburg. Section two of the bill provided funding for the Wisconsin regiments that fought at Gettysburg in the amount of $1,000. Like the states of New York and Pennsylvania, the Wisconsin legislature created rules for the monuments. The legislature expected regimental associations to follow the recommendations of the monument commission for placement and further expected the monuments to be made of Wisconsin granite.[4] The associations of Wisconsin's six regiments and one company of sharpshooters followed the legislature's rules.

One regiment that used the Wisconsin legislature's funding was the 26th Wisconsin Infantry. The regiment mustered into service in September 1862 and served in the Army of the Potomac at Fredericksburg and Chancellorsville. At Gettysburg the regiment was attached to the 2nd Brigade, 3rd Division, XI Corps, and deployed north of town on July 1, lengthening the line started by the I Corps, which was already engaged. The regiment arrived at Gettysburg with 446 men,[5] and was at the end of the brigade's line of battle. The regiment's original order was to make contact with General Francis Barlow's division in the fields north of Gettysburg, where an attack by Confederates of Richard Ewell's Corps, marching down from Carlisle, was imminent.

In the early afternoon of July 1, the 26th Wisconsin faced a tremendous onslaught of Rebel troops. During the fighting, the movement of Barlow's division farther forward exposed the regiment's flank, forcing the 26th to fight in two directions. The regiment "was furiously attacked by vastly superior numbers but held its position until ordered to retreat."[6] The 26th fell back through the streets of Gettysburg and formed on Cemetery Hill south of town with other units of the XI Corps. During the fighting, the 26th Wisconsin suffered 217 casualties, almost half the regiment. It held a reserve position for the rest of the battle and suffered no further losses. After Gettysburg, the 26th continued to serve in the Union army until the war's end.

After the war, the 26th Wisconsin Regiment Association held an annual reunion for its surviving members and their families. The regiment had been recruited from Milwaukee and consisted of nearly all German immigrants. Once the state legislature announced its intentions to fund regimental monuments at Gettysburg, the 26th responded quickly with a design. The association decided on a memorial-type monument in the shape of an obelisk. Each side of it contained historical data about the regiment from the entire Civil War, including the casualty count for the battle of Gettysburg. The monument was placed on the brigade battle line north of Gettysburg. On June 28, 1888, approximately 50 survivors of the regiment departed from Milwaukee for Gettysburg.[7] They followed other Wisconsin regiment association groups to Gettysburg for "Wisconsin Day," scheduled for June 30, 1888.

The regimental associations would not stage a dedication ceremony for each regiment. Instead, the dedication exercises and speeches at Gettysburg would include all seven Wisconsin monuments.[8] The U.S. senator from Wisconsin, John Spooner, gave the primary dedication speech. The delegation chose an area near where General John Reynolds, the I Corps commander, was killed on the first day of battle for the dedication speeches. This spot was chosen because several Wisconsin units, part of the Union's Iron Brigade, fought near this location.

The themes of Senator Spooner's speech focused on abolishing slavery and preserving the Union. Spooner explained that "the proclamation of the freedom of slaves had been at length reluctantly issued. It proved that the war was waged to destroy an institution rather than preserve the union of states."[9] Later in his speech, Spooner returned to his claim that the war was not about preserving the union. Spooner closed his address with, "Let us not fail in our devotion to the Union in defense of which they left all that was dear to them and under whose flags so many marched with stately, intrepid tread to death."[10] Spooner highlighted two critical factors that contributed to the sacrifices made by Union soldiers during the Civil War. Regiments formed later in the war, such as the 26th, were established after the Emancipation Proclamation became known, providing another reason to fight in the war. The second factor related to the casualty counts listed in papers during the war. Men who had not signed up to fight felt it was the right thing to do since so many went before them to fight in the war.

26th Wisconsin Infantry Regiment Monument, north of Gettysburg, Gettysburg National Military Park.

During the Civil War, Wisconsin, like other Midwest states that sent troops to Washington, was considered "western." In today's understanding of the geography of the United States, Wisconsin is not considered part of the West, but at the time the label applied to every state on the other side of Ohio. It is also essential to note the social differences between the various parts of the country in the 1860s. Many Wisconsin troops had probably not left their town, let alone their state, until they signed up to fight. These men almost certainly did not have the same experiences as Northern factory workers or businessmen. This is an essential distinction, in that even though the men of the North had very little in common, what they fought for was of great importance. The commonality of keeping the Union whole allowed many groups of people to come together to fight for a common cause.

The 26th Wisconsin monument is a tall, obelisk-shaped structure located near what is now Barlow's Knoll. While it has a simple design, the monument stands out when driving through the battlefield. Its unique look also breaks up the sight line of the different monuments in the area where the 26th fought. Of course, in the case of many of these monuments, beauty is in the eye of the beholder. The crescent moon symbol of the XI Corps is prevalent on the 26th's monument. While this may seem trivial to the modern visitor, it was a significant symbol to display prominently for the regiment's veterans. Each corps in the Union Army of the Potomac had a different badge or symbol. The purpose of this badge was to enable commanders to quickly identify a unit, while at the same time it generated unit pride among the soldiers themselves. Like many of the XI Corps in the fall of 1863, the 26th Wisconsin shifted to fighting in the Western Theater. However, when deciding to build a monument, the veterans of the 26th did not choose a battlefield in the West; instead, they came to Gettysburg.

The same day of Wisconsin's dedication speeches, 11 regimental monuments for the state of New Jersey were dedicated, bringing to fruition three years of planning and organizing to honor that state's veterans at Gettysburg. As stated at the beginning of chapter four, the New Jersey legislature began acquiring funds for regimental monuments in 1885.[11] New Jersey would also contribute to the GBMA's needs. In 1886, the New Jersey legislature passed a bill providing the organization with $3,000 to help maintain the battlefield and acquire more property.[12] The period between passing legislation for funds and the dedication of its monuments gave New Jersey regimental associations over three years to plan, design, and build their monuments.

One uniquely designed New Jersey monument at Gettysburg is that of the 7th New Jersey Infantry Regiment. The 7th New Jersey was a veteran regiment formed in the fall of 1861, and its men had seen combat in almost every significant engagement since the Peninsula Campaign in 1862. During the Gettysburg campaign, the 7th was attached to the 3rd Brigade, 2nd Division, III Corps of the Army of the Potomac. The regiment would arrive at Gettysburg early on the morning of July 2 and deploy in front of the main Union line, along with the rest of the III Corps, near the Peach Orchard, with 275 men.[13] However, the 7th would not be fighting with its brigade on the afternoon of July 2.

On July 2, the 7th New Jersey was assigned to support Battery B, 1st New Jersey Light Artillery, near the eastern side of the Peach Orchard. During this support detail, General Longstreet's Confederate corps assaulted across the line, hitting both sides of Sickles's salient position. Confederate artillery fire caused most of the regiment's casualties during the fight at the Peach Orchard, and once the Rebel infantry assault started, the 7th New Jersey was flanked from both sides.[14] During the assault, the 7th attempted a counterattack to push back the enemy, but it was unable to amass enough men to mount an effective movement. The regiment made a fighting withdrawal back to Cemetery Ridge on the evening of July 2. On the third day of the battle, the 7th was held in reserve but came under heavy artillery fire for a short time during the assault on the Union center.

Like many Union units of the III Corps, the 7th suffered heavily during the fight at the Peach Orchard. The regiment suffered 114 casualties, nearly half of its number, though the 7th continued to serve in the Army of the Potomac until the end of the war. At Gettysburg, the 7th would be the only New Jersey regiment to lose its commander, Colonel Louis Francine. This loss would play into where the regiment placed its monument 25 years later.

The uniqueness of the 7th New Jersey Infantry monument is in the design. The monument is a large, polished granite piece shaped like a minié ball, the type of bullet used in most infantry rifles during the Civil War. This memorial type of funerary monument also served as a marker for where Colonel Francine fell. Instead of placing the monument on the brigade line or at the location where the regiment was initially sent to protect Union batteries, the regimental association chose a site associated with a death. The regiment had to obtain permission from the GBMA to place the monument in the designated location, as it did not follow the standard protocol for organizing battle line placement. However, since the unit was detached from its brigade to protect Union batteries, the organization made an exception in the 7th New Jersey's favor.

7th New Jersey Infantry Regiment Monument, Peach Orchard, Gettysburg National Military Park.

The dedication ceremonies for New Jersey on June 30, 1888, featured the attendance of both Union and Confederate veterans. Former Confederate General James Longstreet and Union General Dan Sickles exchanged handshakes during the ceremonies.[15] The reconciliatory tone in the crowd would also play a role in the 7th New Jersey's dedication ceremony, the fourth ceremony of the day. Sergeant Edward McDonald, a veteran of the regiment, gave the dedication speech.

McDonald's speech included themes of remembrance for the dead, the preservation of the Union, and the country's reconciliation since the Civil War ended. McDonald spoke of the battle of Gettysburg as the most significant event in the history of the Republic, the victory won during the great struggle to preserve our Union and its flag upon the field we stand today.[16] McDonald continued by explaining how the country benefited from the Union victory at Gettysburg and its effect on the Civil War. McDonald said that veterans must "commemorate events in the great struggle so that those who come after us may know and understand that our republican form of government is no experiment and that its brave defenders will meet those who seek to assail its stability."[17] The defense of the Union was a central theme for all the New Jersey dedication speeches. The only speech that addressed slavery was during the 11th New Jersey Infantry's dedication. Colonel John Schoonover, a veteran of the regiment, concluded his address by explaining what the assembled veterans should be proud of in their service. Schoonover stated, "We are a part of the grandest army that ever struck for liberty, nationality, and the rights of man."[18]

While the country would eventually see the Civil War as a fight to end slavery, this was not always the case in 1863 or when veterans built their monuments. This by no means meant that they did not feel for the enslaved people who lived in the South. Many accepted that the Union was fighting for the preservation of its government and the commercial attachment between the South and North. This is why modern visitors should try to research the monuments they plan to visit at Gettysburg. Visitors will find that the dedication of the monuments varied from unit to unit. While abolishing slavery was a key point in many dedication speeches, preserving the Union and defeating traitors were also common themes.

The shaped bullet used in the design of the 7th New Jersey's monument was one of the deadliest instruments on the battlefield during the Civil War. The minié ball added both accuracy and lethality to the round balls used in previous wars, making the use of the bullet as a monument interesting and macabre. While the shape differs from most monuments, it is an example of violence creating a piece of art. The use of a bullet draws attention to the monument because of the detail of the monument itself. The bullet has so much detail that it looks like the monument could be split off its base and used in a massive gun. The monument also has the three rings that make up the bullet's base worked into the sculpture. The monument, viewed from a distance, could also be mistaken for an artillery round due to the proximity of artillery units to the regiment's battle line. The result is an example of what bullets looked like when used by soldiers in the Union army at Gettysburg.

Another group of Union veterans that prided itself on fighting to preserve the Union was from the state of Maryland. The Union veterans of the border state led a grassroots effort to convince the Maryland legislature to fund the construction of monuments at Gettysburg and to provide funding for the GBMA. The effort began in 1886 but was not formally debated in the Maryland legislature until January 11, 1888. After two months of debate, the legislature passed a bill allocating funds to Maryland's five units in the Army of the Potomac to construct monuments at Gettysburg. The bill stated, "The sum of five thousand dollars, or so much thereof as may be necessary, be and the same is hereby appropriated out of any money in the treasury not otherwise appropriated, to pay for the purchase of said tablets or monuments and having the same properly erected."[19] The money would equal $1,000 per monument at Gettysburg. The bill also provided funds for the GBMA for $1,000 for land purchase and infrastructure.

Maryland regimental associations had been working behind the scenes, preparing to build their monuments as soon as the legislature secured the money. The associations spent the rest of 1888 constructing monuments, having selected October 25, 1888, as "Maryland Day" at Gettysburg. One of the regiments that dedicated a monument was the 1st Maryland Eastern Shore Infantry Regiment. As the name implies, it recruited loyal Union men from the eastern half of Maryland. The regiment's first commander, Colonel James Wallace, was, in fact, an enslaver who did not think the South should have seceded. The regiment was formed in September 1861 but for two years was primarily used for garrison duty in Maryland and parts of Virginia. With the need for reinforcements after Chancellorsville, the regiment was attached to the 2nd Brigade, 1st Division, XII Corps of the Army of the Potomac during the Gettysburg campaign. When the regiment took its position on Culp's Hill, it deployed with 532 men.

In one of the ironic twists of the battle, the 1st Maryland Eastern Shore Regiment of the Army of the Potomac would be attacked by the 2nd Maryland

Infantry of the Confederate army (at the time of the battle called the 1st Maryland Battalion). Both regiments were recruited from the same area of Maryland, and their commanders were cousins. On the morning of the third day of the battle, the 1st Maryland Eastern Shore Infantry was ordered to relieve front-line units. During the transition to the front, a Union veteran of the 1st Maryland recalled, "The enemy attempted to rush upon our works and then delivered a very effective volley over the heads of the men occupying the position we were ordered to relieve."[20] The regiment completed the move into its new position and continued engaging the enemy until they withdrew from the slope of the hill. During the battle, the regiment suffered 25 casualties.[21] The 1st Maryland also had to assist with burying and capturing neighbors and friends. Many of these men were "credibly informed that the enemy we fought was the First Maryland [rebel] Regiment [Battalion]."[22] After the battle, the regiment returned to garrison duty, mustering out of service in 1864. The regiment's first commander, Colonel Wallace, resigned his commission in December 1863 due to the new policy of the federal government that allowed black male citizens to enlist in the Union army.

The dedication exercises for all Union Maryland regiments occurred at the base of Culp's Hill near Spangler's Spring. After several remarks from dignitaries, the 1st Maryland Eastern Shore dedicated its monument. Lieutenant Colonel William Comegys, a veteran of the regiment, gave the dedication speech. Comegys gave a general synopsis of the regiment's history and exploits at Gettysburg. Comegys also spoke of the regiment being committed to the Union and opposed to the creation of the Confederacy. He explained that Gettysburg was "where we met and beat back the adversaries of our government and the bold champions of the Southern cause."[23] The speech did not discuss the state's internal strife, of citizens fighting each other over the issue of slavery. The object of the speech and monument was to show that men loyal to the Union were living in Maryland during the Civil War.

The monument dedicated by the regimental association serves as both a memorial and a sentinel. The monument is a five-by-eight-foot rectangle made of granite, depicting a Union soldier lying in a prone position, ready to fire. On the front is the star emblem of the XII Corps and the inscription "Maryland's Tribute To Her Loyal Sons." The monument is near the regiment's position on the third day of battle when it relieved other Union regiments. It is also not far from where the Confederate 2nd Maryland Infantry Regiment dedicated its monument a few years earlier. However, the Union Maryland veterans did not contest the GBMA's placement of the Confederate Maryland monument.

1st Maryland Eastern Shore Infantry Regiment Monument, Culp's Hill, Gettysburg National Military Park.

The late 1880s saw many states scrambling to erect monuments at Gettysburg for their veterans. Maryland became a part of this movement, even though a Rebel Maryland monument had been placed on the battlefield well before the state legislature got to the business of funding Union ones. The constant tug of war between Maryland's identity as a border state influenced the amount of time it took the state government to allocate funds for monument building. It is unclear why Union Maryland veteran associations did not pool their resources to build monuments sooner, as some veteran groups had. Ironically, in the case of the 1st Maryland Eastern Shore, they would spend a significant portion of the battle fighting men from their own state on Culp's Hill during the battle.

The monument went through recent cleaning and restoration, and the details of the soldier are remarkable. The face of the unnamed soldier is clear, and the uniform details are very sharp. The soldier's position on the monument also indicates how the regiment used earthworks, rocks, and boulders to find better firing positions while on Culp's Hill. The monument also states and distinguishes itself from the Rebel one by clearly stating in granite that its men were the loyal sons of the state to the Union. These sentiments were also stressed during the dedication speeches. In the dedication of this Maryland monument, visitors can see a physical embodiment of the phrase that describes what happened in the American Civil War: brothers fighting brothers.

In 1887, several states passed legislation to build regimental monuments at Gettysburg. While Maryland debated their state funding through much of 1887, the state of Michigan passed its legislation quickly. The act, passed on June 22, 1887, provided "the sum of twenty thousand dollars be, and the same is hereby appropriated from any amounts of money in the State treasury not otherwise appropriated, to erect monuments to mark the places occupied on the battlefield at Gettysburg."[24] Michigan fielded seven infantry regiments, four cavalry regiments, an artillery battery, and a handful of sharpshooter rifle companies at Gettysburg. Money was also allocated to the GBMA to help maintain the monuments and, if necessary, purchase land to conserve parts of Gettysburg. The bill provided more money than most because the state was willing to purchase land, if it had to, for a monument. The monument and parcel of land would then be donated to the GBMA. The two-year process would send funds to Michigan regimental associations for the drafting, contracting, and construction of the monuments. Like New York and Pennsylvania, the monument built by a regimental association had to receive approval from the Michigan Gettysburg Monument Commission.[25] The state of Michigan placed all its monuments by November 1888 and scheduled their collective dedication for June 12, 1889.

One of the Michigan regiments that dedicated their monument in June 1889 was the 24th Michigan Infantry Regiment. The regiment formed in Detroit in August 1862 and was assigned to the "Iron Brigade, made up of regiments from Michigan, Indiana and Wisconsin. General George McClellan gave the brigade its moniker during the battle of South Mountain because the western troops hit the enemy like iron.[26] The regiment joined the brigade for the battle of Fredericksburg but had seen little action until Gettysburg. The regiment entered the battle with a strength of 496 men.[27] It was attached to the 1st Division, I Corps when the regiment moved into position near McPherson's Ridge on July 1 to block the advancing Confederate force north of Gettysburg.

Initial contact with the enemy was a success for the 24th Michigan. The regiment "dashed up and over the hill and down into the ravine, through which flows Willoughby's Run where we captured many prisoners being a part of General [James] Archer's brigade."[28] General Archer himself was taken prisoner, the first time in the war the Army of Northern Virginia had one of its generals captured. The 24th then pulled back across the run and held on with the rest

24th Michigan Infantry Regiment Main Monument, Herbst's Woods, Gettysburg National Military Park.

of the brigade until the afternoon. Once the enemy came again, they came with superior numbers. The Confederates "advanced in two lines of battle, their right extending beyond and overlapping our left."[29] With the brigade flanked, the 24th had to fight desperately to keep its position, eventually withdrawing through the town with the rest of the I and XI Corps.

The regiment would eventually fall back through town and regroup on Culp's Hill. With more Union troops arriving, the 24th was sent to Steven's Knoll, a small hill near Culp's Hill, for the rest of the battle. The regiment suffered 363 casualties during the intense fighting on the first day of battle.[30] Every man who carried the colors of the regiment on July 1 was killed. The rest of the color guard was either wounded or killed. The regiment remained with the Army of the Potomac until January 1865, when it was transferred to Illinois for garrison duty.

The dedication of the 24th Michigan monument occurred on the afternoon of June 12, 1889. At the dedication were 115 men who had fought at Gettysburg. The monument is a sentinel type, standing over 14 feet high. It contains historical information about the regiment and the number of casualties it suffered during the battle. The monument faces in the direction where the men charged over Willoughby's Run and includes a bronze statue of the Michigan seal. This would not be the only monument to the 24th Michigan. The second marker for the regiment marked their position on Steven's Knoll during the second and third days of the battle.

Major Edwin Wight, a veteran of the unit, delivered the dedication speech for the monument. The focus of Wight's dedication was that it was important for veterans and their families to visit Gettysburg to remember the sacrifices of the dead and how their sacrifice affected the war's survivors. Wight compared

24th Michigan Infantry Regiment Marker, Steven's Knoll, Gettysburg National Military Park.

the trip to those "of the Moslem faith [who] shall at least once at least during their lives, make a pilgrimage thither."[31] Wight continued by giving a synopsis of the regiment's history and its actions at Gettysburg. He concluded his address by explaining what patriotism means to veterans. Wight stated, "Patriotism is that lofty, loyal spirit which places love of country and devotion to that country's best interests far above and beyond all petty sectional feeling and party success."[32] Wight wanted veterans and guests to understand that they fought to unite the nation. He felt that the biggest lesson to be learned at Gettysburg was that people came together after the war and moved forward together.

The location selected for the 24th Michigan Infantry's primary monument is where the Iron Brigade initially deployed near Herbst's Woods. Like the 110th Pennsylvania Infantry monument, the sentinel on top of the monument stands watch over their location. The carvings are deep into the granite, glistening in the sunlight. Modern-day visitors will notice contemporary Rebel monuments on the side of the park road, located near the Michigan monument. While these Rebel monuments were not present during the Union dedications, their presence does tie into what Wight discussed in his speech.

Maine continued to pass legislation funding regimental monuments at Gettysburg in 1887. The Maine legislature passed a bill providing "two thousand five hundred dollars to the Gettysburg Battlefield Memorial Association to purchase land, construct avenues, and otherwise care for and beautify the Gettysburg battlegrounds."[33] Later in the bill, funds were also allocated for Maine monuments at Gettysburg. The bill provided a "sum of twelve thousand five hundred dollars to build monuments to commemorate the valor of Maine soldiers on that battlefield."[34] Like the regimental associations in Michigan, the Maine associations would take two years to decide on the design and placement of their monuments.

The 19th Maine Infantry Regiment was formed in August 1862 and consisted of men from all over the state. The Maine men served with the Army of the Potomac in every engagement after the battle of Fredericksburg. The regiment was attached to the 3rd Brigade, 2nd Division, II Corps, and arrived at Gettysburg with 439 men.[35] The regiment was positioned on Cemetery Ridge on the second day of battle when it was ordered to shift left to help cover the retreating III Corps. The regiment's commander, Colonel Francis Heath, ordered his men into a position that extended the II Corps line from Cemetery Ridge toward Little Round Top. Colonel Heath ordered his men to lie down once they reached their covering position. This order was given to "not get caught up in the spirit of the defeated troops and to allow the broken and disorganized troops to pass over us to the rear."[36] Once the III Corps troops passed, the 19th Maine stood and engaged the enemy.

The regiment engaged the advancing Rebels under the direct supervision of General Winfield Scott Hancock. While a corps commander taking direct control of a single regiment was not a common sight during the Civil War, Hancock did this multiple times during the fight at Gettysburg. It was a day of multiple crises, and every time a Confederate thrust was stopped, another threatened to break the line. Hancock was forced to fling his units left and right to plug gaps and launch counterattacks. The 19th Maine was assaulted by a Florida brigade until, seeing an advantage, Colonel Heath ordered his men forward to push back the Confederate line. The advance worked. The regiment "took quite a few prisoners and retook four Napoleon guns abandoned by some of our forces that had been posted to the front."[37]

The third day of battle saw the 19th subject to part of the massive artillery barrage that preceded Pickett's Charge. During that Confederate attack on the Union center, the 19th was once again in the thick of the fighting and helped to repel the advancing enemy. However, the 19th lost "very heavily, especially in non-commissioned officers. Members of the regiment took two battle flags of the enemy."[38] Colonel Heath was not exaggerating when he reported losing heavily. The 19th Maine lost 203 men during its two days of fighting at Gettysburg.

The dedication ceremonies for the Maine monument on October 3, 1889, were sporadic. Most regimental associations decided to let the day's main speakers provide tributes for the 15 regiments dedicating monuments. Reverend George Palmer, a veteran of the regiment, gave the benediction at the dedication ceremonies. In his prayer, Palmer stated, "As we dedicate these monuments in honor of our loyal men who saved liberty on this field, and many of whom laid down their lives, help us to consecrate ourselves to thee and the accomplishment of their unfinished work."[39] References to liberty and freedom were a constant theme in the speeches throughout the day. General Charles Hamlin, a native of Maine, discussed liberty in his dedication speech. Hamlin stated that patriotic and generous people have caused these monuments, made from the enduring granite of our hills, to be erected to the memory of their sons who fell here.[40]

The Governor of Maine, Edwin Burleigh, also discussed liberty in his speech. Burleigh said the monuments "marked where Maine men fell in the bloody struggle for the Union of the states and constitutional liberty."[41] Burleigh used the term "constitutional liberty" to refer to what the country became after the American Revolution. The colonies fought off the British king to become their own country. Eventually, the law of the land became the Constitution, allowing people to live as they wished while also adhering to a prescribed set of rules.

The final version of the 19th Maine monument was a memorial type. It is a roughly 12-foot pyramid made of polished and rough-cut granite. The monument features the II Corps symbol and the regiment's casualty data from the battle. Also included on the monument is a synopsis of the regiment's actions during both days of the battle. The 19th Maine monument is in the battle line with the rest of its brigade on Cemetery Ridge.

The pyramid shape of the 19th Maine monument gives the monument a three-dimensional appearance. Several other monuments surrounding it also have unique shapes that differentiate the line of monuments along Cemetery Ridge. Many of the monuments along this part of the line include a version of

19th Maine Infantry Regiment Monument, Cemetery Ridge, Gettysburg National Military Park.

a pyramid or obelisk. While there is no direct evidence that the units planned on copying one another, it is an interesting catch when walking the battlefield. The dedication speech was also meant to tie the fight at Gettysburg with the Revolutionary War. The North and the South would attempt to utilize the same imagery of the Revolution to illustrate their respective plights during the Civil War. However, after the Civil War, Union veterans were more likely to use the Revolution to tie the helplessness soldiers experienced during the Revolutionary War during some of the battles of that conflict to the same struggle they faced at Gettysburg.

Dedication speeches during this period were example-laden, connecting the past with the present day. Union veterans struggled and fought a great battle at Gettysburg. While it did not end the war outright, it led to the Union army's eventual defeat of the Rebel Army of Northern Virginia at Appomattox Courthouse less than two years later. Modern visitors can now connect with the veterans who placed monuments on the field by reading the inscriptions they left. The 19th Maine was engaged on July 2 and again on July 3. The fighting on Cemetery Ridge, in both cases, was extremely hot as the Confederate army was looking to split the Union lines. Many people think the fighting on the second day of the battle stopped after the engagements on Little Round Top and in the Peach Orchard. In fact, the battle continued to roll up parts of Cemetery Ridge, where the 19th Maine was deployed. The Rebels would then repeat this attack the next day, with the attack preceded by a large enemy artillery barrage. In both cases, the Maine men held fast and were memorialized by the large pyramid monument on Cemetery Ridge.

Toward the south end of the battlefield, another group of Maine men and their families gathered on two round hills to dedicate their monuments. The 20th Maine would become one of the most discussed regiments in the battle of Gettysburg's historical record. The regiment holding the end of Colonel Strong Vincent's brigade on July 2, 1863, would hold the left flank of the Union line until the battle's end. The 20th Maine would enter the battle on July 2 with 386 men.[42] When the army withdrew from Gettysburg, the regiment would have a fighting strength of around 261 men. Upon returning to Little Round Top in the fall of 1889, the regiment's famous former commander, Joshua Chamberlain, delivered the main dedication speech for the three monuments the unit would dedicate on the field.

Beyond the accolades and the status he assumed after the battle of Gettysburg, Chamberlain understood the importance of public speaking. He conveyed the goal of Union veterans returning to the battlefield and dedicating monuments to the living and dead. Chamberlain remarked:

> In great deeds, something abides. On great fields, something stays. Forms change and pass; bodies disappear, but spirits linger to consecrate ground for the vision-place of souls. And reverent men and women from afar, and generations that know us not and that we know not of, heart-drawn to see where and by whom great things were suffered and done for them, shall come to this deathless field to ponder and dream; And lo! The shadow of a mighty presence shall wrap them in its bosom, and the power of the vision pass into their souls.[43]

The great deed was the Union Army of the Potomac's victory over the Confederate Army of Northern Virginia, and the great field was Gettysburg. Chamberlain hoped that by dedicating monuments to an essential battlefield of the Civil War, future generations would understand the sacrifices made by his men during the battle and the war.

Each of the three monuments dedicated by the 20th Maine is a memorial type, and the regiment's exploits on July 2 and July 3 are depicted. The main battle monument marks the regiment's position on July 2 on Little Round Top. The monument, constructed of granite, marks the center of the regiment's line. Chiseled on the main face of the monument is the unit's identifying information, including the V Corps insignia. Also included on the monument is a brief description of the unit's actions on July 2 and the regiment's casualty list.

The regiment's second monument, situated a few hundred yards behind the main one, marks where the regiment's Company B was held in reserve. While this company of the 20th Maine was not part of the primary action on the afternoon of July 2, it was responsible for keeping Rebel movements in check and protecting the main body's left flank from an attack from Big Round Top. Joined by a group of Regular Army sharpshooters, Company B held its position until relieved on the night of July 2. The monument is a small granite square that explains the company's assignment on July 2.

The 20th Maine's last monument, on Big Round Top, is a marker showing the unit's position on July 3. Like the primary monument on Little Round Top, the marker on Big Round Top also serves as a marker for the extreme left flank of the Army of the Potomac on July 2 and 3. The monument itself is a taller, skinnier version of the primary monument on Little Round Top. Made of granite, it encapsulates the regiment's loss and commemorates its commander during the battle.

Many people, including myself, usually make their first visit to Gettysburg centered around the 20th Maine monument on Little Round Top.

20th Maine Infantry Monument, Little Round Top, Gettysburg National Military Park.

20th Maine Company B Marker, Little Round Top, Gettysburg National Military Park.

The novel *The Killer Angels* by Michael Shaara and the 1993 movie *Gettysburg* (based on the book) help encapsulate the battle for many, driving avid interest. As a child, trying to recreate the charge down the hill toward the Rebel position was interesting because the movie version sure seemed to last a lot longer than when I tried it in real life! However, there is more to the monumentation and memorialization of this regiment beyond its famous commander and what popular culture has made people believe. The first is that the regiment held an entire company in reserve behind the line toward Big Round Top.

The men of the 20th Maine, Company B, were able to hear the battle but still held their line, just in case the Rebels tried to flank the main body. I did not know the monument they created existed until I followed a path behind the primary monument. The last monument is on Big Round Top, where the 20th Maine spent the last day of the battle. Contrary to what the movie and book would have you believe, they were not pulled from their position and placed in the Union center, far from their own division and corps. Regardless of what current scholarship and popular depictions tell us about how important their fight was on the flank of the Union Army, these men from Maine fought a great fight. They also went to great lengths to ensure that they left markers at every spot where they were stationed to show that they were there and that some of them had died for their country.

20th Maine Monument, Big Round Top, Gettysburg National Military Park.

As the country rolled into a new decade in 1890, the number of states that had not added monuments to Gettysburg had dwindled to only a few. The drum for nationalizing Civil War battlefields continued to gain momentum as other veterans sought to build monuments in places other than Gettysburg. The battlefields of Shiloh, Vicksburg, Antietam, Chattanooga, and Chickamauga were discussed in Congress.[44] Gettysburg was not initially discussed as a national site because of the GBMA's control of the property. During these discussions of who would control Civil War battlefields, states continued to provide funding for regimental monuments at Gettysburg.

Illinois was the next state to appropriate regimental monuments, in May 1889. The Union veterans of the state had pushed for state funds for several years. The states surrounding Illinois had already built several monuments to their veterans at Gettysburg, and the Illinois veterans felt left out. Most of the units raised in Illinois fought in the Western Theater of the war, while only a few traveled east to fight in the Eastern Theater. Also driving this push for state funding was that Illinois was the state of Abraham Lincoln, and it seemed fitting to the state's veterans that they place monuments where the 16th president gave one of his most famous speeches. The state finally declared that "six thousand dollars is hereby appropriated to procure and erect a suitable mark upon the spot where the Illinois troops opened the battle of Gettysburg."[45] The law's language focused on where the troops "opened the battle" because all three Illinois regiments at Gettysburg engaged the enemy on the battle's first day.

One Illinois regiment that would build a monument at Gettysburg was the 8th Illinois Cavalry Regiment. The regiment formed in St. Charles, Illinois, and mustered into service in September 1861.[46] It served with the Army of the Potomac beginning with the Peninsula Campaign in 1862. During the battle of Gettysburg, the regiment was attached to the 1st Brigade, 1st Division of the Union Cavalry Corps and fielded 470 troopers.[47] Elements of the 8th Illinois were sent several miles north of the main cavalry position to act as a skirmish line. These elements would be part of the opening actions of the battle of Gettysburg.

On June 30, the regiment deployed north of Gettysburg, waiting for contact with Confederate forces. On July 1, Company E of the 8th Illinois Cavalry would become part of one of the contested stories of the battle of Gettysburg: *who fired the first shot.* According to the regiment's official history and eyewitness accounts, Lieutenant Marcellus Jones of Company E fired at advancing Confederates near Mash Creek on the morning of the first day. Surgeon Abner Hard, who wrote the regiment's official history, supports this claim. Hard said, "Captain Dana was in command of the picket line on the Chambersburg Road where they first appeared; here, as in many other great battles, 8th Illinois received the first fire and shed the first blood."[48] Hard refers to Captain Amasa Dana, who commanded Company E of the 8th Illinois Cavalry at Gettysburg. Lieutenant Jones was one of the junior officers under Dana's command.

Another account of the 8th's skirmish line on July 1 comes from Captain Dana himself, as recorded in his diary. He stated, "On the 1st of July the report came in from Lieutenant Jones that he fired a shot at the advancing enemy a little bit before sunrise."[49] After firing the shot, the regiment regrouped along its main line on McPherson's Ridge, delaying the enemy until the Union I Corps arrived. The regiment, having suffered seven casualties, would be held in reserve for the rest of the action at Gettysburg.[50] The actions of the 8th Illinois Cavalry on the first day of the battle would be a point of unit pride for many veterans after the war ended.

The claim of firing the first shot would be controversial because other members of John Buford's cavalry division claimed to have fired the first shot north of Gettysburg on July 1. The most prominent claim was that of the 9th New York Cavalry. In that regiment's official history, one of the 9th's advance guards stated, "They fired several shots at the advancing enemy. This occurred at about 530 A.M. This exchange of shots is believed to be the first shots fired at the battle of Gettysburg on July 1, 1863."[51] According to reports, the 9th was positioned north of Gettysburg on skirmish duty. The enemy did not advance in that direction until later on July 1. The movements of the enemy and other accounts make the 9th New York Cavalry reports inaccurate.[52]

Lieutenant Jones believed so strongly in his account of firing first at Gettysburg that he commissioned a monument with funds he raised himself. On July 1, 1887, Jones and three others placed the monument near the position where he fired his shot.[53] The significance of stating who fired the first shot lies in the battle's historical context. Almost all Union monuments dedicated to Gettysburg emphasized the battle's significance to the country and its impact on the outcome of the Civil War. For veterans, being recognized for who started the fight was a point of personal and unit pride. The significance of firing the first shot at Gettysburg would not be lost on the 8th Illinois Cavalry when they dedicated their monument.

The dedication ceremonies for all three Illinois regiments at Gettysburg occurred on September 3, 1891, and Illinois Governor Joseph Fifer gave the main dedication speech. In the address, Fifer stated that the victorious

Lieutenant Marcellus Jones's "First Shot" Marker, outside of Gettysburg National Military Park.

Union army at Gettysburg "broke the chains of bondage and brought a union of American interests under a single flag."[54] After Fifer's address, the delegation traveled to each Illinois monument for individual dedication speeches. Major John Beveridge gave the speech for the 8th Illinois, as he commanded the regiment at Gettysburg.

8th Illinois Cavalry Regiment Monument, north of Gettysburg, Gettysburg National Military Park.

Beveridge spent most of his dedication defending Jones as the first to fire a shot at Gettysburg. Beveridge concluded the defense portion of his speech: "I am satisfied, that Capt. Jones was honored to fire the first gun at Gettysburg on the morning of July 1, 1863, as the enemy advanced to give battle. He opened the fight."[55] Beveridge then discussed what the battle and war meant to the men of the 8th. Beveridge summarized their Civil War combat experience at Gettysburg: "The battle is fought. The victory is won. The Nation lives. Here on Gettysburg field, the wave of the rebellion culminated."[56] The themes of Beveridge's speech touched on defending the Union and defeating the rebellion but focused mainly on personal glory for the regiment. Few other dedication speeches attack other regimental histories or veteran recollections.

The 8th Illinois Cavalry monument stands on the battle line the regiment took on McPherson's Ridge on the first day of battle. The monument is made of granite and stands roughly 13 feet high. The monument's text includes the regiment's movements during the battle. The monument also features bronze crossed sabers, the state seal of Illinois, and a granite sculpture depicting a horse saddle and a rolled army blanket. The monument also includes the inscription, "Lieut. Jones, Co. E, fired the first shot as the enemy crossed Marsh Creek Bridge."

While the 8th Illinois Cavalry and "First Shot Marker" were not part of the same dedication day, they both serve an essential purpose of Union veteran documentation at Gettysburg. While many veterans and units attempted to be the first to engage the enemy, the 8th Illinois could substantiate its claims with facts and support them with documentation from various sources. Veterans wanted to be able to tell their stories and remember how they fought in the battle, but they also wanted to tell the story correctly. By establishing the correct location of the first shot and explaining how the 8th Illinois was able to have taken the shot with their monument, a better explanation of the battle could occur by comparing the terrain followed by both armies and a timeline set by reports and reminiscences of the veterans that wrote their stories down.

Visiting the "First Shot Marker" used to be an adventure, as the property on which the marker sits did not have parking on the correct side of the road. Visitors used to have to park on the other side of a busy road and sometimes dodge traffic that would usually be traveling at a high rate of speed to get close to the monument. However, the NPS has since restored houses near the marker and created a parking area on the same roadside. Visiting the marker and looking in the direction from which the Rebels came, visitors can easily visualize the small group of cavalrymen standing at their posts, waiting for the enemy to become visible. Once they could identify the direction of advance, these same men could gallop back to their command and communicate the enemy's position. Thanks to veterans of the 8th Illinois, modern-day visitors no longer have to guess where these locations are, as they have been marked and identified in granite.

Most regimental monuments built during this period focus on remembering the fallen at Gettysburg. However, one monument that several states funded would help mark Gettysburg as the high-water mark of the rebellion. The idea for a monument marking the climax of the battle came from John Bachelder. In his guidebook, *Gettysburg: What to See and How to See It*, Bachelder discusses the various troop movements and actions that occurred over the three days of the battle of Gettysburg. When discussing the attack on the Union center on the third day, Bachelder called the attack "unquestionably the high-water mark of this battle and the war!"[57] Bachelder's statement would be the foundation for a monument.

Even with Bachelder on the GBMA board and the official historian of the battle and battlefield, the monument would take years to plan and get funding. During the February 1887 meeting of the GBMA, it was resolved that Bachelder should "prepare an appropriate and suitable tablet descriptive of the engagement and the commands engaged at the 'Copse of Trees' where Pickett's Division assaulted the Union line, said tablet to be placed upon a metallic post thereat."[58] Over the next several years, Bachelder requested money from Northern states to create a monument near the "Copse of Trees" on Cemetery Ridge. By the beginning of 1891, money had been received from Maine, New Hampshire, Vermont, Massachusetts, Rhode Island, Connecticut, New York, New Jersey, Delaware, Pennsylvania, West Virginia, Ohio, Michigan, and Minnesota. Not coincidentally, the states that provided money had units that helped repel the July 3 assault.

The final monument design and dedication speech would provide a comprehensive summation of what Union veterans felt about the Civil War, the battle of Gettysburg, and the war's impact on the United States. The monument's placement was decided by where Bachelder thought the focal point of the Confederate assault was intended. After interviews with Confederate commanders, Bachelder selected the "Copse of Trees" at the center of the Union Cemetery Ridge line as the monument's location.[59] The monument itself is made of granite and bronze. On top of a granite pedestal is a bronze book open in the center. The heading across the top of the left page reads, "The High Water Mark of The Rebellion," and the heading across the top of the right page reads "Repulse of Longstreet's Assault." On the left side of the book is a list of Confederate units that participated in the assault, and on the right are the Union units that repelled it. On either side of the book are full-size cannons and stands of cannon balls.

The symbolism of a book on a pedestal, the name given to the monument, and the placement of unit names collectively help identify the monument's intended meaning. The book being raised above the granite base symbolizes the event's importance. The book signifies a collection of important events,

High Water Mark of The Rebellion Monument, Cemetery Ridge, Gettysburg National Military Park.

Close-up of the High Water Mark of The Rebellion Monument, Cemetery Ridge, Gettysburg National Military Park.

with the pages opened to the Confederate assault on July 3. The name of the monument is also indicative of its importance. The monument was not called "The High Water Mark of the Confederacy" but "The High Water Mark of The Rebellion." From the federal government's point of view, the official name for the Civil War was the War of The Rebellion. This is confirmed by the name of the government's 128-volume Official Records created after the war ended.[60] Even with reconciliation, a key theme in many reunions in the late 1880s and 1890s, the monument's language reached back to earlier antipathy for the Confederate cause and labeled it a rebellion.

Finally, the placement of the names of the units of both armies involved in the assault can also be seen as symbolic. The Army of the Potomac units are on the right-hand page of the open book, and Confederate units are on the left. Verses from the Bible suggest that being on God's right side is preferable to being on the left. In the Bible, the Book of Ecclesiastes states that a wise man's heart directs him toward the right, but the foolish man's heart directs him toward the left. However, even with the symbolism inherent in the monument, the dedication speeches accompanying the monument altered its meaning.

The dedication of the High Water Mark of The Rebellion monument occurred on June 2, 1892. Former Pennsylvania Governor James Beaver delivered the main oration at the monument. In his remarks, Beaver focused on reconciliation rather than the monument's physical form. Beaver stated that people should try to understand the Confederates' motives for fighting: "We can admire their courage, fortitude, and endurance. We can acknowledge that they were at least our equals in all that constitutes a soldier and makes him worthy of our steel."[61] Even though Beaver himself fought against the Confederates at Gettysburg almost thirty years previously, his speech was one of admiration for his former enemy.

John Bachelder spent a long period of his life writing, drawing, and mapping the Gettysburg landscape. He steered the GBMA to help preserve the battlefield and place monuments in their correct location with the help of veterans. In many ways, the construction of this monument was an homage to his leadership and dedication to the battlefield. While scholars and other historians can point out that the war did not end after Gettysburg, it was, in fact, the beginning of the end. The Army of Northern Virginia would never again fight north of Maryland during the Civil War. Bachelder firmly believed that Gettysburg was the tipping point, and this monument reflects that idea. The monument's prominent position near the Union center, and its supposed rallying point during the failed Rebel attack on the third day of battle, also makes it a final act of visiting the battlefield.

Minnesota was the last western state to dedicate a monument at Gettysburg. The 1st Minnesota Infantry Regiment was the only regiment from Minnesota in the Army of the Potomac during the battle. Most of the regiments from Minnesota fought in the Western Theater or were deployed against Native Americans.[62] During most of the Civil War, Native American tribes in Minnesota and the Dakota Territory were in disputes with settlers that often led to violence, requiring military intervention. The 1st Minnesota was also the first regiment to be formed when President Abraham Lincoln called for 75,000 volunteers after the firing on Fort Sumter. The Governor of Minnesota, Alex Ramsey, was in Washington when the announcement was made, and he promptly informed Secretary of War Simon Cameron that Minnesota had immediately dispatched 1,000 men to defend the government.[63] The regiment fought in every significant Union battle in the Eastern Theater, starting with First Manassas.

During the Gettysburg campaign, the regiment was attached to the 1st Brigade, 2nd Division, II Corps of the Army of the Potomac. When the regiment arrived at Gettysburg on the night of the first day of battle, it deployed 330 men.[64] During the second day of the battle, the 1st Minnesota was initially held in a reserve position on Cemetery Ridge. However, as the III Corps moved off Cemetery Ridge and into the Peach Orchard, the gap they left behind had to be filled, and the 1st Minnesota was moved up. Unfortunately for the small regiment, it had to occupy the ground that an entire corps had previously occupied. However, the 1st would not be left alone. The regiment would support Battery C of the Fourth U.S. Army Artillery.[65]

On July 2, the Confederate advance shifted toward Cemetery Ridge after devastating the III Corps. In the panic to move reserves into the breach and hold the line, General Hancock ordered the 1st Minnesota to charge into an oncoming Confederate brigade.[66] The regiment would do so, slowing the Confederates, if only for a few moments. Veterans of the regiment remembered that "the ferocity of our onset seemed to paralyze them for a time, and though they poured in a terrible and continuous fire from the front and enveloping flanks, they kept at a respectful distance from our bayonets."[67] Eventually, the regiment received the reinforcements they needed to push back the Confederate line. The tab that the 1st Minnesota paid to buy the II Corps time to bring up reinforcements was the sacrifice of 224 men. However, the loss of men does not compare to the loss's effect on the survivors. The aftermath of the second day's fight was described as "nearly every officer was dead, or lay weltering with bloody wounds, only 47 men who made the charge were in line."[68] The regiment would be held in reserve on the third day of the battle but would join the fight again during Pickett's Charge. After the war, the survivors of the regiment would do their best to memorialize the sacrifice of their fallen comrades.

The planning for the 1st Minnesota Infantry Regiment monument began in 1891. During that year's legislative session, a bill was passed appropriating "the sum of twenty thousand dollars to be expended on the construction and erection of a suitable monument to the First Regiment of Minnesota Volunteers."[69] A planning committee created two monuments for the regiment. The first would be where the regiment charged at the oncoming Confederate force. The second monument would align with where the regiment held on the battle's third day. The first is a sentinel monument standing 32 feet tall, adorned with a bronze figure of a soldier running toward the enemy. The monument includes historical data of the regiment and its total losses at Gettysburg. The second monument to the regiment is a memorial type in the form of an obelisk. On the obelisk is a bronze bas-relief of the regiment assisting with the countercharge on the third day of the battle.

Both monuments, built by the state of Minnesota, were installed in their positions in early October 1893.[70] Combined with the 1st Minnesota Memorial Urn dedicated in the 1860s (discussed in Chapter 1), the regiment had three different monuments on the field. However, the state monuments were not

1st Minnesota Infantry Regiment Monument, Cemetery Ridge, Gettysburg National Military Park.

dedicated during their placements in 1893. Instead, the state waited until July 2, 1897. The dedication ceremonies were attended by 150 veterans and their families and several prominent members of the Minnesota government. Veterans wanted to pick a time when most could attend and did not want to deal with the large number of visitors on the field during the battle's 30th anniversary.[71]

1st Minnesota Infantry Regiment July 3 Monument, Cemetery Ridge, Gettysburg National Military Park. The monument is situated on a slight slope, which orients it at an angle.

A closeup of the bas-relief on the 1st Minnesota Infantry Regiment July 3 Monument, Cemetery Ridge, Gettysburg National Military Park.

The theme of reconciliation was central to the dedication speech for the 1st Minnesota monuments. United States Senator Cushman Davis, a veteran of the regiment, sent mixed messages about what the veterans of the 1st fought for at Gettysburg and in the Civil War as a whole. Davis's speech focused on the fact that while slavery was wrong and needed to end, both sides needed to get over the past and move forward. He also discussed in his speech the correct way people should move forward and heal the wounds of the Civil War. Davis concluded his speech by saying, "We can leave censure to the jurisdiction of history. Recrimination and reconciliation cannot coexist. The victor does not need to recriminate, least of all on this spot. All civil wars end and must end in forbearing reconciliation."[72] Like most politicians of the era, Davis wanted to acknowledge the past but move the country forward. By the end of the 1890s, the United States was moving forward onto the world stage.

The 1st Minnesota monuments tell a tale of sacrifice. Each day at the battle of Gettysburg, the Union army had one or two regiments that stalled the enemy, buying time for tactical withdrawals or reinforcements. On Cemetery Ridge, General Winfield Scott Hancock utilized the 1st Minnesota to buy time for troops to move up and fill gaps in the line, thereby keeping the ridge position intact. Although the regiment was the size of only a couple of full-sized companies, it attacked a significantly larger enemy force. A painting in the Heritage Series of the Army National Guard, entitled "The First Minnesota," by Don Troiani, depicts the regiment's advance.

The monuments of the 1st Minnesota Infantry serve as a potent reminder for the veterans who survived, marking where they stood their ground. In the meantime, between the completion of the 1st Minnesota monuments on Cemetery Ridge at Gettysburg and their dedication in 1897, control over the battlefield changed. The GBMA sold its property to the federal government, and Gettysburg was now under the control of the War Department. It would soon be seen that the new property administrators would change the rules regarding how and where monuments could be placed on the battlefield.

CHAPTER 6

Transitioning to New Management and Monuments, 1895–1913

The middle of the 1890s would mark a transition for the Gettysburg battlefield and its monumentation. Through the War Department, Civil War battlefields were "acquired, marked, and monumented with great emphasis given on accuracy. Studying, documenting, mapping, and marking every troop position in specific detail on the ground was considered highly desirable."[1] Historians during the late 19th and early 20th centuries focused on mapping and detailing specific movements of armies because it served history and military science. Military academies worldwide studied past campaigns to help teach future generations of soldiers how to develop new ideas in military thought. With dozens of battles to choose from during the Civil War, the War Department had to decide which battlefields the government would purchase and begin to mark.

The decision in the early 1890s to federalize Civil War battlefields initially focused on battles that were significant victories for the principal Union armies that fought in the Civil War. In 1890, the battlefields of Chickamauga and Chattanooga were acquired to memorialize the Union Army of the Cumberland. In 1894, the government bought property around the battlefield of Shiloh for the Union Army of the Tennessee and Army of the Ohio. After purchasing land that was considered the battlefield from farmers and business owners in Gettysburg, the federal government approached the GBMA about acquiring its land. The GBMA needed to determine if selling battlefield sections was a better option than allowing the government to utilize eminent domain to take the properties over.[2] The interest in buying tracts of the Gettysburg battlefield could not come at a better time for the GBMA. Even though several states had provided funds to support the association when dedicating monuments, the funds were not given continuously. The result was that the GBMA could not financially provide for the upkeep of the battlefield. The

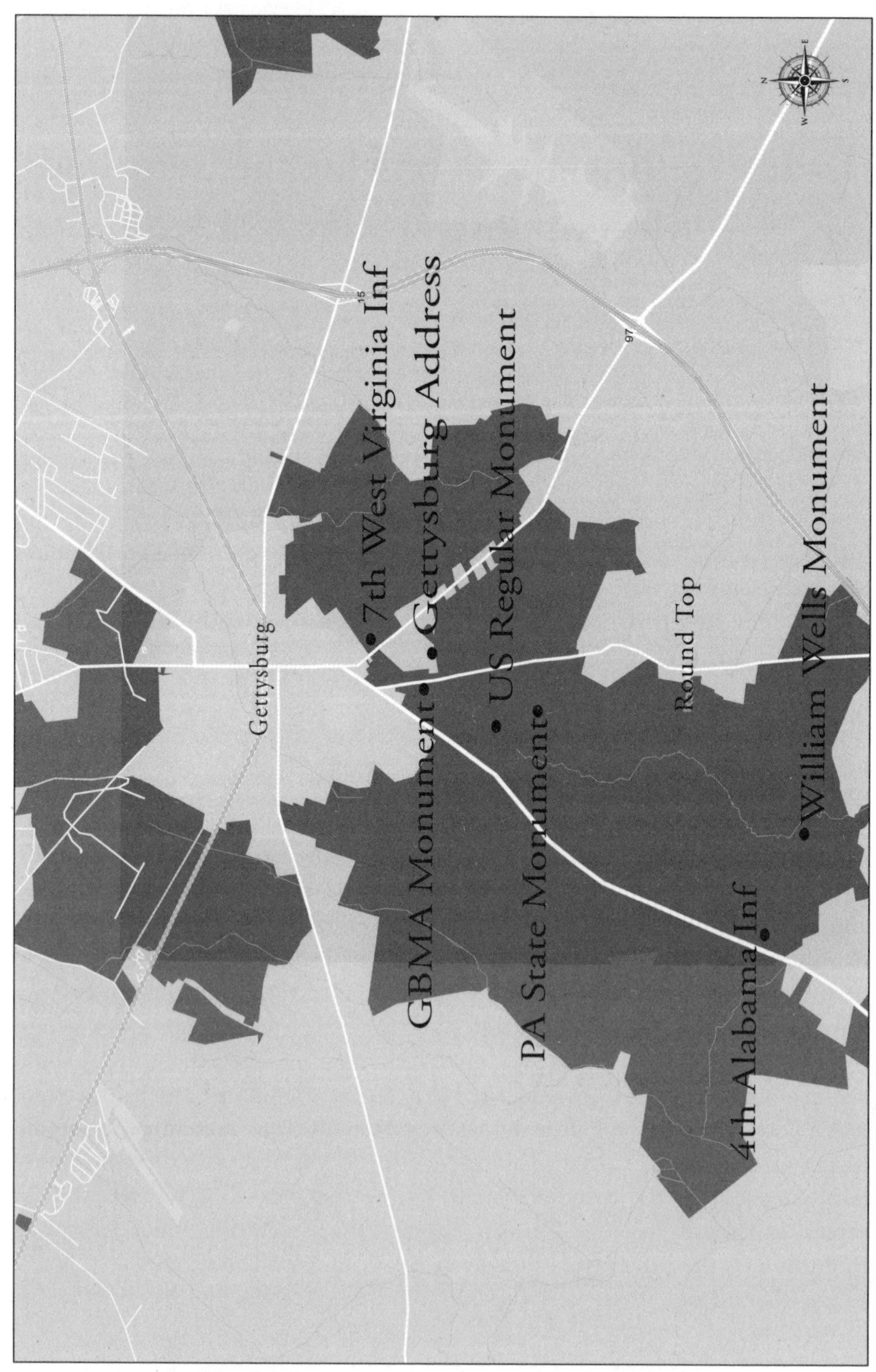

Location of monuments 1895–1913. (Created using ArcGIS Pro by Esri)

inability to pay for the upkeep of existing monuments, combined with the national push to mark and identify all positions of both armies at Gettysburg put the federal government in a position to take over the land owned by the GBMA.

The idea to federalize the Gettysburg battlefield started in 1890 with House Resolution 1868. However, there were not enough votes to pass in the House of Representatives. The most significant obstacle to passing the bill was acquiring GBMA-held land. A congressman who ardently believed in reconciliation pointed out that the GBMA was "a work of love and grateful pride to the loyal states; there is something due to history as well as to patriotism; there were two armies at Gettysburg."[3] However, in 1894, former Union General Daniel Sickles, now a congressman from New York, worked with the GBMA and the House to broker a deal. On December 6, 1894, House Resolution 8906 passed and was sent to the Senate.[4] The major hurdle in acquiring GBMA land was solved by the GBMA's agreement to sign a deed of conveyance. The deed was for 800 acres of land owned by the association, including all improvements and access to federal government services.

On February 11, 1895, President Grover Cleveland signed the Sickles legislation. The law ceded the Gettysburg battlefield to the federal government, designating it as the Gettysburg National Military Park. The government wasted no time in administration, assigning a commission of former Union and Confederate officers to oversee the improvements and monuments placed on the battlefield. This same commission had been working with the GBMA to survey the U.S. Army Regulars' positions at Gettysburg. The commission's goal was "to preserve and restore features of the battlefield as they existed at the time of the battle."[5] While the battlefield was under new management, several of the preexisting rules from the GBMA remained in place.

The first rule was the line-of-battle policy, which stated that unit monuments had to be placed in their battle line. Another GMBA rule that carried over was the placement of Confederate monuments. The War Department would not allow Confederate monuments in the units' advanced positions on the battlefield. After all, many advance Rebel positions were on or beyond the Union lines. Confederate unit markers were now allowed on the battlefield, but only in positions of the basic Confederate line. The unit markers could not be placed near the Union lines where they often fought.

The unit markers were made of metal and included simple inscriptions of the unit and its actions on the field. The markers could not have flourishing language or discuss the unit's motivation for fighting. With these rules in place, the new commission took over administering the battlefield; and it would have

Lieutenant Colonel John P. Nicholson. (Missouri History Museum Photographs and Print Collection)

Major William M. Robbins. (Library of Congress)

its work cut out for it as regimental requests to place monuments came in from both sides. The increase in regimental requests was largely due to the age of the veterans. By the 1890s, the Civil War veteran population had declined due to old age and death from war wounds. Veterans wanted to build monuments to mark where they fought and sacrificed before passing away.

Lieutenant Colonel John P. Nicholson and Major William M. Robbins were prominent battlefield commissioners from 1895 to 1913. Nicholson was a former Union officer from Pennsylvania and a veteran of the war. Before being appointed to the battlefield commission, he helped organize the Pennsylvania Monuments Commission for the battle of Gettysburg. At the onset of his appointment to the Battlefield Commission, Nicholson was named the chairman. Robbins was a former Confederate officer assigned to the 4th Alabama Infantry at Gettysburg. He was a congressman from North Carolina from 1873 to 1879 before becoming a battlefield commissioner. When a position opened on the Gettysburg Commission, President Grover Cleveland wanted to select a Democrat from North Carolina to fill the position. However, Robbins did not seek out the position. In his journal, he wrote about his appointment as something that "was made without application or knowledge on my part though was influenced by Senator Matt Ransom."[6] Robbins continued as a commissioner until he died in 1905.

Both Robbins and Nicholson worked tirelessly to improve the battlefield and create more accessible ways to reach monuments and battle lines. Most of the roads that now run through the battlefield were constructed under the direction of these two men. The other battlefield commissioner during this initial period of federal control was Charles Richardson, who served in the Union army during the battle. Richardson also served with the New York Battlefield Monuments Commission before assuming his position as a federal battlefield commissioner.

One of the primary reasons for constructing new roads and avenues along the battlefield was to facilitate Confederate access to the battlefield. The commission wanted to "invite surviving Confederate officers and soldiers to visit the field as well as authorities of Southern States to point out positions."[7] In the North, there was a strong appreciation for sharing the entire story of the battlefield with visitors. The public and veterans generally accepted the commissioner's approach of marking the battle lines of both armies. However, they did not want Confederate monuments added, as from the park's inception they were never intended to be included.[8] The federal government did not want to change preexisting rules set by the GBMA, even if they alienated Confederate associations. In the South, Confederate veteran organizations pushed for more to be done for Confederate monumentation. Confederate veterans went so far as to vote on and petition for more status at Gettysburg.[9] However, no concrete decisions were made about Confederate monuments in the first few years of the commission. This did not mean that Confederate positions would not be marked on the battlefield. Starting in May 1894 and continuing through 1895, Confederate and Union officers who fought at Gettysburg helped mark Confederate infantry and artillery positions. Edward Porter Alexander, a former artillery officer in the First Corps of the Army of Northern Virginia, and Emmor Cope, an engineer for the Army of the Potomac, toured the battlefield together to mark positions. Both men would be responsible for identifying 65 different Confederate positions.[10] Another commission task involved accepting applications for new monuments and determining their placement.

During the Federal Battlefield Commission era, West Virginia was one of the first states to request the placement of monuments at Gettysburg. One of the reasons for the state's delay in creating monuments was that the state government was still learning how to function and be of use to the people of West Virginia. By the end of the Civil War and during Reconstruction, West Virginia was still figuring out how to function as a state government. What is now West Virginia was part of Virginia during the first year of the Civil War. The western part of the state was not a firm believer in slavery, while the influence of nearby Pennsylvania and Ohio influenced the opinion of Virginians living in that region. The western part of the state was dominated by mountains, so that communities there did not share the same lifestyle or values as the plantation owners in the east.

After war broke out, the western counties of Virginia seceded from their state, disagreeing with the secession and wanting to remain in the Union. The result was the creation of a new state, but it did not receive official recognition until June 20, 1863. As West Virginia stabilized its state government and raised revenue through taxes, funds became available for the state to build monuments commemorating its actions during the Civil War. Eventually, the legislature passed a bill allowing the "sum of two thousand dollars to erect tablets and monuments to be placed on the positions occupied by the West Virginia troops."[11] One of the monuments that the funds helped build was for the 7th West Virginia Infantry Regiment.

The 7th West Virginia was formed in December 1861 and was initially tasked with defending the railroad system in western Virginia from Confederate attacks. Eventually, the regiment moved to Washington in 1862. During the battle of Gettysburg, the regiment, which totaled 234 men, was assigned to the 1st Brigade, 3rd Division of the II Corps.[12] The regiment would not see fighting until late on the second day of the battle when General Hancock ordered the 7th and two other regiments to reinforce East Cemetery Hill. When the West Virginians arrived, Rebel infantry had reached the top of the hill and had even overrun a pair of Union batteries. The 7th charged upon the enemy and completely routed the attacking force, driving the enemy back down the hill and capturing several prisoners."[13] The 7th held a line down the slope of East Cemetery Hill until the end of the battle. For their actions on the field, the regiment suffered 47 casualties. When it was time to stay in the army or go home after their enlistment, most of the men chose to remain, and the regiment continued to serve until the war's end.

When the West Virginia legislature approved state funding in 1897, the survivors of the regiment decided to mark every location they held at Gettysburg. The main monument, located at the top of East Cemetery Hill, is a sentinel-type with a soldier standing at rest, facing the enemy. The monument is orientated so that the soldier faces the rear of the monument, looking down the hill. The rest of the monument features historical data about the regiment and an inscription detailing the narrative of events at Gettysburg. The regiment would also build stone markers at the bottom of the hill to mark where it held the line after its success on the evening of July 2.

7th West Virginia Infantry Regiment Main Monument, Cemetery Hill, Gettysburg National Military Park.

Second Position Marker, 7th West Virginia Infantry, Ziegler's Grove, Gettysburg National Military Park.

Third Position Marker, 7th West Virginia Infantry, Cemetery Hill, Gettysburg National Military Park.

The dedication for all West Virginia monuments occurred on September 28, 1898. At the dedication ceremony for the 7th West Virginia, Governor George Atkinson, a veteran of the battle, spoke about the loss of West Virginia men and the significance of their sacrifice at Gettysburg. Atkinson stated, "On this blood-red field of Gettysburg, the Union soldier held and kept the key to the nation's life, the key that must unlock the immortal destiny of eons yet to come."[14] The governor wanted to convey that only a Union victory at Gettysburg could secure the country's path after the Civil War. Something to consider when visiting the West Virginia monuments is that, since they were built later than most, the granite appears more recent. Ironically, the newest state in the Union during the Civil War would be one of the last to build monuments at Gettysburg.

As the 19th century gave way to the 20th, the federal administration continued to improve the battlefield landscape and restore the field near to its appearance in July 1863. Overgrowth from trees was removed, and the land was restored to resemble how it looked to the veterans who fought there. Roads continued to be improved, and more land was purchased to preserve the battlefield. Union and Confederate battle lines continued to be marked, identifying troop placements and movements. To this end, the commission established 462 unit tablets and markers.[15] However, only one Confederate regimental marker was placed at Gettysburg during this period.

The Confederate marker followed all the rules of the battlefield commission and was placed at its original line of battle. It was for the 4th Alabama Infantry, the regiment to which William Robbins was assigned at Gettysburg. During the battle of Gettysburg, the 4th Alabama fought in General Evander Law's brigade, which was part of General John Bell Hood's division assigned to Longstreet's First Corps of the Army of Northern Virginia. The regiment was one of several Alabama regiments assigned to attack the Union position on Little Round Top. Like the rest of Law's brigade, they had marched most of the day to get to the battlefield, assigned the farthest position on the Rebel right, and then were ordered to attack uphill. One the attack kicked off late in the afternoon, the regiment fought until the evening before withdrawing to their original position on Warfield Ridge.

The 4th Alabama brought 392 men into Gettysburg, and during the battle near the Round Tops suffered 92 casualties. The unit would continue fighting until the end of the war with William Robbins as an officer. With Robbins a battlefield commissioner decades later, he arranged for a monument to his old regiment.

4th Alabama Infantry Regiment Marker, Warfield Ridge, Gettysburg National Military Park.

Following federal protocols, Robbins constructed an identifying plaque, similar to those placed by the War Department on the battlefield. However, the 4th Alabama Regiment marker is physically smaller than its Union counterparts. The marker also sits on a round base, unlike Union markers, which are typically on square bases. The tablet includes a narrative of what happened to the regiment, compiled from official reports. The monument is on Warfield Ridge near the brigade marker for General Law's brigade. Robbins used his own money to build the monument and placed it in its correct position on the battle line.

Ironically, the 4th Alabama Infantry Regiment marker was placed before the United States Army Regulars had a monument dedicated to their sacrifices on the battlefield. While the majority of the Army of the Potomac, like most of the Union army during the Civil War, consisted of volunteers from states loyal to the Union, there were also Regular Army troops in the ranks. The total troop strength of the U.S. Regular Army at Gettysburg was approximately 7,100 men. The Regulars' units included infantry, cavalry, artillery, and engineers, and collectively suffered 1,175 casualties during the battle.

While not having a monument to these men may seem like a slight to their sacrifice, this was not the case. As the charter of the GBMA explained, the focus of monumentation at Gettysburg was on state volunteers. Regimental monuments of volunteers were more critical than monuments that focused on professional soldiers. This placed even Confederate regimental monuments in front of United States Army Regulars. A monument for the Regulars had been in the works since the late 1880s, but the GBMA was unable to secure the funds to build it independently.[16] Eventually, once the federal government took ownership of the battlefield, money was appropriated for the monument. Congress allocated funds to construct "markers on the battlefield of Gettysburg,

United States Regular Army Monument, Cemetery Ridge, Gettysburg National Military Park.

Pa., to commemorate the valorous deeds of certain regiments and batteries of the United States Army."[17] To this end, Congress appropriated funds within the budget of the Gettysburg National Military Park to construct monuments for the United States Regular Army.

The United States Regular Army monument is located on Cemetery Ridge near the center of the Union line. It is a memorial obelisk, approximately 35 feet tall, and each of the Regular Army units is identified on the monument. President William Taft gave the dedication speech during the monument's dedication ceremony. The speech was filled with nationalism and pride in the soldiers defending the Union. Taft called the monument "a tardy recognition of the nation's debt to its brave defenders, whose allegiance was purely to the nation, without local color or strengthening of state or municipal pride."[18]

The pride that President Taft expressed in the United States Regulars was extended beyond the large monument on Cemetery Ridge. Coinciding with the construction of the main monument, each position held by a Regular Army unit at Gettysburg was adorned with a plaque. Each one includes the name of the regiment, troop disposition, any casualties suffered during the battle, and a synopsis of the unit's contributions to the battle.

Additionally, during this period, the Gettysburg National Military Park wanted to highlight the significance of the battle in United States history as well as the contributions of the GBMA. They did so by erecting a monument specifically to the organization. Dedicated in 1908, this memorial-style monument describes the formation of the National Military Park and the efforts of the GBMA from 1864 to 1895. It explained how the mission of the GBMA and the new Gettysburg Park Commissioners, who were all Union and Confederate veterans, was to "ascertain and mark the lines of battle of all troops engaged in the battle of Gettysburg within the limits of the Park or adjacent thereto subject to the approval of the Secretary of War." While the monument is a simple tablet of bronze and granite, it lays out the commissioners' goals and aspirations for the park and what it should convey to the public.

While the GBMA monument's location seems random in the park's current layout, it was not considered so during its placement. Located near the current parking lot for the National Cemetery, the monument was adjacent to the original National Park Visitor Center. When the new Visitor Center was opened, the old one was demolished in 2008, returning the area to its natural state with the monument in place. Keeping the monument in its original location perfectly exemplifies one of the park's goals. By not building anything

Monument to GBMA formation of Gettysburg National Military Park, National Cemetery Parking Lot, Gettysburg National Military Park.

over the existing structure, the area was restored to its original state during the battle and the effort remains a significant milestone in the park's history.

While the United States Regular Army monument was being dedicated, the state of Pennsylvania broke ground on its state monument. In its final form it would dominate the landscape on Cemetery Ridge and be the centerpiece of the battle's 50th anniversary. The allocation of funds for a Pennsylvania memorial monument at Gettysburg was announced in February 1909 when the state legislature appropriated $150,000 dollars for the project.[19] The War Department designated four acres of property on Hancock Avenue, near Cemetery Ridge, for the memorial, and work began in the spring of 1909.

The goal of the Pennsylvania monument was to acknowledge every Pennsylvanian who fought in the battle, living and dead. The Monument Commission also sought to build a structure that would be the largest on the field. By 1909, the tallest monument, at 90 feet, was the New York State monument in the National Cemetery. The design of the Pennsylvania monument called for a granite terrace measuring about 100 feet on each side. The exterior walls contain bronze tablets for each Pennsylvania unit, as well as a roster for each.[20] On top of the terrace are granite arches, creating a victory arch on all four sides, with a granite dome and observation deck. The monument stands approximately 100 feet tall and was initially dedicated on September 27, 1910; the dedication was accelerated from the planned date due to the project running out of funds.

The Pennsylvania monument constructed in September 1910 was not the complete monument that was originally designed. The project ran out of money, and the Pennsylvania Monument Commission was unable to secure the necessary funds. The dedication ceremony was sparsely attended and offended most veterans due to the lack of respect shown to those who did attend.[21] Many Pennsylvania veterans could not understand why the state legislature couldn't complete the monument to the specifications agreed to. To many Pennsylvania veterans, their state monument had to be the largest and most ornate on the battlefield, as it was within their home state.

The veterans' feelings carried over into one of the dedication speeches for the monument. General Henry Huidekoper, who had lost an arm on the first day of Gettysburg, oversaw the Pennsylvania Monument Commission. In his address, he stated, "We hoped the money would allow us to include bronze statues, but they had to be abandoned early in the project. We hope that some legislature in the future would incline to authorize the moderate cost of these statutes and enlarge our plan for the monument."[22]

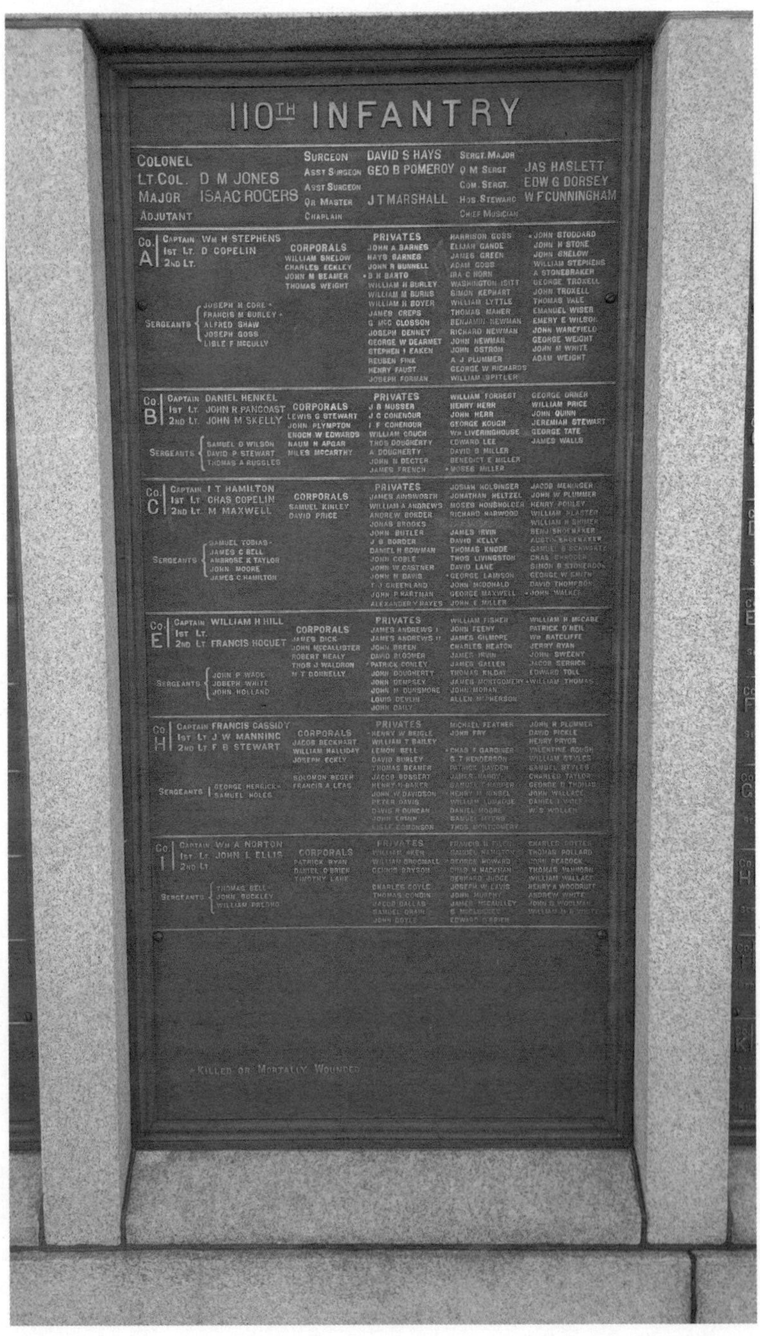

Example of a Pennsylvania Monument Bronze Unit Tablet, Cemetery Ridge, Gettysburg National Military Park.

Pennsylvania State Memorial, Cemetery Ridge, Gettysburg National Military Park.

Future goals of the monument included adding bronze statues of Pennsylvania generals at Gettysburg and installing additional bronze tablets to commemorate Pennsylvanians who fought in the battle. The additions to the monument would require more funding from the Pennsylvania state legislature. Eventually, funding was secured, and additions were made to the monument in 1913.

Beyond apologizing to veterans, the theme of dedication speeches for the Pennsylvania Memorial emphasized the significance of the battle within the context of the Civil War. General David Gregg told the assembled crowd, "Had the Army been defeated, in all probability, the National Capitol would have fallen into the hands of the enemy, the foreign powers would have recognized the Confederacy, and the Union would have been dissolved with consequences too evil to be described."[23]

Following General Gregg, Pennsylvania Governor Edwin Stuart explained how the monument would help future generations learn about the battle and Pennsylvania's role. Stuart proclaimed that the monument "will always inspire the succeeding generations and remind them of deeds that made this place immortal."[24]

In 1913, one of the final Union regimental monuments placed by veterans at Gettysburg was dedicated to General William Wells, who was a major in the 1st Vermont Cavalry during the Gettysburg campaign. Older veterans decided to build a monument in his honor for two reasons: first, Wells was awarded a Medal of Honor for his actions on the third day of the battle; second, it would give the 1st Vermont Cavalry another monument on the battlefield and help commemorate where the Farnsworth charge occurred. When Vermont first passed legislation for state monuments in 1890, the GBMA rule was that regimental monuments could not be dedicated to an individual, and were only to identify where a unit was fighting. By 1913, however, the regulation was no longer strictly in force.

The monument would be placed in the saddle between the Round Tops, directly in line with the dangerous charge ordered by General Judson Kilpatrick and led by Captain Elon Farnsworth. Wells rode at the head of the charge and somehow survived, though Farnsworth and many others were killed. The sentinel-type monument is made of granite and bronze and features a bronze statue of Wells in full uniform, gazing toward the enemy. The monument's granite base features the actions of the 1st Vermont Cavalry during the charge and the casualty data associated with the attack. Also included on the monument is a bas-relief of the Vermont troopers charging toward the enemy.

The dedication ceremonies for the monument were conducted on July 3, 1913. Although the monument was dedicated to a single individual, the funds were provided by the Vermont state legislature. The legislature provided "the sum of six thousand dollars to perpetuate the memory of General William Wells and the officers and enlisted men of the First Regiment, Vermont Cavalry."[25] Private Myron Parker, the president of the First Vermont Cavalry Association, who also fought at Gettysburg, delivered the dedication speech for the monument.

Parker's theme focused on the courage of the 1st Vermont and William Wells, but it also contained reconciliatory tones. Parker stated, "Each side participating in that sanguinary conflict displayed equal valor. Though both sides are now united in loyalty to a common country, each fought for a principle they believed right."[26] Included in the ceremony was an address by Evander Law, the commander of the Confederate brigade which the 1st Vermont Cavalry attacked. Law stated in his address that the battle of Gettysburg was "the culminating point of the Civil War, which marked an epoch in American history. I feel justified in the assertion that the meeting of the two hostile armies on this field fifty years ago was scarcely more important in its results than the meeting now being held by those same armies on this same field will be in its influence on the American people."[27] Parker's and Law's speeches matched the festivities surrounding the monument's dedication during the battle's 50th anniversary.

Major William Wells and 1st Vermont Cavalry Monument, Big Round Top, Gettysburg National Military Park.

Bas-relief of the 1st Vermont Cavalry Charge, Big Round Top, Gettysburg National Military Park.

The Gettysburg Reunion, planned for 1913, marked the culmination of 50 years of battle of Gettysburg monumentation and memorialization. Initial plans for the reunion were announced during the dedication of the Pennsylvania Monument in 1910. Commissioners were requested from every state and territory to meet in Harrisburg, Pennsylvania, in October 1910 to plan a grand reunion of Union and Confederate veterans at Gettysburg.[28] The reunion was one of the last large-scale gatherings of Civil War veterans in the United States. Events during the reunion included battle walks, banquets, and other festive gatherings celebrating the reconciliation of veterans from the North and South.[29]

Many dedication speeches embraced the idea of reconciliation and acceptance that the country had mainly healed since the battle's end. The United States had learned from its civil strife and, by the early 1900s, established itself on the world stage. Many speeches during the reunion expanded on the status of Americans since the end of the Civil War. An example of these themes can be found in the speech given by President Woodrow Wilson, whose focus was on accepting the past and moving forward. Wilson told the assembled veterans, "Lift your eyes to the great tracts of life yet to be conquered in the interest of righteous peace, of that prosperity which lies in a people's hearts and outlasts all wars and errors of men."[30]

Many who attended the reunion echoed the theme of looking forward, not backward. Pennsylvania Congressman James Logue stated about the reunion,

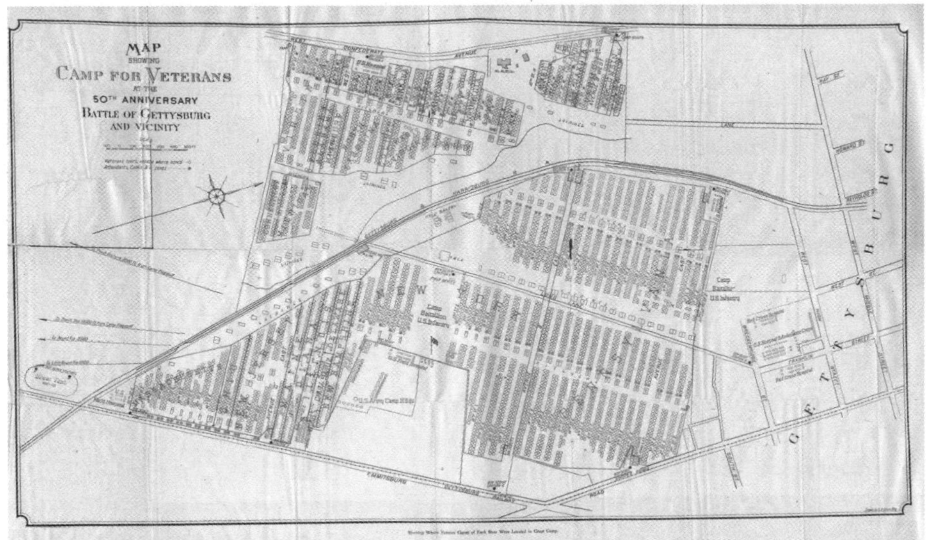

Map of the 50th Gettysburg Anniversary Campground. (*Pennsylvania at Gettysburg, Volume 3*, map insert)

"Both North and South of our great land join in jubilation. Looking backward, no one speaks of a lost cause."[31] While this observation by Logue speaks of the camaraderie between veterans and forgetting the past, discussion of the "lost cause" would continue in the South. Interestingly, Logue's statement highlights the difference between veterans and those who were brought up after the war ended. People who lived after the Civil War ended were raised in a country grappling over control of how the war would be remembered. However, for Civil War veterans in their old age, such concerns were overshadowed by the allure of connecting with others who shared the seminal experience of the great battle.

The 1913 reunion enabled many participants to visit another monument located within the Gettysburg National Cemetery. Completed in 1912, several states from the North joined to build a monument to President Abraham Lincoln and his Gettysburg Address in November 1863.[32] This memorial-type monument features a bronze bust of President Lincoln, the date of his address, and a copy of the address etched in bronze. The monument did not get the attention it deserved because people felt it was not grand enough. However, the monument memorialized the importance of Lincoln's "few appropriate remarks." The monument proved that Lincoln resonated with veterans and the public, helping to establish Gettysburg as a preeminent location for memorialization and remembrance.

President Lincoln's Gettysburg Address Monument, Gettysburg National Cemetery, Gettysburg National Military Park.

Confederate and Union veterans shaking hands. Cemetery Ridge, Gettysburg National Military Park. (Library of Congress)

During the 1913 reunion, the feelings of reconciliation were so high that an event more than 20 years in the making occurred at the Angle on Cemetery Ridge near the High Water Mark monument. Veterans of the Philadelphia Brigade met Confederate veterans at the stone wall and shook hands. The image captured at that moment encapsulated the mood of reconciliation that dominated the reunion. During the week surrounding the anniversary, 3,361 Confederate veterans joined 41,051 Union veterans on the fields of Gettysburg.[33]

A sticking point for Confederate veterans at the 1913 reunion was the push for applying for federal government pensions. Only Union veterans were allowed to apply for pensions after the Civil War. While Confederate veterans were allowed admittance back as United States citizens, they were not afforded money from the government. Reconciliation had reached a critical point in the United States when Southern politicians began discussing the idea with their counterparts in Washington. The hope was that the reunion would be a tipping point for this cause. While talks continued during the reunion regarding the inclusion of Confederate veterans in applying for federal pensions, the idea lost traction after the reunion concluded.[34]

One of the more memorable moments of the 1913 reunion came from a speech by former Union officer John Brooke. During the battle of Gettysburg, Brooke was a brigade commander in the II Corps, and he explained in his speech the importance of Gettysburg and its impact on the Civil War: "On this ground was fought the battle that assured the maintenance of the Great Republic. Many battles were fought after Gettysburg, and it was not until upon the plains of Appomattox that the union of states was assured, but Gettysburg was the turning point of the war."[35]

The 1913 reunion would mark the end of the Battlefield Commission following rules about monumentation that had been in place since the GBMA. Voices in the Southern states increasingly pushed for Confederate monuments to be placed on their side of the battlefield. The road infrastructure created by William Robbins would ultimately be utilized to construct the monuments that he envisioned in the late 1890s. Though many Confederate veterans did not live to see it, monuments to their deeds started to dot the landscape, beginning with the Virginia State Monument, dedicated in 1917. The federal administration of the park finally began to fulfill its promise to interpret and allow monumentation on both sides of the battlefield. However, this did not occur until most Union veterans had passed away, leaving the task to be carried out by others.

One of the primary reasons for the success of the 1913 reunion was the federalization of the battlefield. Though the War Department adhered closely to the GBMA's monumentation approach, which involved preserving battle lines during July 1863, one of the assets of federalizing the battlefield was funding. The battlefield would always have the necessary money and oversight to improve roads and maintain monuments, a critical need that was lacking under the GBMA. The resilience to maintain the battlefield under different conditions allowed veterans to visit and share their stories with later generations.

One way the Gettysburg National Military Park would honor the memory of veterans was by creating a dedicated group of battlefield guides for visitors. Visitors to Gettysburg after the battle were known to hire locals to show them the landmarks and highlights. While this was a common practice after 1863, there was no standardization in how these guides explained the battle; nor was there a system in place to verify the information they provided. Even though the GBMA attempted to streamline the information provided to visitors on the land it owned, there was no effective way to prevent individuals from offering their own tours of the battle and generating a profit.

With the government taking control of the battlefield, freelance guiding at Gettysburg would eventually come to an end. This occurred because of rules put in place by the government for the National Military Park to protect the battlefield and provide a standard narrative of the battle. The other reason was to prevent price gouging and to stop guides from trying to make a profit. This came to a head after several instances of guides fighting for business in the streets of Gettysburg.[36] These scuffles led to legislation that defined licensed battlefield guiding in Gettysburg, which continues to the present day.

The law, written and passed in the summer of 1913, set the framework for how the National Military Park would select and retain battlefield park guides. The bill passed quickly through Congress and serves as the founding document for becoming a guide at Gettysburg. The Battlefield Licensed Guides would become the foundation for touring the battlefield, enduring to this day. To follow the new rules for becoming a Licensed Battlefield Guide at Gettysburg, a written test was created to test a potential guide's knowledge of the battlefield. While initial tests to become a guide started with a basic comprehension of the battle, the modern version requires intensive study.

To become a guide at Gettysburg, an individual must be prepared to undergo a rigorous testing process. The first part of the process is taking a comprehensive written exam about the battle, the campaign, and the Civil War in general. The most recent administration of the written exam included over 180 written questions. If an individual passes the written exam, there are still two more stages to pass to become a guide. The first is a panel interview with current guides and the National Park Service, followed by a mock two-hour battlefield tour. If, at any point, a prospective guide fails a section of the process, they will be asked either to redo the failed section or restart the process from the beginning. This process aims to ensure that a guide can answer most questions visitors have about the battle, providing a solid link to the past.

CHAPTER 7

What Do Union Monuments at Gettysburg Tell Us?

Gettysburg is the most memorialized battlefield in American history. This memorialization includes hundreds of monuments and more tablets dedicated to the men who fought for three days in and around Gettysburg in July 1863. The voluminous historical research about tactics, command decisions, and fighting at Gettysburg reflects the interest in the battle from the Civil War until today. The monumentation and the continued interest in Gettysburg grew out of Union veterans' desire for the battle to be remembered by future generations. The reasons why Union men fought during the Civil War and the effect of combat on their lives drove them to commemorate what they did at Gettysburg. The park became so central to Americans' sense of their history that once the federal government took over, it was deemed a National Military Park.

The reasons for fighting for the Union in the Civil War mostly came from personal choice and conviction. Many dedication speeches echoed sentiments from early colonial days and the Revolution to drive their points home. The analysis of monuments and speeches presented in this book highlights similarities between speakers' themes across different eras of Union monumentation. The largest group of monument dedications centered on preserving the Union—veterans felt the need to explain the importance of protecting the Union from dissolving.

Veterans did not ask the federal government for help when the opportunity arose to build monuments at Gettysburg. The monumentation movement started as a grassroots effort at the local level. As veteran organizations like the Grand Army of the Republic built local monuments to commemorate hometown heroes, they began to look for more significant opportunities to memorialize Union soldiers on battlefields. Working with the Gettysburg Battlefield Memorial Association, regimental organizations could dedicate

Location of monuments post-1913. (Created using ArcGIS Pro by Esri)

monuments to their units at Gettysburg. However, as costs began to rise, veterans went to state legislatures to help raise funds for their monuments. With this shift in funding came more constraints on how monuments were designed and built. State memorial commissions expected detailed accounting and specific plans from regimental associations for the state to help build their monuments.

Another important theme for Union veterans when dedicating monuments was honoring the sacrifice of those who fell. People needed a place to remember where and why their family members and friends died. The Gettysburg Battlefield Memorial Association and the Gettysburg National Cemetery were established within a year of the battle's end to address this need. Furthermore, the speech given by President Lincoln set the benchmark for why Gettysburg was so important, and remembering the fallen on the field became an imperative for the entire country. In many cases, preserving the Union and commemorating the dead went hand in hand with the designs of monuments and the speeches dedicated to them.

The total number of casualties between both armies for three days of fighting at Gettysburg fell roughly around 50,000 men. After the battle, many Union regiments were no longer on the rolls of the Union army. Several regiments were sent home due to the expiration of enlistments, or they were so diminished by casualties they were absorbed into other units. The battle also marked the end of two corps in the Army of the Potomac. In September 1863, the XI and XII Corps were deployed west to join the Union army in the Western Theater, where they would remain until the war's end. Even though many of those units would continue fighting in brutal battles in the West, they chose to return to Gettysburg to honor their unit's heritage and their dead.

Cultural shifts in the United States during the 1880s and 1890s prompted Americans to move beyond the sectional struggle and heal the country. At the end of the 19th century, the United States was becoming a major player on the world stage. America was expanding its global economic reach, bringing wealth and prosperity to the country. By 1898, the United States was willing to fight Spain to remove European influence from the Americas, thereby solidifying the country's position as a global power with a forward foreign policy. Excited about the possibilities during this period, nationalism in the United States began to rise, and this required the infighting of previous generations to be put to bed. An acknowledgment of the fighting spirit on both sides prevailed in many of the speeches given at Gettysburg. The third theme presented in dedication speeches by Union veterans was reconciliation with former Confederates who fought at Gettysburg. While defeating the treasonous

South was a common theme in early dedication speeches at Gettysburg, this changed in later speeches.

Veterans on both sides wanted to share everyday experiences in the 1890s and early 1900s. In their advanced age, Union and Confederate veterans wanted to heal old wounds that could still be open from the Civil War. Starting with local conventions, veterans from both sides met to commiserate. Eventually, these local gatherings would build to a national stage. The desire for reconciliation between Union and Confederate veterans hit its zenith during the 1913 Reunion at Gettysburg. Most reunions at that time centered on bringing both armies together to acknowledge how far the United States had come 50 years since the battle.

While this reconciliation was a reason for the growth of monuments at Gettysburg in the 1880s and 1890s, state and unit pride continued to be important. As regimental monuments began to fill the Gettysburg landscape, veterans began to take notice. States did not want to be left behind if neighboring states dedicated monuments to their veterans and fallen heroes. An example of the influence of state pride can be seen in the speed at which legislatures passed bills to free up funds for monumentation on the battlefield. However, many states followed the lead of New York and Pennsylvania by ensuring that Union monuments were built to withstand the test of time and were placed with historical accuracy. The monuments built by Union veterans provided a roadmap for troop positions and movements. They allowed older veterans to remember where they fought when returning to the field decades later.

Over time, other monuments would be designed and created to memorialize the men who helped create the memorializations on the field. Nestled between the II Corps monuments on Cemetery Ridge is a monument dedicated to John Nicholson, erected in 1925. The former Chairman of the Gettysburg National Military Park died in 1922. The monument is single-faced and includes all of Nicholson's military and postwar veteran affairs accomplishments. Made from granite and bronze, the tribute seamlessly blends in with the rest of the surrounding monuments. During the week that the monument was to be dedicated, the *Gettysburg Times* ran a three-part series chronicling Nicholson's military record and dedication to veterans' affairs.

My first introduction to this monument occurred in 2019 during a Gettysburg Licensed Battlefield Guide tour. While the construction is simple and unassuming compared to other monuments dedicated to individuals on the battlefield, the accomplishments listed are a testament to Nicholson's tireless work for Union veterans after the war. Nicholson sought to bring recognition to all veterans who fought at Gettysburg and for the Union during

Monument to Lieutenant Colonel John P. Nicholson, Cemetery Ridge, Gettysburg National Military Park.

the American Civil War. I found it fitting that the monument was simplistic yet packed with information about the man himself. While the monument addresses Nicholson's bona fides as a soldier of the 28th Pennsylvania Infantry, it focuses mainly on what he did after the war.

This also raises an observation about monument placement, which was a persistent issue for many Union veterans. Most monuments to individuals at Gettysburg are placed where they fell or near where their unit was in the front line. However, this is not the case for Nicholson's monument. As discussed in an earlier chapter, the monuments to the 28th Pennsylvania are located on Culp's Hill, not on Cemetery Ridge. It was decided to place Nicholson's own monument in a central location where he had a hand in authorizing veteran groups to place their works. By blending in with the surrounding monuments, the Nicholson monument serves as a testament to his contributions to the veterans of Gettysburg, identifying and explaining the actions of the men themselves on the battlefield.

Veterans also turned to Gettysburg to establish what the Civil War meant beyond veterans who fought on the field. A GAR monument to the last surviving Union Civil War veteran, Albert Woolson, is located not far from Nicholson's monument, near the current Bryant farm building. The monument pays tribute to all Union military personnel during the Civil War and features a bronze likeness of Woolson as an older man seated. The monument is a memorial type that commemorates Woolson's accomplishments as Senior Vice Commander-in-Chief of the Grand Army of the Republic. On the other side of the granite base, an inscription reads, "Last Survivor." Due to his death in the modern era, there are pictures, audio, and visual recordings of Woolson and his reminiscences.

Given the time Woolson had to reflect on his military service, he could watch the country deal with the social changes created by the Civil War. During this period, Woolson worked tirelessly with GAR, supporting other Union veterans, and he rose within the organization's leadership. While many older veterans remembered service details in ways that read like an adventure novel, Woolson took a different approach. When asked why he joined to fight at such a young age, he is quoted later in life as saying that the only reason to fight was "for our brothers and in that there is no glory." While the monument is a fitting tribute to the last Union veteran (and the last from either side), who died in 1956, Woolson did not participate in the Gettysburg campaign.

Albert Woolson enlisted in the 1st Minnesota Heavy Artillery at the age of 17 in 1864. The unit was not at Gettysburg in 1863 and certainly not when Woolson enlisted a year later. However, with Woolson being the last recognized

The "Last Survivor" GAR Monument, Cemetery Ridge, Gettysburg National Military Park.

surviving member of the Union army alive by the 1950s, the organization replacing the GAR, the Sons of Union Veterans of the Civil War, sought to place the monument at a battlefield that was heavily traveled and featured a wide variety of monuments. The GAR monument is in Ziegler's Grove, near the Nicholson monument built 30 years ago. During the dedication speech for the monument, Woolson's life was summed up with, "He also was the son of a veteran.... Here we have a statue of a man ... who symbolizes all the great virtues of the common, ordinary citizen; the citizen who becomes a soldier and then returns to ordinary life."[1] Even though Woolson never fought in the battle of Gettysburg, he embodied the spirit of Union veterans in the years after the war, wanting to acknowledge what his comrades had fought for.

Very few speeches and monument dedications mention removing slavery from the United States with the Union victory at Gettysburg and, eventually, the Civil War. The instances where the issue of slavery is mentioned typically involve regiments that formed during and after President Lincoln issued the Emancipation Proclamation, or else the regiments themselves were staunchly abolitionist. The lack of discussion of slavery in dedication speeches did not mean that Union veterans were not concerned with abolishing the institution. For many Union veterans, it was apparent that a necessary consequence of defeating the Confederacy would be the eradication of slavery from the United States.

However, when building monuments to their accomplishments during the war, they usually chose to honor sacrifice and duty to their country. The ideals of honor, sacrifice, and duty, as reflected in the monuments at Gettysburg, are products of the era in which most monuments were erected. Throughout the Gilded Age, Americans sought to commemorate the positive achievements that enabled the country to move forward, while downplaying negative aspects. The Civil War nearly destroyed the country and devastated regions of the South, so as the country moved past the end of the war and began to focus on rebuilding itself, the stigma of secession and the central role slavery played in it were marginalized.

Supplanting these issues were ideas of American exceptionalism, specifically the honor of fighting for a cherished cause, an attribute that began to be assigned to both North and South. People wanted to believe that both sides fought for what they believed in. Eventually, the federal government would prioritize the concept of honor and sacrifice in the commissioning of monuments when it acquired the Gettysburg battlefield. Where previously only Union monuments were allowed, Confederate state monuments and markers were eventually added as Union veterans warmed to reconciliation.

Over time, Gettysburg became a place where both sides were honored to explain their sacrifice during the Civil War.

During the federal takeover and administration of the park, political influences looked to add Confederate monuments and interpretations to the setting. The battlefield that started as a place to commemorate a great Union victory, turned into a commemoration of reconciliation. This change in interpretation and addition of Confederate monuments has not deterred visitors from coming to the park on a consistent basis. To this day, Gettysburg is one of the most visited National Parks in the country. The efforts of Union veterans to show the importance of the battlefield through memorialization and monumentation is one of the reasons for the park's popularity. The work of Union veterans allows modern-day visitors to stand where the armies stood and see the sight lines and geography of the battle in the same way they did in 1863. The ground and adjoining signs explain the battle and the tactics used in July 1863. The monuments on the battlefield, however, tell another story, one of how war and a battle can shape individuals for the rest of their lives and inspire their desire for future generations to remember those deeds. General Ulysses Grant summed up what many veterans believed future generations would think about the Civil War as a whole. Grant wrote:

> I would not have the anniversaries of our victories celebrated, nor those of our defeats made fast days and spent in humiliation and prayer; but I would like to see truthful history written. Such history will do full credit to the courage, endurance, and soldierly ability of the American citizen, no matter what section of the country he hailed from or in what ranks he fought … For the present, and so long as there are living witnesses of the great war of sections, there will be people who will not be consoled for the loss of a cause they believed to be holy. As time passes, people, even of the South, will begin to wonder how it was possible that their ancestors ever fought for or justified institutions which acknowledged the right of property in man.[2]

From my experiences walking the battlefield as a young boy, a teenager, and now an adult, those deeds remain poignant. Walking through the forest of granite outside a small Pennsylvania town, there is always something to find and a new story to uncover. Each monument tells a story of a group that came together to fight. While historians and society grapple with what that fight meant and how it defines people in the modern day as interpretations change, there is a more straightforward way to understand what happened at Gettysburg in July 1863. Read the inscriptions on the monuments and find the stories of the men who fought at Gettysburg. In those words, and by looking at the battle through their eyes, we can see what Union veterans thought of their service.

APPENDIX I

Union Troop Strength at Gettysburg Ranked by State

Rank	State	Strength
1	Pennsylvania	24,067
2	New York	23,374
3	Massachusetts	6,104
4	Vermont	4,444
5	Ohio	4,402
6	New Jersey	4,073
7	Michigan	3,899
8	Maine	3,752
9	Wisconsin	2,155
10	Indiana	2,035
11	Maryland	1,953
12	Connecticut	1,268
13	Illinois	1,021
14	Rhode Island	960
15	New Hampshire	843
16	West Virginia	788
17	Delaware	485
18	Minnesota	378

APPENDIX 2

Union Casualties at Gettysburg Ranked by Total Loss

Rank	State	Total Loss
1	New York	6,752
2	Pennsylvania	5,891
3	Massachusetts	1,537
4	Ohio	1,271
5	Michigan	1,111
6	Maine	1,027
7	Wisconsin	806
8	New Jersey	634
9	Indiana	552
10	Vermont	415
11	New Hampshire	368
12	Connecticut	340
13	Minnesota	224
14	Delaware	161
15	Maryland	140
16	Illinois	139
17	Rhode Island	97
18	West Virginia	67

APPENDIX 3

Union Casualties at Gettysburg Ranked by Loss Percentage

Rank	State	Percent Loss
1	Minnesota	59.3
2	New Hampshire	43.7
3	Wisconsin	37.4
4	Delaware	33.2
5	New York	28.9
6	Ohio	28.9
7	Michigan	28.5
8	Maine	27.4
9	Indiana	27.1
10	Connecticut	26.8
11	Massachusetts	25.2
12	Pennsylvania	24.5
13	New Jersey	15.6
14	Illinois	13.6
15	Rhode Island	10.1
16	Vermont	9.3
17	West Virginia	8.5
18	Maryland	7.2

APPENDIX 4

Total Number of Monuments at Gettysburg Ranked by State

Rank	State	Number Of Monuments
1	Pennsylvania	138
2	New York	123
3	Massachusetts	35
4	Ohio	24
5	Maine	23
6	New Jersey	14
7	Connecticut	14
8	Michigan	11
9	Vermont	11
10	Wisconsin	10
11	Indiana	8
12	West Virginia	7
13	Rhode Island	6
14	Maryland	6
15	New Hampshire	5
16	Illinois	4
17	Delaware	4
18	Minnesota	3

APPENDIX 5

Locations of Selected Monuments

Coordinates given in Decimal Degrees (DD)

Gettysburg National Cemetery

Soldiers' National Monument
Location: Center of Gettysburg National Cemetery
Coordinates: 39.81979316352177, -77.23121924594466

1st Minnesota Infantry Urn
Location: Southwest of National Soldiers' Monument
Latitude and Longitude: 39.81961201211299, -77.23166147362878

President Lincoln's Gettysburg Address
Location: Inside West Side entrance of Cemetery
Coordinates: 39.81755087062916, -77.23184864242099

New York State Memorial
Location: Inside East Side entrance of Cemetery
Coordinates: 39.8208212796117, -77.23056656337131

North of Gettysburg

1st Shot Marker
Location: Route 30 & Knoxlyn Road
Coordinates: 39.85076662054227, -77.28103306941092

8th Illinois Cavalry
Location: Route 30 & South Reynolds Avenue
Coordinates: 39.8357712649406, -77.2494672597577

24th Michigan Infantry Regiment
Location: Route 30 & Stone-Meredith Avenue
Coordinates: 39.83488973994174, -77.25438106655743

3rd Indiana Cavalry
Location: Route 30 & North Reynolds Avenue
Coordinates: 39.83789676469948, -77.24783647682213

157th New York Infantry Monument
Location: Mummasburg Road & Howard Avenue
Coordinates: 39.84015269274726, -77.23650661677347

157th New York Infantry, Secondary Monument
Location: Howard Avenue & Biglerville Road
Coordinates: 39.84303950151158, -77.2313210934491

157th New York Infantry Advance Marker
Location: Biglerville Road south of Table Rock Road
Coordinates: 39.84553133839005, -77.23137473764137

26th Wisconsin Infantry Regiment
Location: East Howard Avenue
Coordinates: 39.84340204200503, -77.22943255140763

12th Massachusetts Infantry Regiment
Location: Doubleday Avenue & Robinson Avenue
Coordinates: 39.843687326644684, -77.24206625985596

Stevens Knoll

24th Michigan Infantry Regiment, Secondary Marker
Location: Williams Avenue & Slocum Avenue
Coordinates: 39.819546584180166, -77.22402398892565

East Cemetery Hill

7th West Virginia Infantry Regiment
Location: Baltimore Street
Coordinates: 39.82170834904346, -77.2289790800298

7th West Virginia Infantry Regiment, Third Marker
Location: East of Main Monument
Coordinates: 39.822065898400304, -77.22838621800202

7th West Virginia Infantry Regiment, Fourth Marker
Location: Wainwright Avenue
Coordinates: 39.822080319009885, -77.22760004685645

Culp's Hill

2nd Massachusetts Infantry Regiment
Location: Colgrove Avenue & Carmen Avenue
Coordinates: 39.813333333333333, -77.215861111111111

2nd Maryland Infantry Regiment (CSA)
Location: Slocum Avenue
Coordinates: 39.81667490658924, -77.21823676159114

2nd Maryland Infantry Regiment (CSA) Advance Marker
Location: Geary Avenue & Slocum Avenue
Coordinates: 39.81662835655152, -77.2194041924812

20th Connecticut Infantry Regiment
Location: Slocum Avenue
Coordinates: 39.815802700630634, -77.2177295989653

66th Ohio Infantry Regiment
Location: Crest of Culp's Hill
Coordinates: 39.820074671916785, -77.21955685502613

Major Joshua Palmer Wound Site
Location: Near Main Monument
Coordinates: 39.82006379193373, -77.21954926523492

66th Ohio Infantry Regiment Left Flank Marker
Location: East of Main Monument on Large Stone
Coordinates: 39.820376675325065, -77.21824209407048

123rd New York Infantry Regiment
Location: Slocum Avenue
Coordinates: 39.81597214970374, -77.21787919878702

123rd New York Infantry Regiment Advance Marker
Location: East of Main Monument
Coordinates: 39.81627500112016, -77.21732934596638

1st Maryland Eastern Shore Infantry Regiment
Location: Slocum Avenue
Coordinates: 39.81917684486177, -77.21967472441696

Cemetery Ridge

7th West Virginia Infantry Regiment, Secondary Marker
Location: West of Taneytown Road
Coordinates: 39.81589403508446, -77.23277584716675

12th Massachusetts Infantry Regiment, July 2 Marker
Location: Hancock Avenue & Humphrey Avenue
Coordinates: 39.80672392784096, -77.23511118637568

12th Massachusetts Infantry Regiment, July 3 Marker
Location: North side of National Cemetery Parking Lot
Coordinates: 39.8171784826276, -77.23344387935009

1st Delaware Infantry Regiment
Location: Hancock Avenue
Coordinates: 39.81459787028292, -77.2354198137074

2nd Rhode Island Infantry Regiment Advance Marker
Location: Emmitsburg Road
Coordinates: 39.80983290497637, -77.24219679941172

1st Independent New York Battery
Location: Hancock Avenue
Coordinates: 39.812368104530826, -77.23562213630531

71st Pennsylvania Infantry Regiment
Location: Hancock Avenue
Coordinates: 39.813362108491724, -77.23631035219645

99th Pennsylvania Infantry Regiment, Secondary Marker
Location: Hancock Avenue
Coordinates: 39.81350056921091, -77.23516647624547

19th Maine Infantry Regiment
Location: Hancock Avenue
Coordinates: 39.81107763178905, -77.23612332167342

1st Minnesota Infantry Regiment
Location: Hancock Avenue
Coordinates: 39.806647442655034, -77.23500875337587

1st Minnesota Infantry Regiment, July 3 Marker
Location: Hancock Avenue
Coordinates: 39.81048057345297, -77.2360737289207

Gettysburg Battlefield Memorial Association Monument
Location: Cyclorama Drive and Hancock Avenue
Coordinates: 39.8170846264782, -77.23461930246812

Grand Army of the Republic Monument
Location: Hancock Avenue
Coordinates: 39.81611957143775, -77.23482131763146

Lieutenant Colonel John P. Nicholson Monument
Location: Hancock Avenue
Coordinates: 39.81462224069575, -77.23521280470044

Pennsylvania State Memorial
Location: Hancock Avenue & Humphreys Avenue
Coordinates: 39.80760131435045, -77.23529133223684

United States Regular Army Monument
Location: Hancock Avenue
Coordinates: 39.81121966215719, -77.23570286730212

Warfield Ridge

4th Alabama Infantry Regiment
Location: South Confederate Avenue
Coordinates: 39.78756949216722, -77.25419848033621

Peach Orchard

2nd New Hampshire Infantry Regiment
Location: Emmitsburg Road & Birney Avenue
Coordinates: 39.800512878907746, -77.25034675142996

New York Excelsior Brigade
Location: Sickles Avenue & Excelsior Field
Coordinates: 39.801778828543654, -77.24750134131538

73rd New York Infantry Regiment Stone Marker
Location: Sickles Avenue & Excelsior Field
Coordinates: 39.80182305886423, -77.24769824600598

73rd New York Infantry Regiment
Location: Sickles Avenue & Wheatfield Road
Coordinates: 39.80211074597423, -77.24815343194783

7th New Jersey Infantry Regiment
Location: Sickles Avenue & Wheatfield Road
Coordinates: 39.80149296731111, -77.24674201260582

Wheatfield

Colonel Charles Frederick Taylor Death Monument
Location: Ayers Avenue
Coordinates: 39.79558501116786, -77.24124482928566

27th Connecticut Infantry Regiment
Location: Wheatfield Road & Ayers Avenue
Coordinates: 39.7970623300767, -77.24156300182705

27th Connecticut Infantry Regiment Advance Marker
Location: Brooke Avenue
Coordinates: 39.795308174036535, -77.24693482482118

27th Connecticut Infantry Regiment, Secondary Marker
Location: Brooke Avenue & Cross Avenue
Coordinates: 39.795342550695864, -77.24708866462872

Colonel Henry Merwin Death Site
Location: Wheatfield Road West of Ayers Avenue
Coordinates: 39.79757747152398, -77.24092688539642

Captain Jedediah Chapman Death Site
Location: DeTrobriand Avenue
Coordinates: 39.79617758570377, -77.24545887216968

110th Pennsylvania Infantry Monument
Location: DeTrobriand Avenue
Coordinates: 39.79653023053422, -77.2460619935418

2nd Rhode Island Infantry Regiment
Location: Sedgwick Avenue & Wheatfield Road
Coordinates: 39.79560225712185, -77.23410695727344

Devil's Den

99th Pennsylvania Infantry Regiment
Location: Sickles Avenue & Devil's Den area
Coordinates: 39.792381084849886, -77.24226935266537

Little Round Top

20th Maine Infantry Regiment
Location: Southeast side of Little Round Top
Coordinates: 39.7895005528874, -77.2361689112842

20th Maine Infantry Regiment, Company B Marker
Location: 100 Yards east of main Monument
Coordinates: 39.78875169326387, -77.23477470540301

Colonel Vincent's Rock
Location: Crest of Little Round Top
Coordinates: 39.791307960426266, -77.23701254229618

Colonel Vincent's Wound Marker
Location: South slope of Little Round Top
Coordinates: 39.79066727128891, -77.23691691885051

140th New York Infantry Regiment
Location: Crest of Little Round Top
Coordinates: 39.7914408259491, -77.23703484523735

Big Round Top

20th Maine Infantry, Secondary Monument
Location: Summit of Big Round Top
Coordinates: 39.78625842123949, -77.24099058474157

9th Massachusetts Infantry Regiment
Location: S. Confederate Avenue & Warren Avenue
Coordinates: 39.788532948208506, -77.23782257415452

Major William Wells and the 1st Vermont Cavalry
Location: South Confederate Avenue
Coordinates: 39.7848312197857, -77.24560098005334

East Cavalry Field

General Gregg's Cavalry Shaft
Location: Cavalry Field Road
Coordinates: 39.826398208961265, -77.1630114373374

Endnotes

Introduction

1 War of The Rebellion: A Compilation of the Official Records of the Union and Confederate Armies, Series 1, Volume 27, Part 1 (Washington, DC: Government Printing Office, 1889), 118–19.
2 Calvin Haynes, "Letter to Wife, July 19, 1863," Letters 1862–1863, Manuscripts and Special Collections, New York State Library, Albany, New York.
3 Official Records, Vol. 27, pt. 1, 477.
4 "Gettysburg Victory," *Burlington Daily Times*, July 8, 1863.
5 "Eastern News," *The Placer Herald*, July 11, 1863.
6 "Terrible Defeat of The Invincibles," *The Daily Bee*, July 9, 1863.
7 "Bull Run Dedication of Monuments," *Washington Evening Star*, June 12, 1865.
8 *Maine at Gettysburg: Report of Maine Commissioners* (Portland: Lakeside Press, 1898), 568.
9 William Hardee, *Manual for Rifle and Light Infantry Tactics* (Philadelphia: Lippincott Grambo & Co., 1855).
10 John Busey and David Martin, *Regimental Strengths and Losses at Gettysburg* (Highstown: Longstreet House, 2005).
11 Philip St. George, *The U.S. Cavalry Tactics: Instructions, Formations, Maneuvers* (Washington, DC: Government Printing Office, 1862).
12 War Department, *Instruction for Field Artillery* (Philadelphia: Lippincott, 1860).

Chapter 1

1 Andrew Curtin, "The Enemy Is Approaching, June 16, 1863," I-Original-1862–3, Archives and Special Collections, Dickinson College, Carlisle, PA.
2 William Bayly, "Memoirs of a Thirteen Year Old Boy Relating to the Battle of Gettysburg," *Gettysburg Compiler*, October 30, 1939.
3 Amelia Harmon, "Burning of the Mclean House," *Gettysburg Compiler*, July 3, 1915.
4 "Terrible Accident," *Adams County Sentinel*, November 24, 1863.
5 Commonwealth of Pennsylvania, Department of the Auditor-General, Damage Claims under the Acts of April 23, 1863, April 9, 1869, and May 27, 1871, Adams County, William Bliss, 4110.
6 "To All Citizens," *Adams County Sentinel*, July 7, 1863.
7 Leonard Gardner, "Sunset Memories," *Gettysburg Times*, September 10, 1940.
8 Robert McClean, "A Boy in Gettysburg in 1863," *Gettysburg Compiler*, June 30, 1909.
9 Michael Jacobs, *Notes on the Rebel Invasion of Maryland and Pennsylvania, and the Battle of Gettysburg* (Philadelphia: J. P. Lippincott & Co., 1864), 47.

10 Robert E. Nale and Jean A. Suloff, eds., *The 36th Regiment, Pennsylvania Volunteer Militia: July and August 1863*, Copy in Gettysburg National Military Park Library, V6-PA36 MIL.
11 "Gov. Curtin Notes," *Adams County Sentinel*, July 28, 1863.
12 Theodore Dimon, *From Auburn to Antietam: The Journal of a Battlefield Surgeon Who Served with the Army of the Potomac 1861–1865*, V-5 Theodore S. Dimon, Gettysburg National Military Park Archives, Gettysburg, PA, 135–41.
13 David Wills, Letter to Governor Andrew Curtin July 24, 1863, Executive Correspondence, RG 26, Department of State, Secretary of The Commonwealth, Pennsylvania State Archives, Harrisburg, PA.
14 War of The Rebellion: A Compilation of the Official Records of the Union and Confederate Armies, Series 1, Volume 27, Part 3 (Washington, DC: Government Printing Office, 1889), 162, 370.
15 David McConaughy, "Our Heroic Dead," *Adams County Sentinel*, June 24, 1862.
16 D. H. Buehler and Edward G. Fahnestock, Letter to Governor Andrew Curtin, August 14, 1863, Vertical File 10-5 David Wills Correspondence, Gettysburg National Military Park Archives, Gettysburg, PA.
17 *Revised Report of the Select Committee Relative to the Soldiers National Cemetery* (Harrisburg: Singerly & Myers, 1865), 8.
18 *Revised Report of the Select Committee Relative to the Soldiers National Cemetery*, 168–169.
19 Abraham Lincoln, Letter from David Wills to Abraham Lincoln, November 2, 1863, Abraham Lincoln Papers: Series 1, General Correspondence. 1833 to 1916, Library of Congress, Washington, DC.
20 Edward Everett, *An Oration Delivered on the Battlefield of Gettysburg* (New York: Baker & Godwin Printers, 1863), 29–32.
21 Abraham Lincoln, Draft of the Gettysburg Address: Nicolay Copy, November 1863; Series 3, General Correspondence, 1837–1897; The Abraham Lincoln Papers at the Library of Congress, Manuscript Division, Washington, DC.
22 *Revised Report of the Select Committee Relative to the Soldiers National Cemetery*, 160.
23 Ibid., 166.
24 John Bartlett, *The Soldiers' National Cemetery at Gettysburg: With the Proceedings at Its Consecration, at the Laying of the Corner-Stone of the Monument, and at Its Dedication* (Providence: Providence Press Company, 1874), 63.
25 "Another Great Day In Gettysburg," *Adams County Sentinel*, July 11, 1865.
26 Bartlett, *The Soldiers' National Cemetery at Gettysburg*, 68.
27 Ibid., 86.
28 "Dedication of the Monument," *Gettysburg Compiler*, July 9, 1869.
29 "Soldiers Monument," *Gettysburg Star and Sentinel*, October 16, 1867.
30 John Busey and David Martin, *Regimental Strengths and Losses at Gettysburg* (Hightown: Longstreet House, 2005), 129.
31 David McConaughy, Letter to Governor Andrew Curtin, July 25, 1863, Executive Correspondence, RG 26, Department of State, Secretary of The Commonwealth, Pennsylvania State Archives, Harrisburg, PA.
32 McConaughy, Letter to Governor Andrew Curtin, July 25, 1863.
33 "An Act to Incorporate the Gettysburg Battlefield Memorial Association," Gettysburg Battlefield Memorial Association, Civil War Vertical File Manuscripts, Gettysburg College Special Collections, Gettysburg, PA.
34 John Vanderslice, *Gettysburg Then and Now* (New York: G. W. Dillingham Co., 1897), 204.

35 Vanderslice, *Gettysburg Then and Now*, 363.
36 David McConaughy, Letter to Reverend Charles Krauth, August 14, 1863, MS-022 David McConaughy Papers, Special Collections and College Archives, Gettysburg College, Gettysburg, PA.
37 "An Act to Incorporate the Gettysburg Battlefield Memorial Association," April 30, 1864.
38 Robert Lee, Letter to David McConaughy, August 4, 1869, MS-022 David McConaughy Papers, Special Collections and College Archives, Gettysburg College, Gettysburg, PA.
39 "Army Reunion At Gettysburg," *New York Times*, July 27, 1869.
40 Minute Book Gettysburg Battlefield Memorial Association 1872–1895, Vertical File 11 Park History, Gettysburg National Military Park Archives, Gettysburg, PA.

Chapter 2

1 "Order creating the United States Sanitary Commission, by the Secretary of War and approved by the President, June 13, 1861," Manuscripts and Archives Division, The New York Public Library, New York City, NY.
2 Charles Stillé, *History of the United States Sanitary Commission During the War of the Rebellion* (Philadelphia: J. B. Lippincott & Co., 1866), iii–iv.
3 *Statutes at Large of the United States of America from March 1871 to March 1873*, Vol. 1 (Boston: Little, Brown and Company, 1873), 566–77.
4 Robert Beath, *The Grand Army Blue-book Containing the Rules and Regulations of the Grand Army of the Republic* (Philadelphia: Burk & McFetridge Printers, 1884), iii.
5 Beath, *Rules and Regulations of the Grand Army of the Republic*, 1.
6 William Ward, *Records of Members of the Grand Army of the Republic* (San Francisco: H. S. Crocker & Co., 1886), 7–10.
7 "The Encampment," *Gettysburg Compiler*, July 19, 1878.
8 There are very few studies of General Strong Vincent. A biography called *What Death More Glorious: A Biography of General Strong Vincent* by James Nevins and William Style provides a comprehensive biography of Vincent. Recently another biography, *The Lion of Round Top* by H. G. Myers, focuses on his military accomplishments before and during Gettysburg.
9 Oliver Norton, *Strong Vincent and His Brigade at Gettysburg* (Chicago: Private Printing, 1909), 6.
10 War of The Rebellion: A Compilation of the Official Records of the Union and Confederate Armies, Series 1, Volume 27, Part 1 (Washington, DC: Government Printing Office, 1889), 616–617.
11 John Busey and David Martin, *Regimental Strengths and Losses at Gettysburg* (Highstown: Longstreet Publishing, 2005), 134.
12 Official Records, Vol. 27, Pt. 1, 618.
13 Issac Moorhead, *The Occasional Writings of Issac Moorhead with a Sketch of His Life, ed. Andrew Caughey* (Erie: A. H. Caughey Publisher, 1882), 84.
14 Ibid., 84–85.
15 "The GAR Encampment," *Gettysburg Compiler*, July 26, 1878.
16 "GAR Encampment," *Gettysburg Compiler*, August 2, 1878.
17 "Grand Army Encampment," *Gettysburg Star and Sentinel*, August 1, 1878.
18 Oliver Norton, *Army Letters 1861–1865* (Dayton: Morningside Press, 1990), 373.

19 Charles Hobson and Arnold Shankman, eds., "Colonel of the Bucktails: Civil War Letters of Charles Frederick Taylor," *The Pennsylvania Magazine of History and Biography* 97, no. 3 (July 1973): 360, https://journals.psu.edu/pmhb/article/view/42971/42692.
20 Official Records, Vol. 27, Pt. 1, 654.
21 Hobson and Shankman, eds. "Civil War Letters of Charles Frederick Taylor," 360.
22 Busey and Martin, *Regimental Strengths and Losses at Gettysburg*, 135.
23 "Grand Army Reunion," *Philadelphia Inquirer*, July 24, 1878.
24 "Bucktails Dedication Monument," *Gettysburg Compiler*, October 11, 1905.
25 Osmund Thompson and William Rauch, *History of the Bucktails* (Philadelphia: Electric Printing Company, 1906), 447.
26 Thompson and Rauch, *History of the Bucktails*, 444.
27 "Brieflets," *Boston Evening Transcript*, September 9, 1879.
28 Official Records, Vol. 27, Pt. 1, 766–67.
29 Charles Morse, "The Twelfth Corps at Gettysburg," Papers of the Military Historical Society of Massachusetts, Vol. 14 (Boston: Cadet Armory, 1918), 26.
30 Official Records, Vol. 27, Pt. 1, 813–14.
31 Alonzo Quint, *The Record of the Second Massachusetts Infantry 1861–65* (Boston: James Walker, 1867), 180.
32 Busey and Martin, *Regimental Strengths and Losses at Gettysburg*, 142.
33 "The Massachusetts Second," *Boston Evening Transcript*, December 23, 1879.
34 Ibid.
35 The themes of reconciliation and how the country moved past the Civil War is discussed in detail in David Blight's *Race and Reunion: The Civil War in American Memory.*
36 Official Records, Vol. 27, Pt. 2, 697.
37 Ibid., 699.
38 Ibid., 696.
39 William Rawle, *History of the Third Pennsylvania Cavalry in the American Civil War* (Philadelphia: Franklin Printing Company, 1905), 555.
40 Gregg Cavalry Shaft Record Book 1883–1918, Group 2, Series 8, Box 48, Folder17, MOLLUS Archives, The Union League Legacy Foundation, Philadelphia, Pennsylvania.
41 Rawle, *History of the Third Pennsylvania Cavalry in the American Civil War*, 656.
42 "The Cavalry Shaft," *Gettysburg Compiler*, October 21, 1884.
43 "Gen. Gregg's Command at Gettysburg," *Reading Times*, October 16, 1884.
44 William Rawle, "Gregg's Cavalry Fight at Gettysburg," *Journal of the United States Cavalry Association*, Vol. 4 (Leavenworth: Ketchenson & Reeves, 1889), 257.
45 Rawle, "Gregg's Cavalry Fight at Gettysburg," 275.
46 William Rawle, *Gregg's Cavalry Fight at Gettysburg* (Philadelphia: William Brooke-Rawle, 1884), 29.
47 "Cavalry Reunion at Gettysburg," *The Marion Times-Standard*, October 15, 1884.
48 "On To Gettysburg," *Baltimore Sun*, November 19, 1886.
49 The economics of rebuilding after the Civil War and making money from its memory is discussed in *Buying and Selling Civil War Memory in Gilded Age America*, edited by James Marten and Caroline Janney.
50 Official Records, Vol. 27, Pt. 2, 571.
51 Busey and Martin, *Regimental Strengths and Losses at Gettysburg*, 280.
52 Minute Book, Gettysburg Battlefield Memorial Association, 129.
53 Ibid., 126.

54 "Rebel Monuments Offensive," *Pittsburgh Dispatch*, October 24, 1889.
55 "Dedicating The Monument," *Baltimore Sun*, November 20, 1886.
56 Bradley Johnson, "The Maryland Confederate Monument at Gettysburg," Southern Historical Society Papers, Vol. 14 (Richmond: William Jones Printers, 1886), 435.
57 "The Maryland Confederate Monument at Gettysburg," 436.
58 "Dedicating the Monument," *Baltimore Sun.*
59 "The Maryland Confederate Monument at Gettysburg," 429.
60 John Bachelder, *Bachelder Papers: Gettysburg In Their Own Words*, Vol. 3, David and Aubrey Ladd eds. (El Dorado Hills: Savas Beatie, 2021), 1461.
61 *Pennsylvania at Gettysburg: Ceremonies at the Dedication of the Monuments,* Vol. 1 (Harrisburg: E. K. Meyers, 1893), 471–72.

Chapter 3

1 "Kent County Soldiers," *Detroit Free Press*, August 31, 1885.
2 Acts of the Legislature of the State of New Jersey, 1885 (Camden: Courier Publishing Association, 1885), 273.
3 Minute Book Gettysburg Battlefield Memorial Association, 74.
4 *Massachusetts Soldiers, Sailors, and Marines in the Civil War*, Vol. 1 (Norwood: Norwood Press, 1931), 617–18.
5 David McNamara, *History of the Ninth Regiment Massachusetts Volunteer Infantry* (Boston: E. B. Stillings & Co., 1899), 306–7.
6 McNamara, *History of the Ninth Massachusetts*, 320.
7 *Harrisburg Daily Independent*, June 7, 1885.
8 War of The Rebellion: A Compilation of the Official Records of the Union and Confederate Armies, Series 1, Volume 27, Part 1 (Washington, DC: Government Printing Office, 1889), 793.
9 John Storrs, *Twentieth Connecticut: A Regimental History* (Ansonia: Naugatuck Valley Sentinel Press, 1886), 93.
10 Official Records, Vol. 27, Pt. 1, 794.
11 Storrs, *Twentieth Connecticut: A Regimental History*, 175.
12 Ibid., 178.
13 Ibid., 177.
14 "Battlefield Monuments," *Gettysburg Compiler*, July 7, 1885.
15 Storrs, *Twentieth Connecticut: A Regimental History*, 190.
16 *Massachusetts Soldiers, Sailors, and Marines in the Civil War*, Vol. 2 (Norwood: Norwood Press, 1931), 3.
17 John Bachelder, *Bachelder Papers: Gettysburg In Their Own Words*, Vol. 1, David and Aubrey Ladd eds. (El Dorado Hills: Savas Beatie, 2021), 108.
18 Official Records, Vol. 27, Pt. 1, 309.
19 *Massachusetts Legislative Acts, 1884* (Boston: Wright & Potter Printing Co., 1885), 375.
20 "Their Glory: Dedicating the Monuments at Gettysburg," *Boston Globe*, October 9, 1885.
21 "Battlefield Memorials," *Philadelphia Inquirer*, October 9, 1885.
22 "Their Glory," *Boston Globe*.
23 Ibid.
24 Winthrop Sheldon, *The Twenty-Seventh: A Regimental History* (New Haven: Morris & Benham, 1886), 10–11.

25 "St. Johnsbury At Gettysburg," *St. Johnsbury Caledonian*, September 17, 1885.
26 "27th C.V. Memorial," *The Morning Journal-Courier*, October 19, 1885.
27 "The Monument Dedicated," *The Morning Journal-Courier*, October 23, 1885.
28 Ibid.
29 Dedication of Monument of the 27th Connecticut Volunteers (New Haven: Price, Lee & Co. Printers, 1886), 16.
30 John Busey and David Martin, *Regimental Strengths and Losses at Gettysburg* (Highstown: Longstreet Publishing, 2005), 106.
31 Official Records, Vol. 27, Pt. 1, 927.
32 "Indiana's Monument at Gettysburg," *Pittsburgh Daily Post*, October 29, 1885.
33 "Monuments at Gettysburg," *Indianapolis Journal*, October 29, 1885.
34 Ibid.
35 Stephen Rockenbach, *War Upon Our Border: Two Ohio Valley Communities Navigate the Civil War* (Charlottesville: University of Virginia Press, 2016), 11.
36 Indiana's post-Civil War economic policy with Southern states is discussed in Emma Thornbrough's book, *Indiana in the Civil War Era.*
37 Frederick Dyer, *A Compendium of the War of the Rebellion* (Des Moines: Dyer Publishing Company, 1908), 1016–18.
38 *Journal of the House of Representatives of the State of Delaware* (Wilmington: Henry Eckel Printer, 1861), 102–3.
39 Official Records, Vol. 27, Pt. 1, 469.
40 *Report of the Joint Committee to Mark the Positions Occupied by the 1st and 2nd Delaware Regiments at Gettysburg* (Dover: Delawarean Press, 1887), 16.
41 Busey and Martin, *Regimental Strengths and Losses at Gettysburg*, 130.
42 "The Legislature," *Delaware Gazette and State Journal*, April 16, 1885.
43 *Report of Delaware Monuments*, 4.
44 Ibid., 5.
45 Ibid., 17.
46 Ibid., 5.
47 "Delaware's Dead Heroes," *News Journal*, June 11, 1886.
48 "Some Impressions," *Morning News*, June 14, 1886.
49 The actions of Daniel Sickles have been a constant topic of debate in Gettysburg historiography and continues in the present. Almost every work written about Gettysburg analyzes the decisions made by General Sickles.
50 Official Records, Vol. 27, Pt. 1, 574–75
51 "The Granite State," *The National Tribune*, July 22, 1886.
52 Ibid.
53 "Rhode Island's Day," *Newport Mercury*, October 23, 1886.
54 Busey and Martin, *Regimental Strengths and Losses at Gettysburg*, 138.
55 Whitelaw Reid, *Ohio in the War: Her Statesmen, Her Generals, Her Soldiers*, Vol. 2 (Cincinnati: Moore, Wilstach & Baldwin, 1886), 387.
56 Official Records, Vol. 27, Pt. 1, 828–29.
57 Busey and Martin, *Regimental Strengths and Losses at Gettysburg*, 142.
58 *Report of the Ohio Gettysburg Memorial Commission* (Columbus: Nitschke Brothers Press, 1887), 4–5.
59 "Ohio Monuments," *Cincinnati Inquirer*, September 15, 1887.
60 *Report of the Ohio Gettysburg Memorial Commission*, 35–36.

61 Official Records, Vol. 27, Pt. 1, 844.
62 "Ohio Monuments."
63 Ibid.
64 *Special Acts and Resolutions of the State of Connecticut*, Vol. 10 (Hartford: Case, Lockwood & Brainard Press, 1890), 1043–44.
65 *17th and 27th Connecticut Volunteers at Gettysburg: October 22, 1889 Order of Exercises and Addresses* (Bridgeport: Standard Association Printers, 1889), 12.
66 "Local Finishes," *Gettysburg Compiler*, November 8, 1887.

Chapter 4

1 "Legislative Brevities," *Democrat and Chronicle*, May 12, 1886.
2 New York Monuments Commission, *Final Report of the Battlefield of Gettysburg*, Vol. 1 (Albany: J. B. Lyon Printers, 1902), 2.
3 *Laws of the State of New York Passed at the 110th Session* (Albany: Banks & Brothers Publishing, 1887), 339.
4 Ibid., 340.
5 Frederick Phisterer, *New York in the War of the Rebellion*, Vol. 5 (Albany: J. B. Lyon Company, 1912), 3831.
6 John Busey and David Martin, *Regimental Strengths and Losses at Gettysburg* (Highstown: Longstreet Publishing, 2005), 90.
7 Albert Barlow, *Company G: A Record of the Services of One Company of the 157th N.Y. Vols. in the War of the Rebellion* (Syracuse: A. W. Hall Publishing, 1899), 137.
8 Barlow, *Company G*, 136–37.
9 "Throughout Pennsylvania," *The Valley Spirit Daily*, September 10, 1886.
10 New York Monuments Commission, *Final Report of the Battlefield of Gettysburg*, Vol. 3, 1060.
11 The scholarship on the assault is enormous. Recently, James Hessler and Wayne Motts *Pickett's Charge at Gettysburg: A Guide to the Most Famous Attack in American History* and Carl Reardon's *Pickett's Charge in History and Memory* cover the overall picture of the assault.
12 Busey and Martin, *Regimental Strengths and Losses at Gettysburg*, 82.
13 War of The Rebellion: A Compilation of the Official Records of the Union and Confederate Armies, Series 1, Volume 27, Part 1 (Washington, DC: Government Printing Office, 1889), 690.
14 The use of artillery and its tactics at Gettysburg are covered in detail by George Newton in *Silent Sentinels: A Reference Guide to the Artillery at Gettysburg* and *"Double Canister at Ten Yards": The Federal Artillery and the Repulse of Pickett's Charge, July 3, 1863*, by David Shultz.
15 Official Records, Vol. 27, Pt. 1, 690.
16 "Cowan's Battery Monument," *Philadelphia Times*, July 4, 1887.
17 New York Monuments Commission, *Final Report of the Battlefield of Gettysburg*, Vol. 3, 1273.
18 "Cowan's Battery Monument," *Philadelphia Times*, July 4, 1887.
19 "Honoring American Heroism," *Philadelphia Times*, July 10, 1887.
20 Minute Book, Gettysburg Battlefield Memorial Association, 159.
21 Busey and Martin, *Regimental Strengths and Losses at Gettysburg*, 96.
22 "Three More New York Monuments Dedicated at Gettysburg," *The Record-Union*, September 6, 1888.
23 New York Monuments Commission, *Final Report of the Battlefield of Gettysburg*, Vol. 2, 852.
24 Ibid., 852–853.

25 Ibid., 852.
26 "The 140th in the Late Fight," *Rochester Evening Express*, July 11, 1863.
27 Busey and Martin, *Regimental Strengths and Losses at Gettysburg*, 135.
28 Official Records, Vol. 27, Pt. 1, 593.
29 "Four Monuments Dedicated," *The Morning Journal-Courier*, September 18, 1889.
30 New York Monuments Commission, *Final Report of the Battlefield of Gettysburg*, Vol. 3, 952.
31 Ibid., 952.
32 Ibid., 953.
33 Ibid., 958.
34 Phisterer, *Final Report of the Battlefield of Gettysburg*, Vol. 4, 2751
35 Busey and Martin, *Regimental Strengths and Losses at Gettysburg*, 54.
36 John Downey, "Second Regiment, Excelsior Brigade." *New York Daily Tribune*, July 14, 1863.
37 Frank Moran, "Reminiscences of a Fire Zouave," *The National Tribune*, October 16, 1890.
38 "New York's Dead Heroes," *The Sun*, July 3, 1893.
39 New York Monuments Commission, *Final Report of the Battlefield of Gettysburg*, Vol. 2, 585.
40 "73d REG. N.Y. Volunteers," *Gettysburg Compiler*, September 7, 1897
41 New York Monuments Commission, *Final Report of the Battlefield of Gettysburg*, Vol. 2, 602.
42 "The New York State Monument at Gettysburg," *Frank Leslie's Illustrated Newspaper*, March 21, 1891.
43 New York Monuments Commission, *Final Report of the Battlefield of Gettysburg*, Vol. 1, 236.
44 Ibid., 238.
45 Frank Moore, ed., *The Rebellion Record: A Diary of American Events* (New York: G. P. Putnam, 1861), 45.
46 New York Monuments Commission, *Final Report of the Battlefield of Gettysburg*, Vol. 2, 911.
47 New York Monuments Commission, *Final Report of the Battlefield of Gettysburg*, Vol. 3, 978.
48 Laws of the General Assembly of the Commonwealth of Pennsylvania Passed at the Session of 1887 (Harrisburg: Edwin K. Meyers State Printer, 1887), 409.
49 Ibid.
50 George Beodelman, "Letter to father, October 24, 1861," MS 43: George Beodelman Collection, Box 1, Folder 7. Gettysburg College Special Collections, Gettysburg College.
51 Busey and Martin, *Regimental Strengths and Losses at Gettysburg*, 40.
52 Official Records, Vol. 27, Pt. 1, 432.
53 "The Pickett Reunion at Gettysburg," *Gettysburg Compiler*, July 12, 1887.
54 *Pennsylvania at Gettysburg: Ceremonies at the Dedication of the Monuments Erected by the Commonwealth of Pennsylvania*, Vol. 1 (Harrisburg: William Stanley Printers, 1904), 410.
55 Ibid., 416.
56 Samuel Bates, *History of the Pennsylvania Volunteers 1861–1865*, Vol. 3 (Harrisburg: B. Singerly, 1870), 978–981.
57 Busey and Martin, *Regimental Strengths and Losses at Gettysburg*, 52.
58 James Hamilton, "The 110th Regiment in the Gettysburg Campaign," *Philadelphia Weekly Press*, February 24, 1896.
59 George Hillyer, *My Gettysburg Battle Experiences* (Gettysburg: Thomas Publications, 2005), 16
60 Manuscript History of the 110th Pennsylvania Volunteers, 1805.002.031, MOLLUS Archives, The Union League Legacy Foundation, Philadelphia, Pennsylvania.
61 Busey and Martin, *Regimental Strengths and Losses at Gettysburg*, 132.
62 *Pennsylvania at Gettysburg*, Vol. 1, 597–98.
63 Ibid., 597.

64 Busey and Martin, *Regimental Strengths and Losses at Gettysburg*, 50.
65 Official Records, Vol. 27, Pt. 1, 513.
66 Busey and Martin, *Regimental Strengths and Losses at Gettysburg*, 131.
67 *Pennsylvania at Gettysburg*, Vol. 1, 537.
68 Ibid., 545.
69 Ibid., 531.
70 Official Records, Vol. 27, Pt. 1, 502.
71 *Pennsylvania at Gettysburg*, Vol. 2, 539.

Chapter 5

1 "A Great Battlefield," *New York Times*, July 16, 1888.
2 George Kilmer, "Gettysburg Wordy Controversies," *Weekly News-Democrat*, June 14, 1888.
3 *Laws of Wisconsin Passed by the Biennial Session of the Legislature of 1887*, Vol. 1 (Madison: Democrat Printing Company, 1887), 53.
4 *Laws of Wisconsin*, Vol. 1, 54.
5 John Busey and David Martin, *Regimental Strengths and Losses at Gettysburg* (Highstown: Longstreet Publishing, 2005), 91.
6 War of The Rebellion: A Compilation of the Official Records of the Union and Confederate Armies, Series 1, Volume 27, Part 1 (Washington, DC: Government Printing Office, 1889), 746.
7 "Veterans Off to Gettysburg," *Milwaukee Sentinel*, June 29, 1888.
8 "Wisconsin's Monuments," *Salt Lake Herald*, July 1, 1888.
9 "Tributes to the Brave," *Gogebic Iron Tribune*, July 7, 1888.
10 Ibid.
11 *State of New Jersey Final Report of the Gettysburg Battlefield Commission* (Highstown: Longstreet House Publishing, 1997), 15.
12 *Acts of the Legislature of the State of New Jersey 1886* (Trenton: MacCrelish & Quigley Publishing, 1886), 299.
13 Busey and Martin, *Regimental Strengths and Losses at Gettysburg*, 55.
14 Official Records, Vol. 27, Pt. 1, 578.
15 "Wisconsin's Monuments."
16 *State of New Jersey Final Report of the Gettysburg Battlefield Commission*, 52.
17 Ibid., 53.
18 Ibid., 56.
19 *Laws of The State of Maryland Made and Passed 1888* (Annapolis: James Young State Printer, 1888), 164.
20 Official Records, Vol. 27, Pt. 1, 808.
21 Busey and Martin, *Regimental Strengths and Losses at Gettysburg*, 142.
22 Official Records, Vol. 27, Pt. 1, 809.
23 *Report of the State of Maryland Gettysburg Monument Commission* (Baltimore: William K. Boyle & Son, 1891), 52.
24 *Public Acts of the Legislature of the State of Michigan Passed at the Regular Session of 1887* (Lansing: Thorp & Godfrey State Printers, 1887), 256.
25 "Monument Contracts and Deeds," Record Group 44, Box 68, Folder 7, Gettysburg Battlefield Commission, Michigan State Archives, Lansing, MI.
26 George McClellan, *McClellan's Own Story* (New York: Charles L. Webster, 1887), 582.

27 Busey and Martin, *Regimental Strengths and Losses at Gettysburg*, 23.
28 Official Records, Vol. 27, Pt. 1, 267.
29 Official Records, Vol. 27, Pt. 1, 268.
30 Busey and Martin, *Regimental Strengths and Losses at Gettysburg*, 125.
31 *Michigan at Gettysburg* (Highstown: Longstreet House, 1998), 116.
32 Ibid., 126.
33 *Resolves of the State of Maine 1887* (Augusta: Sprague & Son Printers of the State, 1887), 29.
34 Ibid.
35 Busey and Martin, *Regimental Strengths and Losses at Gettysburg*, 39.
36 Silas Adams, *"The Nineteenth Maine at Gettysburg" in War Papers Read Before the Commandery of the State of Maine*, Vol. 4 (Portland: Lefavor-Tower Company, 1915), 242.
37 Official Records, Vol. 27, Pt. 1, 422.
38 Ibid.
39 *Maine at Gettysburg* (Portland: Lakeside Press, 1898), 581.
40 *Maine at Gettysburg*, 561.
41 Ibid.
42 Busey and Martin, *Regimental Strengths and Losses at Gettysburg*, 134.
43 *Maine at Gettysburg: Report of Maine Commissioners* (Portland: Lakeside Press, 1898), 559.
44 Ronald Lee, *The Origin and Evolution of the National Military Park Idea* (Washington, DC: Office of Park Historic Preservation, 1973), 6.
45 *Laws of the State of Illinois Passed by the Thirty-Six General Assembly* (Springfield: H.W. Rokker Printer and Binder, 1889), 24.
46 Abner Hard, *History of the Eighth Cavalry Regiment of Illinois Volunteers* (Aurora: Abner Hard Publisher, 1868), 34.
47 Busey and Martin, *Regimental Strengths and Losses at Gettysburg*, 106.
48 Hard, *History of the Eighth Cavalry Regiment of Illinois Volunteers*, 256.
49 "Who Fired the Opening Shots," *Philadelphia Weekly Times*, February 2, 1878.
50 Busey and Martin, *Regimental Strengths and Losses at Gettysburg*, 143.
51 Newel Chaney, *History of the Ninth Regiment New York Volunteer Cavalry 1861–1865* (Foland Center: Martin Merz & Son, 1901), 103.
52 Official Records, Vol. 27, Pt. 1, 939.
53 "Trip To Gettysburg," *The Naperville Clarion*, July 20, 1887.
54 "Illinois Monuments," *Alton Evening Telegraph*, September 4, 1891.
55 *Illinois Monuments at Gettysburg* (Springfield: H. W. Rokker Printer and Binder, 1892), 19.
56 Ibid., 22.
57 John Bachelder, *Gettysburg: What to See and How to See It* (Boston: John Bachelder Publishing, 1876), 56.
58 Minute Book, Gettysburg Battlefield Memorial Association, 146.
59 John Bachelder, *Bachelder Papers: Gettysburg In Their Own Words*, Vol. 3, David and Aubrey Ladd eds. (El Dorado Hills: Savas Beatie, 2021), 1854–1855.
60 Official Records, Vol. 1, Pt. 1, iii.
61 "The Blue and Gray," *Carlisle Weekly Herald*, June 9, 1892.
62 *Minnesota in the Civil and Indian Wars 1861–1865* (St. Paul: Pioneer Press Company, 1890), iii.
63 Ibid., 2.
64 Busey and Martin, *Regimental Strengths and Losses at Gettysburg*, 39.
65 William Lochner, "The First Minnesota at Gettysburg" in *Glimpses of the Nation's Struggle Third Series: 1889–1892* (St. Paul: D. D. Merrill Co, 1893), 48.

66 Official Records, Vol. 27, Pt. 1, 425.
67 Lochner, "The First Minnesota at Gettysburg," 50.
68 Ibid.
69 *General Laws of the State of Minnesota 1891* (St. Paul: Pioneer Press Company, 1891), 293.
70 "Most Memorable Charge," *New Ulm Review*, October 4, 1893.
71 "Minnesota's Gettysburg Monument," *Allentown Ledger*, July 3, 1897.
72 *History of the First Regiment Minnesota Volunteer Infantry 1861–1864* (Stillwater: Easton & Masterson, 1916) 435–36.

Chapter 6

1 Ronald Lee, The *Origin and Evolution of the National Military Park Idea* (Washington, DC: Office of Park Historic Preservation, 1973), 6.
2 Gettysburg Battlefield Military Park Commission, Annual Report 1893 (Washington, DC: Government Printing Office, 1894), 10.
3 House Committee on Military Affairs, Battle Lines at Gettysburg, Report No. 3024 (Washington, DC: Government Printing Office, 1890), 4.
4 H.R. 8096, "A Bill to establish a National Military Park at Gettysburg, Pennsylvania" (December 6, 1894), 53rd Congress, 3rd Session.
5 Annual Reports of the War Department, Vol. 1 (Washington, DC: Government Printing Office, 1900), 206.
6 William Robbins, Journal 1894–1898, March 14, 1894, Folder 19: Volume 5: Diary, William McKendree Robbins, 1894–1898, William M. Robbins Papers, The Southern Historical Collection. University of North Carolina Library, Chapel Hill, NC.
7 1895 Report of the Gettysburg National Military Park (Washington, DC: Government Printing Office, 1895), 23.
8 "The Ex-Editor in New York," *The Philadelphia Inquirer*, May 31, 1896.
9 *Minutes of the Ninth Annual Meeting and Reunion of United Confederate Veterans* (New Orleans: Hopkins' Printing Office, 1900), 137.
10 1895 Report of the Gettysburg National Military Park Commission, 1–2.
11 *Acts of the Legislature of West Virginia 1897* (Charleston: Moses W. Donnally Public Printer, 1897), 37.
12 John Busey and David Martin, *Regimental Strengths and Losses at Gettysburg* (Highstown: Longstreet Publishing, 2005), 42.
13 War of The Rebellion: A Compilation of the Official Records of the Union and Confederate Armies, Series 1, Volume 27, Part 1 (Washington, DC: Government Printing Office, 1889), 464.
14 "The Brave Dead," *The Wheeling Intelligencer*, September 29, 1898.
15 Earnest Garlington, "Gettysburg National Park Inspection Report, November 1904," (Washington, DC: Government Printing Office, 1904), 2–7.
16 Minute Book, Gettysburg Battlefield Memorial Association, 226.
17 Statutes at Large of the United States of America from December 1907 to March 1909 (Washington, DC: Government Printing Office, 1909), 536.
18 "President Taft at Gettysburg," *The State Herald*, June 4, 1909.
19 "Commission Selects Site," *The Gettysburg Times*, February 25, 1909.
20 "Work To Start Immediately," *The Gettysburg Times*, May 3, 1909.
21 "12,000 Witness Dedication of New Monument," *The Gettysburg Times*, September 28, 1910.

22 "The Dedication Ceremony," *Gettysburg Compiler*, September 28, 1910.
23 Ibid.
24 "12,000 Witness Dedication of New Monument."
25 *Acts And Resolves Passed by the General Assembly of the State of Vermont, 1912* (Montpelier: Capital City Press, 1913), 354.
26 *Dedication of the Statue of Brevet Major General William Wells and the Officers and Enlisted Men of the First Vermont Cavalry* (Privately Printed, 1914), 60.
27 Ibid., 85.
28 "Plans For Fiftieth Anniversary," *Gettysburg Compiler*, September 28, 1910.
29 "Veterans to Meet on the Battlefield," *Public Press*, June 27, 1913.
30 Lewis Beitler, *Fiftieth Anniversary of the Battle of Gettysburg, Report of the Pennsylvania Commission* (Harrisburg: William Stanley Ray State Printer, 1913), 176.
31 "Fine Time in Camp," *Washington Post*, July 7, 1913.
32 "New Monument Completed," *Adams County News*, January 27, 1912.
33 "Veteran Vanguard Now in Gettysburg," *New York Times*, June 29, 1913.
34 "Memories of the Civil War Trip to the Re-union at Gettysburg," *Western Carolina Democrat*, July 7, 1913.
35 *Fiftieth Anniversary of the Battle of Gettysburg, Report of the Pennsylvania Commission*, 121.
36 "Guides Altercation," *Gettysburg Times*, July 12, 1913.

Chapter 7

1 "3,000 Attend Dedication of Woolson Statue as Memorial to GAR Here on Wednesday," *Gettysburg Times*, September 13, 1956.
2 Ulysses Grant, *Personal Memoirs of U.S. Grant Volume 1* (New York City: Charles L. Webster & Co., 1885), 170.

Bibliography

Primary Sources

17th and 27th Connecticut Volunteers at Gettysburg: October 22, 1889, Order of Exercises and Addresses. Bridgeport: Standard Association Printers, 1889.

1895 Report of the Gettysburg National Military Park Commission. Washington, DC: Government Printing Office, 1895.

Acts and Resolves Passed by the General Assembly of the State of Vermont, 1912. Montpelier: Capital City Press, 1913.

Acts of the Legislature of the State of New Jersey, 1885. Camden: Courier Publishing Association, 1885.

Acts of the Legislature of the State of New Jersey, 1886. Trenton: MacCrelish & Quigley Publishing, 1886.

Acts of the Legislature of West Virginia, 1897. Charleston: Moses W. Donnally Public Printer, 1897.

Adams County News.

Adams County Sentinel.

Adams, Silas. "The Nineteenth Maine At Gettysburg." War Papers Read Before the Commandery of the State of Maine. Portland: Lefavor-Tower Company, 1915.

Alexandria Gazette.

Allentown Ledger.

Alton Evening Telegraph.

"An Act to Incorporate the Gettysburg Battle-field Memorial Association." Gettysburg Battlefield Memorial Association, Civil War Vertical File Manuscripts. Gettysburg College Special Collections, Gettysburg, PA.

Annual Reports of the War Department, Volume 1. Washington, DC: Government Printing Office, 1900.

Bachelder, John. *Bachelder Papers: Gettysburg in Their Own Words*, Volume 1, David and Aubrey Ladd eds. El Dorado Hills: Savas Beatie, 2021.

———. *Bachelder Papers: Gettysburg in Their Own Words*, Volume 3, David and Aubrey Ladd eds. El Dorado Hills: Savas Beatie, 2021.

Baltimore Sun.

Barlow, Albert. *Company G: A Record of the Services of One Company of the 157th N.Y. Vols. in the War of the Rebellion.* Syracuse: A.W. Hall Publishing, 1899.

Bartlett, John. *The Soldiers' National Cemetery at Gettysburg: With the Proceedings at Its Consecration, at the Laying of the Corner-Stone of the Monument, and at Its Dedication.* Providence: Providence Press Company, 1874.

Bates, Samuel. *History of the Pennsylvania Volunteers, 1861–1865.* Harrisburg: B. Singerly, 1870.

Beath, Robert. *The Grand Army Blue-book Containing the Rules and Regulations of the Grand Army of the Republic.* Philadelphia: Burk & McFetridge Printers, 1884.

Beitler, Lewis. *Fiftieth Anniversary of the Battle of Gettysburg, Report of the Pennsylvania Commission.* Harrisburg: William Stanley Ray State Printer, 1913.

Beodelman, George. "Letter to father, October 24, 1861." MS 43: George Beodelman Collection, Box 1, Folder 7. Gettysburg College Special Collections, Gettysburg College. Gettysburg, PA.

Boston Evening Transcript.

Boston Globe.

Buehler, D. H. and Edward G. Fahnestock. Letter to Governor Andrew Curtin, August 14, 1863. Vertical File 10-5 David Wills Correspondence. Gettysburg National Military Park Archives, Gettysburg, PA.

Buehler, Fannie. *Recollections of the Rebel Invasion and One Woman's Experience During the Battle of Gettysburg.* Gettysburg: Star And Sentinel, 1896.

Burlington Daily Times.

Carlisle Weekly Herald.

Cincinnati Inquirer.

Commonwealth Of Pennsylvania, Department of the Auditor-General, Damage Claims under the Acts of April 23, 1863, April 9, 1869, and May 27, 1871. Adams County, William Bliss, 4110.

Curtin, Andrew. "The Enemy Is Approaching—June 16, 1863." I-Original-1862-3, Archives and Special Collections. Dickinson College, Carlisle, PA.

The Daily Bee.

Dedication of the Statute of Brevet Major General William Wells and the Officers and Enlisted Men of the First Vermont Cavalry. Privately Printed, 1914.

Dedication of Monument of the 27th Connecticut Volunteers. New Haven: Price, Lee & Co. Printers, 1886.

Delaware Gazette and State Journal.

Democrat and Chronicle.

Detroit Free Press.

Dimon, Theodore. *From Auburn to Antietam: The Journal of a Battlefield Surgeon Who Served with the Army of the Potomac, 1861–1865.* V-5 Theodore S. Dimon, Gettysburg National Military Park Archives. Gettysburg, PA.

Ebersole, Jacob. "Incidents of Field Hospital Life in the Army of the Potomac" in *Sketches of War History 1861–1865,* Papers read before the Ohio Commandry of the Military Order of the Loyal Legion of the United States. 1890–1896. Volume 4. Cincinnati: The Robert Clarke Company, 1896.

Everett, Edward. *An Oration Delivered on the Battlefield of Gettysburg.* New York: Baker & Godwin Printers, 1863.

Frank Leslie's Illustrated Newspaper.

Garlington, Earnest. "Gettysburg National Park Inspection Report, November 1904." Washington, DC: Government Printing Office, 1904.

General Laws of the State of Minnesota 1891. St. Paul: Pioneer Press Company, 1891.

Gettysburg Battlefield Military Park Commission. Annual Report 1893. Washington, DC: Government Printing Office, 1894.

Gettysburg Compiler.

Gettysburg Regimental and Individual Monuments. Vertical File 17. Gettysburg National Military Park Library, Gettysburg, PA.

Gettysburg Star and Sentinel.

Gettysburg Times.

Gogebic Iron Tribune.

Grant, Ulysses. *Personal Memoirs of U.S. Grant Volume 1*. New York City: Charles L. Webster & Co., 1885.

Gregg Cavalry Shaft Record Book 1883–1918. Group 2, Series 8, Box 48, Folder17, MOLLUS Archives. The Union League Legacy Foundation. Philadelphia, Pennsylvania.

H.R. 8096, "A Bill to Establish a National Military Park at Gettysburg, Pennsylvania." (December 6, 1894), 53rd Congress, 3rd Session.

Hardee, William. *Manual for Rifle and Light Infantry Tactics*. Philadelphia: Lippincott Grambo & Co., 1855.

Harrisburg Daily Independent.

Haynes, Calvin. "Letter to Wife—July 19, 1863." Letters 1862–1863, Manuscripts and Special Collections. New York State Library, Albany, New York.

Hillyer, George. *My Gettysburg Battle Experiences*. Gettysburg: Thomas Publications, 2005.

House Committee on Military Affairs. Battle Lines at Gettysburgh, Report No. 3024. Washington, DC: Government Printing Office, 1890.

Illinois Monuments at Gettysburg. Springfield: H. W. Rokker Printer and Binder, 1892.

Indianapolis Journal.

Jacobs, Michael. *Notes on the Rebel Invasion of Maryland and Pennsylvania, and the Battle of Gettysburg*. Philadelphia: J. P. Lippincott & Co., 1864.

Johnson, Bradley. "The Maryland Confederate Monument at Gettysburg." Southern Historical Society Papers. Volume 14. Richmond: William Jones Printers, 1886.

Laws of the General Assembly of the Commonwealth of Pennsylvania Passed at the Session of 1887. Harrisburg: Edwin K. Meyers State Printer, 1887.

Laws of the State of Illinois Passed by the Thirty-Six General Assembly. Springfield: H. W. Rokker Printer and Binder, 1889.

Laws of the State of Maryland Made and Passed 1888. Annapolis: James Young State Printer, 1888.

Laws of the State of New York Passed at the 109th Session. Albany: Banks & Brothers Publishing, 1886.

Laws of the State of New York Passed at the 110th Session. Albany: Banks & Brothers Publishing, 1887.

Laws of Wisconsin Passed by the Biennial Session of the Legislature of 1887. Madison: Democrat Printing Company, 1887.

Lee, Robert. Letter to David McConaughy, August 4, 1869. MS-022 David McConaughy Papers. Special Collections and College Archives. Gettysburg College, Gettysburg, PA.

Lincoln, Abraham. Draft of the Gettysburg Address: Nicolay Copy, November 1863. Series 3, General Correspondence, 1837–1897. The Abraham Lincoln Papers at the Library of Congress. Manuscript Division, Washington, DC.

———. Letter from David Wills to Abraham Lincoln, November 2, 1863. Abraham Lincoln Papers: Series 1, General Correspondence. 1833 to 1916. Library of Congress, Washington, DC.

Lochner, William. "The First Minnesota at Gettysburg" in *Glimpses of the Nation's Struggle, Third Series: 1889–1892*. St. Paul: D. D. Merrill Co., 1893.

Maine at Gettysburg: Report of Maine Commissioners. Portland: Lakeside Press, 1898.

Manuscript History of the 110th Pennsylvania Volunteers. 1805.002.031, MOLLUS Archives. The Union League Legacy Foundation. Philadelphia, PA.

The Marion Times-Standard.

Massachusetts Legislative Acts 1884. Boston: Wright & Potter Printing Co., 1885.

Massachusetts Soldiers, Sailors, and Marines in the Civil War. Norwood: Norwood Press, 1931.

McClellan, George. *McClellan's Own Story*. New York: Charles L. Webster, 1887.

McConaughy, David. Letter to Governor Andrew Curtin, July 25, 1863. Executive Correspondence, RG 26, Department of State, Secretary of The Commonwealth. Pennsylvania State Archives, Harrisburg, PA.

———. Letter to Reverend Charles Krauth, August 14, 1863. MS-022 David McConaughy Papers. Special Collections and College Archives, Gettysburg College, Gettysburg, PA.

Michigan at Gettysburg. Highstown: Longstreet House, 1998.

Milwaukee Sentinel.

Minnesota in the Civil and Indian Wars 1861–1865. St. Paul: Pioneer Press Company, 1890.

Minute Book, Gettysburg Battlefield Memorial Association 1872–1895. Vertical File 11 Park History, Gettysburg National Military Park Archives, Gettysburg, PA.

Minutes of the Ninth Annual Meeting and Reunion of United Confederate Veterans. New Orleans: Hopkins' Printing Office, 1900.

"Monument Contracts and Deeds." Record Group 44, Box 68, Folder 7, Gettysburg Battlefield Commission, Michigan State Archives, Lansing, MI.

Moore, Frank, ed. *The Rebellion Record: A Diary of American Events*. New York: G. P. Putnam, 1861.

Moorhead, Issac. *The Occasional Writings of Issac Moorhead with a Sketch of His Life*, ed. Andrew Caughey. Erie: A.H. Caughey Publisher, 1882.

The Morning Journal-Courier.

Morning News.

Morse, Charles. "The Twelfth Corps at Gettysburg." Papers of the Military Historical Society of Massachusetts. Volume 14. Boston: Cadet Armory, 1918.

The Naperville Clarion.

The National Tribune.

Newport Mercury.

News Journal.

New Ulm Review.

New York Daily Tribune.

The New York Herald.

New York Monuments Commission, *Final Report of the Battlefield of Gettysburg*. Albany: J. B. Lyon Printers, 1902.

New York Times.

Norton, Oliver. *Army Letters 1861–1865*. Dayton: Morningside Press, 1990.

"Order creating the United States Sanitary Commission, by the Secretary of War and approved by the President, June 13, 1861." Manuscripts and Archives Division. The New York Public Library, New York City, NY.

Pennsylvania at Gettysburg: Ceremonies at the Dedication of the Monuments, Volume 1. Harrisburg: E. K. Meyers, 1893.

Philadelphia Bulletin.

Philadelphia Inquirer.

Philadelphia Times.

Philadelphia Weekly Times.

Pittsburgh Daily Post.

Pittsburg Dispatch. The Placer Herald.

Public Acts of the Legislature of the State of Michigan Passed at the Regular Session of 1887. Lansing: Thorp & Godfrey State Printers, 1887.

Public Press.

The Record-Union.

Redding Times.

Report of the Joint Committee to Mark the Positions Occupied by the 1st and 2nd Delaware Regiments at Gettysburg. Dover: Delawarean Press, 1887.

Report of the State of Maryland Gettysburg Monument Commission. Baltimore: William K. Boyle & Son, 1891.

Report of the Ohio Gettysburg Memorial Commission. Columbus: Nitschke Brothers Press, 1887.

Resolves of the State of Maine, 1887. Augusta: Sprague & Son Printers of the State, 1887.

Revised Report of the Select Committee Relative to the Soldiers National Cemetery. Harrisburg: Singerly & Myers, 1865.

Robbins, William. Journal 1894–1898, March 14, 1894, Folder 19: Volume 5: Diary, William McKendree Robbins, 1894–1898, William M. Robbins Papers. The Southern Historical Collection. University of North Carolina Library, Chapel Hill, NC.

Rochester Evening Express.

St. Johnsbury Caledonian.

St. George, Philip, *The U.S. Cavalry Tactics: Instructions, Formations, Maneuvers.* Washington, DC: Government Printing Office, 1862.

Salt Lake Herald.

Sheldon, Winthrop. *The Twenty-Seventh: A Regimental History.* New Haven: Morris & Benham, 1886.

Special Acts and Resolutions of the State of Connecticut. Volume 10. Hartford: Case, Lockwood & Brainard Press, 1890. *The State Herald.*

State of New Jersey Final Report of the Gettysburg Battlefield Commission. Highstown: Longstreet House Publishing, 1997.

Statutes at Large of the United States of America from March 1871 to March 1873. Volume 1. Boston: Little, Brown and Company, 1873.

Statutes at Large of the United States of America from December 1907 to March 1909. Washington, DC: Government Printing Office, 1909.

The Sun.

The Valley Spirit Daily.

Ward, William. *Records of Members of the Grand Army of the Republic.* San Francisco: H. S. Crocker & Co., 1886.

War Department. *Annual Report of the Secretary of War 1917.* Washington, DC: Government Printing Office, 1918.

War Department. *Instruction for Field Artillery.* Philadelphia: Lippincott, 1860.

War of The Rebellion: A Compilation of the Official Records of the Union and Confederate Armies. Volume 1. Washington, DC: Government Printing Office, 1880.

War of The Rebellion: A Compilation of the Official Records of the Union and Confederate Armies. Volume 25. Washington, DC: Government Printing Office, 1889.

War of The Rebellion: A Compilation of the Official Records of the Union and Confederate Armies. Volume 27. Washington, DC: Government Printing Office, 1889.

Washington Evening Star.

Washington Post.

Weekly News-Democrat.

Western Carolina Democrat. The Wheeling Intelligencer.

Wills, David. Letter to Governor Andrew Curtin, July 24, 1863. Executive Correspondence, RG26, Department of State, Secretary of The Commonwealth. Pennsylvania State Archives, Harrisburg, PA.

Secondary Sources

Abroe, Mary. "'All The Profound Scenes': Federal Preservation of Civil War Battlefields 1861–1990." PhD Thesis, Loyola University Chicago, 1996. ProQuest Dissertations & Theses Global.

Ainsworth, Scott. "Electoral Strength and the Emergence of Group Influence in the Late 1800s Grand Army of the Republic." *American Politics Research* 23, no. 3 (July 1995): 319–38. https://doi.org/10.1177/1532673X9502300304.

Bachelder, John. *Gettysburg: What to See and How to See It*. Boston: John Bachelder Publishing, 1876.

———. *History of the Battle of Gettysburg*. El Dorado Hills: Savas Beatie, 2021.

Bates, Samuel. *Battle of Gettysburg*. Philadelphia: T. H. Davis & Co., 1875.

Beecham, Robert. *Gettysburg The Pivotal Battle of the Civil War*. Chicago: A. C. McClurg & Co., 1911.

Beetham, Sarah. "Sculpting the Citizen Soldier: Reproduction and National Memory 1865–1917." PhD Thesis, University of Delaware, 2014. ProQuest Dissertations & Theses Global.

Blight, David. *Race and Reunion: The Civil War in American Memory*. Cambridge: Harvard University Press, 2003.

Brown, Thomas. *Civil War Monuments and The Militarization of America*. Chapel Hill: University North Carolina Press, 2019.

Budiansky, Stephen. *The Bloody Shirt: Terror after the Civil War*. New York: Plume, 2009.

Busey, John and David Martin. *Regimental Strengths and Losses at Gettysburg*. Highstown: Longstreet House, 2005.

Calhoun, Charles. *From Bloody Shirt to Full Dinner Pail: The Transformation of Politics and Governance in the Gilded Age*. New York: Hill and Wang, 2011.

Chaney, Newel. *History of the Ninth Regiment New York Volunteer Cavalry 1861–1865*. Foland Center: Martin Merz & Son, 1901.

Christ, Elwood. *"Over A Wide, Hot … Crimson Plane:" The Struggle for the Bliss Farm*. Baltimore: Butternut and Blue, 1994.

Coddington, Edwin. *The Gettysburg Campaign: A Study in Command*. Norwalk: Easton Press, 1968.

Craven, Wayne. *Sculpture in America*. New York: Crowell Publishing, 1968.

Desjardin, Thomas. *These Honored Dead: How the Story of Gettysburg Shaped American Memory*. Cambridge: Da Capo Press, 2005.

Dixon, Benjamin. "Gettysburg: A Living Battlefield." PhD Thesis, University of Oklahoma, 2000. ProQuest Dissertations & Theses Global.

Dyer, Frederick. *A Compendium of the War of the Rebellion*. Des Moines: Dyer Publishing Company, 1908.

Faust, Drew. *This Republic of Suffering Death and the American Civil War*. New York: Vintage Press, 2009.

Hard, Albert. *History of the Eighth Cavalry Regiment of Illinois Volunteers*. Aurora: Abner Hard Publisher, 1868.

Harris, M. Keith. *Across the Bloody Chasm: The Culture of Commemoration Among Civil War Veterans*. Baton Rouge: Louisiana University Press, 2014.

Hessler, James and Wayne Motts. *Pickett's Charge at Gettysburg: A Guide to the Most Famous Attack in American History*. El Dorado Hills: Savas Beatie, 2015.

History of the First Regiment Minnesota Volunteer Infantry 1861–1864. Stillwater: Easton & Masterson, 1916.

Hobson, Charles and Arnold Shankman, eds., "Colonel of the Bucktails: Civil War Letters of Charles Frederick Taylor." *The Pennsylvania Magazine of History and Biography* 97, no. 3 (July 1973): 333–61. https://journals.psu.edu/pmhb/article/view/42971/42692.

Jordan, Brian. *Marching Home: Union Veterans and Their Unending Civil War*. New York: Liveright Publishing, 2016.

Kammen, Michael. *Mystic Chords of Memory: The Transformation of Tradition in American Culture*. New York: Vintage Press, 1991.

Kennell, Brian. *Beyond the Gatehouse: Gettysburg's Evergreen Cemetery*. Hanover: Sheridan Press, 2000.

Kinsel, Amy. "'From These Honored Dead': Gettysburg in American Culture 1863–1938." PhD Thesis, Cornell University, 1992. ProQuest Dissertations & Theses Global.

Lee, Ronald. *The Origin and Evolution of the National Military Park Idea*. Washington, DC: Office of Park Historic Preservation, 1973.

Leeming, David. *The Oxford Companion to World Mythology*. New York: Oxford University Press, 2005.

Longacre, Edward. *The Cavalry at Gettysburg*. Lincoln: Bison Books, 1993.

Marten, James and Caroline Janney. *Buying and Selling Civil War Memory in Gilded Age America*. Athens: University of Georgia Press, 2021.

McConnell, Stuart. *Glorious Contentment: The Grand Army of the Republic 1865–1900*. Chapel Hill: University of North Carolina Press, 2000.

McNamara. *History of the Ninth Regiment Massachusetts Volunteer Infantry*. Boston: E. B. Stillings & Co., 1899.

Murray, Jennifer. *On a Great Battlefield: The Making, Management, and Memory of Gettysburg National Military Park, 1933–2013*. Knoxville: University of Tennessee Press, 2014.

Myers, H. G. *The Lion of Little Round Top: The Life and Military Service of Brigadier General Strong Vincent in the American Civil War*. Casemate Publishers, 2022.

Neff, John. *Honoring the Civil War Dead: Commemoration and the Problem of Reconciliation*. Lawrence: University of Kansas Press, 2005.

Nevins, James and William Style. *What Death More Glorious: A Biography of General Strong Vincent*. Kearny: Belle Grove Publishing Co., 1997.

Newton, George. *Silent Sentinels: A Reference Guide to the Artillery at Gettysburg*. El Dorado Hills: Savas Beatie, 2017.

Norton, Oliver. *Strong Vincent and His Brigade at Gettysburg*. Chicago: Private Printing, 1909.

Panhorst, Michael. "Lest We Forget: Monuments and Memorial Sculpture in National Military Parks on Civil War Battlefields 1861–1917." PhD Thesis, University of Delaware, 1988. ProQuest Dissertations & Theses Global.

Phisterer, Frederick. *New York in the War of the Rebellion*. Albany: J. B. Lyon Company, 1912.

Quint, Alonzo. *The Record of the Second Massachusetts Infantry 1861–65*. Boston: James Walker, 1867.

Rawle, William. "Gregg's Cavalry Fight at Gettysburg." *Journal of the United States Cavalry Association*. Volume 4. Leavenworth: Ketchenson & Reeves, 1889.

———. *History of the Third Pennsylvania Cavalry in the American Civil War*. Philadelphia: Franklin Printing Company, 1905.

Reardon, Carol. *Pickett's Charge in History and Memory*. Chapel Hill: University of North Carolina Press, 2003.

Reid, Whitelaw. *Ohio in the War: Her Statesmen, Her Generals, Her Soldiers*. Cincinnati: Moore, Wilstach & Baldwin, 1886.

Rockenbach, Stephen. *War Upon Our Border: Two Ohio Valley Communities Navigate the Civil War*. Charlottesville: University of Virginia Press, 2016

Schultz, David. "*Double Canister at Ten Yards:*" *The Federal Artillery and the Repulse of Pickett's Charge, July 3, 1863*. El Dorado Hills: Savas Beatie, 2017.

Sheldon, George. *When the Smoke Cleared at Gettysburg: The Tragic Aftermath of the Bloodiest Battle of the Civil War*. Nashville: Cumberland House, 2003.

Smith, Timothy. *"Altogether Fitting and Proper": Civil War Battlefield Preservation in History, Memory, and Policy, 1861–2015*. Knoxville: University of Tennessee Press, 2017.

———. *The Golden Age of Battlefield Preservation: The Decade of the 1890s and the Establishment of America's First Five Military Parks*. Knoxville: University Of Tennessee Press, 2008.

Spielvogel, John. "Interpreting 'Sacred Ground': The Rhetoric of National Park Service Civil War Historical Battlefields and Parks." PhD Thesis, Pennsylvania State University, 2003. ProQuest Dissertations & Theses Global.

Stillé, Charles. *History of the United States Sanitary Commission During the War of the Rebellion*. Philadelphia: J. B. Lippincott & Co., 1866.

Storrs, John. *Twentieth Connecticut: A Regimental History*. Ansonia: Naugatuck Valley Sentinel Press, 1886.

Thompson, Osmond and William Rauch. *History of the Bucktails*. Philadelphia: Electric Printing Company, 1906.

Thornbrough, Emma. *Indiana in the Civil War Era 1850–1880*. Bloomington: Indiana University Press, 1969.

"Travelers Fortieth Anniversary." *Insurance Monitor* 52, 4. New York: April 1904.

Tucker, Glenn. *High Tide at Gettysburg*. Indianapolis: Bobbs-Merill Publishing, 1958.

Vanderslice, John. *Gettysburg Then and Now*. New York: G. W. Dillingham Co., 1897.

Weeks, Jim. *Gettysburg: Memory, Market, and an American Shrine*. Princeton: University Of Princeton Press, 2011.

Index